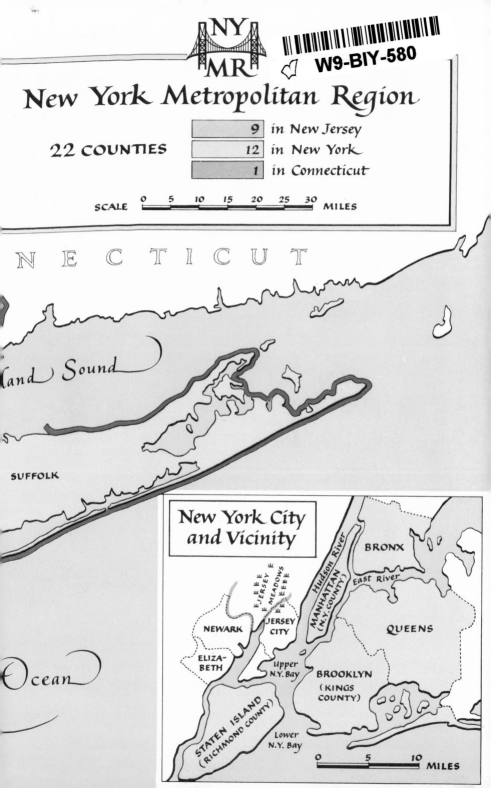

NY MR

New York Metropolitan Region

W9-BIY-580

22 COUNTIES

9	in New Jersey
12	in New York
1	in Connecticut

SCALE 0 5 10 15 20 25 30 MILES

NECTICUT

Iand Sound

SUFFOLK

Ocean

New York City and Vicinity

BRONX

Hudson River

East River

MANHATTAN (N.Y. COUNTY)

JERSEY MEADOWS

NEWARK

JERSEY CITY

QUEENS

ELIZA-BETH

Upper N.Y. Bay

BROOKLYN (KINGS COUNTY)

STATEN ISLAND (RICHMOND COUNTY)

Lower N.Y. Bay

0 5 10 MILES

NEW YORK METROPOLITAN REGION STUDY

RAYMOND VERNON, DIRECTOR

Max Hall, Editorial Director

*A Study undertaken by the Graduate School
of Public Administration, Harvard University,
for Regional Plan Association, Inc.*

1400 GOVERNMENTS

THE POLITICAL ECONOMY OF THE NEW YORK
METROPOLITAN REGION

By Robert C. Wood

with Vladimir V. Almendinger

HARVARD UNIVERSITY PRESS

Cambridge, Massachusetts · 1961

JS
1228
.W6

© Copyright 1961 by Regional Plan Association, Inc.
All rights reserved

Endpaper map by Jeanyee Wong

Charts by H. I. Forman

Designed by Marcia Lambrecht Tate

Library of Congress Catalog Card Number 61-13747
Printed in the United States of America

LIBRARY
WISCONSIN STATE UNIVERSITY
Stevens Point, Wis. 54481

To Peg, who maintained her perspective

148598

Foreword

This is one of a series of books on the forces that shape metropolitan areas. In particular, the series has to do with the forces that shape
the largest and most complex metropolitan area in the United
States, a 22-county expanse which takes in parts of three states but
which, for convenience, we have termed the New York Metropolitan Region. The present volume deals with the impact of local government programs and the political processes which underlie the
pattern of urban development. As such it adds the dimension of
political science to the Study, though obviously it does not treat the
party politics of the Region. Rather, it focuses on those public activities which seem most likely to affect the distribution of firms and
households throughout the Region.

In 1956, the Regional Plan Association, a nonprofit research and
planning agency whose purpose is to promote the coordinated development of these 22 counties, requested the Graduate School of Public
Administration of Harvard University to undertake a three-year
study of the Region. The challenging task was to analyze the key
economic and demographic features of the Region and to project
them to 1965, 1975, and 1985.

The resulting studies are reports to the Regional Plan Association.
At the same time, they are designed to be of service to a much
broader audience. Most Americans now live in metropolitan areas;
indeed ever-increasing proportions of the world's populations are
gravitating to metropolitan clusters. Their well-being depends to a
considerable extent on how these areas develop. Yet the scholar's
understanding of the currents underlying the rise of such areas seems
grossly inadequate.

As a study of these underlying currents, this project is not a blue-
print for action. It has no recommendations to make about the phys-

ical structure of the Region or about the form or activities of the governmental bodies there. At the same time, it is a necessary prelude to future planning studies of the Region and to well considered recommendations for governmental action. Its end product is an analysis of the Region's probable development, assuming that the economic and demographic forces in sight follow their indicated course and assuming that the role of government is largely limited to existing policies.

The results of the Study, it is hoped, will be applied in many ways. Governments and enterprises in the Region should be in a better position to plan their future programs if they become more closely aware of the economic environment in which they may expect to operate. Other metropolitan areas, it is already evident, will benefit from the methodology and the conclusions which the Study has developed.

From the first, there has been a general recognition that the main part of the Study would have to be done by a group located within the New York Metropolitan Region and devoted exclusively to the project. Such a group was assembled in New York. The work that followed was a complex partnership. The New York staff functioned in close harness with members of the Harvard University faculty. It drew on the faculties of other universities, including Columbia University, Fordham University, Hofstra College, New York University, Rutgers University, and the Massachusetts Institute of Technology. It obtained the help of dozens of governmental organizations in the Region, and literally hundreds of private groups and individuals. It made use of the materials which the Regional Plan Association had painstakingly pulled together in prior years.

One cannot easily account for all the elements that went into the making of this book nor of the others in the series. The Regional Plan Association performed an indispensable function in conceiving and sponsoring the idea of a study. The Ford Foundation and the Rockefeller Brothers Fund generously provided the financial support. The usual formula in such a situation obviously applies: credit for the Study's results must be shared with those who helped to bring it about, but the onus of error or omission lies with us.

The several volumes in the series bear the names of their principal authors. In the present instance Professor Wood undertook his research with the help and collaboration of Vladimir V. Almendinger. Mr. Almendinger conceived of and carried out the application of factor analysis used in the second chapter and was responsible for the assembly and summarizing of government financial data. The selection and interpretation of the financial data used throughout the book remain the responsibility of Professor Wood.

The undertaking as a whole has been under the direction of Raymond Vernon. He is responsible for the summary volume, *Metropolis 1985,* which was published in November 1960, and substantial parts of other studies, and his guidance is evident throughout the series.

EDWARD S. MASON
for the Graduate School
of Public Administration,
Harvard University

Contents

Charts

Tables

Author's Acknowledgment

These days no book is the product of a single author, a volume toward the end of a lengthy series least of all. The most substantial assistance came from Vladimir V. Almendinger, who began as a collector of the financial data covering government activities in the New York Region but soon took responsibility for the organization and analysis of this information as well. He first recommended the use of factor analysis in the study of government programs; he designed and executed the research project reported in Chapter 2; after the classification system for studying public expenditures and revenues was established, he prepared all the financial statistics used in the book. Without his imaginative and painstaking efforts, the treatment of public finances would have been a far more prosaic and a far less rewarding endeavor.

Assisting Mr. Almendinger in his work were five talented young ladies who, though working in various periods in the three years of research, uniformly contributed interest, intelligence, precision, and grace to the task. Mrs. Elizabeth Howard, Mrs. Alice Karl, Mrs. Margaret Crim Barry, Mrs. Betty Lou Marple, and Miss Elizabeth Hooper made vital contributions in bringing a mass of data under manageable control.

Within the New York Metropolitan Region Study I am indebted to my associates—in particular Alan K. Campbell, Benjamin Chinitz, Oscar Handlin, Edgar M. Hoover, Robert M. Lichtenberg, and Martin Segal—for stimulation, encouragement, and counsel. Outside the Study, old and distinguished friends gave freely of their time and knowledge. Once again, for guidance and support I thank Wallace S. Sayre of Columbia University, Lucian Pye of the Massachusetts Institute of Technology, Martin Meyerson of Harvard University, Herbert Kaufman of Yale University, Jesse Burkhead of

Syracuse University, Werner Z. Hirsch of Washington University, St. Louis, and Norton E. Long of Northwestern University. I am also grateful to Kirk Petshek of Philadelphia, Lyle C. Fitch of New York, Delphius Goldberg of the House Committee on Government Operations, U. S. Congress, and Matthias E. Lukens of the Port of New York Authority, for providing special insights of scholars-turned-practitioners.

Finally, my wife Margaret Byers Wood deserves special thanks for her help. As before, her patience, encouragement, and thoughtful criticism were major sources of support. But this time, her collaboration involved moving the family to New York City for a summer which became the hottest of a decade, and managing the family unassisted for two other long summer vacations. The price of scholarship ran extraordinarily high.

With all this personal and professional aid gratefully acknowledged, the responsibility for the book—its organization, contents, and conclusions—remains that of the undersigned alone.

Robert C. Wood

1400 Governments

I

The Political Economy of a
Metropolitan Area

On the eastern seaboard of the United States, where the state of
New York wedges itself between New Jersey and Connecticut, ex-
plorers of political affairs can observe one of the great unnatural
wonders of the world: that is, a governmental arrangement perhaps
more complicated than any other that mankind has yet contrived or
allowed to happen. A vigorous metropolitan area, the economic capital of the nation, governs itself by means of 1467 distinct political
entities (at latest count), each having its own power to raise and
spend the public treasure, and each operating in a jurisdiction determined more by chance than design. The whole 22-county area which
we know as the New York Metropolitan Region provides beds for
about sixteen million people and gainful employment for about
seven million of them.* Its growth, which is rapid, takes place almost entirely in its outer, less crowded parts, and this means that
the Region is becoming more alike in the density of its population
and jobs, more alike in community problems. But the responsibility
to maintain law and order, educate the young, dig the sewers, and
plan the future environment remains gloriously or ridiculously frag-
mented.

The state of fragmentation can be defended as carrying on the

* Nine of the counties are in New Jersey, as follows: Hudson, Essex,
Union, Passaic, Bergen, Monmouth, Middlesex, Somerset, and Morris. Twelve
are in New York State; besides the five counties making up New York City,
they are: Nassau, Suffolk, Westchester, Rockland, Orange, Putnam, and
Dutchess. One county, Fairfield, is in Connecticut.

cherished democratic tradition of home rule. It can be deplored as hopelessly unsuited to the realities of modern metropolitan life. Our purpose in this book is neither to defend nor to deplore. It is to observe, dissect, and classify the Region's governments and to estimate their likely impact on the Region's development. We must assess the present nature, functions, and spending habits of political units so diverse that they include both Goshen, New York, and the Port of New York Authority. And then, in order to project their impact on the rapidly changing Region as far ahead as 1985, we must, before we are through, try to predict whether the present governmental structure will undergo revolutionary changes of its own.

This volume of the New York Metropolitan Region Study, then, is concerned with the Region's *political economy*—a good old-fashioned phrase here applied to the relatively new-fangled concept of a metropolitan area. As a general proposition we accept the dictionary definition of the phrase—"the art of managing the resources of a people and a government"—but we also give it two specific meanings. The New York Region's political economy consists, first, of what economists call a "public sector"—the resources allocated to public purposes and the services and products which result. It consists, second, of the political systems which exercise the "art of managing" and make the decisions about what resources are to be made available and what is to be done with them.

The "public sector" is a familiar term in analytical writing these days, but when applied to a metropolitan area it requires some further explanation. We will use it to embrace all revenues made available to, and all expenditures made by, the governments in the Region—permitting revenues to serve as our measure of the resources allocated to public purposes, and expenditures to serve as our measure of the services and products which result. On the revenue side, we will deal with local taxes and charges, state and federal grants, any money which flows to local coffers. On the side of expenditures, we are concerned principally with those made by the Region's governments; on occasion, we will deal with expenditures which state or federal agencies make directly in the Region, but only when these are clearly tied in with programs of Regional development, such as programs for highways and public housing. Expenditures of the Regional establishments of the Post Office Department or the Customs Service or the New York State Employment Service are not part of the public sector that will be placed on exhibit in this book.

As for the *systems* which manage the *sector,* we identify two.

First, we treat as a single system the units of government which are popularly known as "local." These are jurisdictions possessing general public powers—cities, counties, boroughs, towns, villages, and the like—and special-purpose governments covering only a small geographical area, namely school districts, fire districts, water districts, and so on.

Our second system is a handful of metropolitan giants. Their legal origins are various; their responsibilities affect broad parts of the Region; and they influence the pattern of Regional growth in a more positive fashion than the local governments. The center of this system is the Port of New York Authority and the Triborough Bridge and Tunnel Authority, but the system extends to state legislatures, governors, state highway departments, and federal bureaus and agencies whenever they participate in decisions about the use of resources for specified public purposes.

In considering how the systems manage the sector, we focus on public decisions—what impels them, who makes them, by what criteria, and with what results. In particular, we focus on the process for making those decisions which most strongly affect the private sector, that is, affect the location of firms and households or the transportation of goods and people. Such decisions are often "unintentional" in their shaping of the private sector, for they are concerned with resource allocations—taxing and spending—and the avowed purpose is simply the provision of necessary or desirable public services. Some decisions, on the other hand, are deliberately designed to influence land use, to stimulate private development, or to encourage or counteract trends. Both kinds of decisions, the unintentional and the calculated, represent links between the public sector and the private sector of the Region, and we select them from the many facets of Regional political behavior for our special attention.

With this emphasis on "links" between public and private activity, our analysis uncovers the essentials of a feedback mechanism. In the first instance, we search for the forces which motivate the political systems to expand the public sector—to collect larger amounts of taxes and to spend more and more money for public purposes. We also seek to identify the pressures which trigger off the provision of particular kinds of services and the adoption of particular policies. This search takes us of course into the private sector—to the characteristics of the Region's population, their income, occupations, and locational preferences. But it also leads us to consider the behavior of office-holders and public administrators, voters and lobbyists as they try to record the preferences of the population.

Once we have a notion of the forces which generate activity in the public sector, we inquire how the political systems react. How do local governments make decisions about the migration of new residents into their bailiwicks, about the increased number of automobiles on their roads, about the perennial demands for better schools? How do the institutions with broader Regional responsibilities respond to pressures? What calculations enter into their decisions to build a bridge, construct a dam, raise subway fares? How and why do the decisions differ as between the two political systems and as between the way affairs are managed in the public sector and the way they are managed in the private sector?

Finally, we want to know what consequences the public decisions have for the private sector. We must examine whether the amount and level of public expenditures and taxes have an appreciable effect on the trends in the movement of households and industries; whether the decisions of public authorities or governors or Washington officials vitally shape the Region's future in the sense that they disrupt the workings of the marketplace; whether industrial development programs influence the locational choices of manufacturers; whether better schools build better communities or whether it is more accurate to say that better communities build better schools.

Challenge, response, and consequence, then, are what we are looking for as we approach the political economy of the New York Metropolitan Region.

THE SERVICE STATE SETTLES IN

✐ CHRISTMAS BASKETS AND BARBECUES

Fifty years ago, an economic analysis of New York City would not have considered the political economy an appropriate topic for inquiry, and a study of the whole New York Region would have been even less concerned with the subject. Neither in the resources commandeered nor the powers exercised did the governmental apparatus sufficiently affect the course of economic development.

A local system was of course much in evidence in 1910, and its activities could be more easily—and more colorfully—described than those of the modern one.[1] In many ways, the management of the political economy was almost indistinguishable from the direction of a private enterprise. Richard Croker, who had recently retired as leader of Tammany with an estate estimated at five million dollars, had viewed the management of public affairs in no small measure as a personal commercial venture.[2] His successor, Charles Francis Murphy, was already a millionaire, having used his office as dock commissioner to award contracts to the New York Contracting and Trucking Company, of which he happened to be sole owner.[3]

Smaller political and bureaucratic fry emulated the behavior of their betters. Police protection was a commodity to be sold, its principal purchasers being the operators of illegitimate enterprises. Public works employees served simultaneously the municipality and private construction companies. City inspectors were on the payrolls of both the regulator and the regulated. The style of the time was to regard government programs as sources for exploitation and plunder. In 1910, in all but name, the municipality could quite realistically be regarded as a business—distinguished principally by the fact that it could not legally be brought into bankruptcy.

It is true that even in those days the political world was not en-

tirely devoid of impact on the economic world. To the businessmen
who were building the subways, brownstones, railroad stations, and
gas lines, contact with government was essential. They needed transit
franchises, public utility rights, and construction permits—and systematically they entered into Tammany alliances. Similarly in municipal improvement projects, bankers frequently found irresistible
the lure of municipal bonds issued under the liberal terms of the day.
They chose to ignore the circumstance that the terms of repayment
far exceeded the useful life of the facility, and they abetted political
habits of extravagance. Even merchants who personally abhorred
politics often discovered that the purchase of local political good will
was essential to construct new buildings or renew occupational licenses or even to pass goods through customs offices which were legally federal agencies. So regular and routinized were these relations
—not only in New York but also in other cities—that Lincoln Steffens could characterize them in a single term, "the fix," and find
literary fame in chronicling their operations.[4]

The political system of the day also made contact with some households and consumers. There were Thanksgiving and Christmas bas-
kets, buckets of coal for low-income citizens, and jobs on municipal
payrolls—in exchange for the votes which kept the organization in
power. There were free fireworks, barbecues where twenty thousand
glasses of beer washed down five tons of beef, excursion steamers
provisioned with six thousand pounds of candy and fifteen thousand
quarts of ice cream, and promises of recreational piers every half
mile along the Hudson.[5]

Moreover, New York City had performed certain feats that influenced the pattern of settlement for households and industry alike.
After all, the Brooklyn Bridge had made developmental history as
early as 1883.

Yet, though the governmental system absorbed resources, provided
services, and maintained relations with the private sector in ways
colorful or reprehensible depending on one's point of view, its decisions by and large could not be called a major influence on the
economic life of the City. The public sector was simply too small for

that. In spite of the inflated contracts for public improvement, the lavish debt policy, and the granite block scandals, the sum of public activity had little effect on the mainstream of development. At times, the pattern of politics might accelerate the over-all rate of growth in small ways, at times retard it. But even in the words of a passionate reformer, "New York is too rich to be bought into insolvency. Great cities, when badly administered, cannot be sold and abolished; they simply become dirty, unhealthy, unsafe, disgraceful, and expensive." [6]

Statistics confirmed the reformer's impression. In 1910, despite Tammany's reliance on the municipal payroll as the foundation for its political organization, only one person out of every 112 residents worked for the City, less than 4 per cent of the labor force. Annual municipal expenditures amounted to $200 million, and municipal capital assets, as indicated by the gross funded debt of the time, totaled about $800 million. [7]

Moreover, even though government regulation or misregulation could jeopardize the fortunes of an individual businessman, neither industry nor labor normally looked to government for decisions essential to its work. Except for the provision of water, which had only recently been supplied in an adequate amount, and the maintenance of law and order, often at minimum levels, the direct services the City offered to business were few in number. Manufacturers, wholesalers, and retailers relied on other private businessmen to establish the major freight terminal facilities, to transport their workers, to acquire space for their enterprises, to furnish fuel and other utilities, and in many instances, to protect their plants and settle their labor disputes. The system of the dole had proved grossly inadequate in the panic of the 1890's, and systematic care for the poor remained largely in the hands of voluntary charities. Health services were largely limited to sanitary inspections and the control of contagious diseases. Even the public schools enrolled less than half the children of high school age. [8]

Finally, the notion that government could guide and stimulate private development was still in embryonic form. Though the City's powers to restrict private property rights had been sanctioned since the eighteenth century, though offensive trades and industries had long been excluded from residential districts, and though a maximum height for houses had been established in 1855, comprehensive and detailed zoning ordinances were not to appear until 1916.[9] Given the condition of city politics, there was little disposition to rely on government to help shape the economic future. In the newly established New York Bureau of Municipal Research, young researchers like Robert Moses and Luther Gulick, who were later to intervene vigorously in economic affairs in the name of the City, now put first things first. They concentrated their efforts on the reform of the internal machinery of government administration and finance, seeking to reorganize and purify before expanding the scope of governmental operations.

With respect to the importance of local government to economic growth, New York's experience paralleled the nation's. True, oratorical rumblings against the trusts were loud and the Square Deal of the first Roosevelt had been proclaimed almost ten years earlier, but laissez-faire doctrine basked in a golden sunset. "The less government, the better" was still the slogan of the day and though it was proper that "the people should patriotically and cheerfully support their Government, its functions do not include the support of the people." [10]

Local governments accounted for 51 per cent of total public expenditures in the United States at the turn of the century; yet their purchases of goods and services represented less than 2 per cent of the gross national product. The combined capital assets of all governments—federal, state, and local—amounted to something under $7 billion, one-fifteenth of the nation's property, and one worker out of 24 was employed in government service.[11] Having such a puny share of the economy's wealth, offering few services critical to economic development, and seeing few indications that the public seriously desired governmental intervention in business affairs, governments hardly touched the economic life of the typical American. Except in time of crisis, public programs did not figure in the private calculations of producer or consumer.

⁊ GOVERNMENTS IN FLUX

If an analysis of the Region's political economy would not have been required early in the century, it *could* not have been undertaken twenty-five years ago. In 1935, the public sector was big enough to be important—but the governmental systems were in the process of an abrupt and dramatic break with the past. Where, how, and why public decisions were made had become matters of great uncertainty.

The time between 1910 and 1935 had witnessed a sharp and substantial increase in the volume of governmental activities because of pressures from the private sector. During this period, changes in the nation's economy and technology translated themselves into more public expenditures, more taxes, more governmental intervention. The advent of the Model T transformed the automobile from a toy to a reliable means of transportation, and thereby inaugurated a large-scale highway program to get America "out of the mud." Medical advance increased life expectancy and called forth changes in welfare and public health activities. Rising incomes and higher literacy requirements for employment put more children in school and kept them there longer. Some public utilities came under public management. Planning and zoning matured in concept and application. The conscious efforts of municipalities to stimulate private development reached at least the booster stage. As early as 1927, government was coming of age, both as a resource manager and as an influential force upon the private economy.

But the advent of the Great Depression shattered established procedures for government action. As the first stages of the New Deal got under way—its enthusiasm undeniable but its purposes and plans uncertain—a massive reorganization of the structure and philosophy of American government seemed imminent. Businessmen, workers, and consumers expected positive action; they had voted for it. But while one could predict a new era, one could not begin to sketch out its dimensions. America, in the words of Arthur Schlesinger, Jr., was "in a state of extreme shock." At the time of Franklin Roosevelt's inauguration, it seemed to Rexford Tugwell that "we were confronted with a choice between an orderly revolution—a peaceful and rapid departure from past concepts—and a violent and disorderly overthrow of the whole capitalist structure." The mood was such that Governor Alfred M. Landon of Kansas could publicly conclude that "even the iron hand of a national dictator is in preference to a paralytic stroke." [12]

The sense of crisis was even more acute at the state and local levels. There the demands for public action had exploded first and the breakdown in government machinery had been most obvious. For a quarter of a century, state and local governments had shouldered the bulk of new public demands. Expressed as shares of the gross national product, their expenditures almost doubled between 1902 and 1927. Expressed as a proportion of total public expenditures, they rose from 69 to 74 per cent and for nonmilitary functions alone from 88 to 92 per cent. In the two decades between 1903 and 1923, while the federal government was both reducing expenditures and retiring debt, the expenditures of state and local governments rose from $2.25 billion a year to $5.5 billion, and their debt from $2 billion to $15 billion. Particularly at the local level, where demands for education, streets, and health and welfare programs were most immediate—and the capacity to tap new sources of revenue most restricted—the pressure mounted. Throughout the prosperous twenties, local units continued to borrow heavily, their interest payments alone rising from $167 million in 1913 to $1.5 billion by the early thirties.[13]

At the time of the Crash, then, the financial structures of most local governments were already in a weakened condition. Their administrative apparatus and talent were severely extended. The new programs they had undertaken were in only the early processes of assimilation. A few well-to-do suburban units around New York and elsewhere had their financial houses in order, but there was an acute imbalance in responsibilities among the three levels of government, and only the federal establishment apparently possessed the capacity to respond to Depression demands. Local and state governments alike turned to Washington, and four years after Wall Street's Black Thursday it was obvious that Washington would respond. Yet this fact itself made the future of local government even more uncertain.

New York's position was as precarious as any in the nation. The municipality had undergone a period of extraordinary activity. Since 1920, to finance extensions and improvements in transit, water, and other public facilities, the City had increased its gross funded debt from $1.2 to $2.1 billion. By 1932 its operations were second only to the federal government in size, exceeding those of any state government and accounting for 4.5 per cent of all governmental expenditures.[14] Now, with 84 per cent of its revenue dependent on real property, the City's officials watched the tax base tumble in four depression years from an assessed valuation of over $18 billion to barely $13 billion in a precipitous decline that only World War II would arrest.

The unusual Bankers' Agreement of 1932, providing emergency loans to the City, and the special permission granted by the state legislature to reduce teachers' salaries enabled the City to pay current bills. Yet the stringent conditions which were attached by the bankers placed the City in a financial straitjacket, unable to make more than minimum replacements and repairs to its existing plant. Operating at a subsistence level, dependent on the disparate graces of the financial community and the Roosevelt administration, unable to find means which approached self-support, the City seemed to flounder. At times, it appeared that only the verve and dash of the mayor, Fiorello La Guardia, kept the municipal ship of state afloat. It would have been a rash observer indeed who would then have predicted the future of local government in the New York Metropolitan Region, let alone the substance of its programs and the nature of its relation to Washington and the three state capitals, Albany, Trenton, and Hartford.

⁊ The governments today

Today, too, those who describe the role of government in order to speculate about the future must acknowledge a streak of rashness. As New York City and the surrounding jurisdictions which now encompass the metropolitan economy have emerged from their wartime cocoons of frozen payrolls and of minimum public works programs, they have faced pent-up demands upon every one of their major programs. Throughout the Region, local units have taken the buffeting of the restless shifts of population, have struggled to catch up with postponed improvement projects, have assumed a wider array of responsibilities, and have watched the steady erosion of their budgets by inflation. In transportation, water supply, housing, and pollution control, they have undertaken programs of apparently major import to the economy. And in every part of the Region, a burst of planning has occurred and new zoning policies have been adopted. When one compares the municipal operations of the 1950's with those of the 1930's, only the names of the jurisdictions seem constant.

Yet, treacherous as the terrain may be, it is now quite clear that the aggregate figures for public expenditures are too large to ignore. For the nation as a whole, the trend of local government expenditures which had proceeded in almost a horizontal line from the mid-thirties to the mid-forties, and for some functions had actually declined, turned sharply upwards in the next decade. As Chart 1 indicates, the spending of all county and municipal governments in the United States spurted from about $8 billion to more than $30 billion in the first twelve years after the war. Even if the new level were adjusted for price increases, the rise would be impressive. And comparable spending in the New York Metropolitan Region rose almost as impressively. The Region, which was not expanding its population and income quite as fast as the nation during this period, did not match the nation in the rate of spending increase; but even so, its local governments more than tripled their outlays, from $1.2 billion to $3.8 billion. Within the Region, however, there were marked differences. New York City doubled its expenditures. The New Jersey portion of the Region fell short of that. But the New York portion outside New York City more than quadrupled its governmental outlays.*

---

* Statistics on governmental activities involve many problems of coverage and comparability, which are discussed in Appendix A.

Chart 1

Expenditures of Local Governments, U.S. and New York Metropolitan Region,[a] 1945–1957

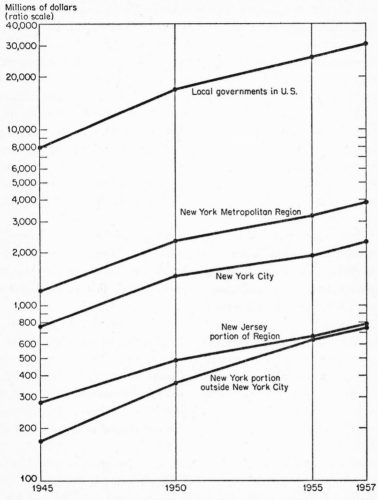

Millions of dollars (ratio scale)

Local governments in U.S.

New York Metropolitan Region

New York City

New Jersey portion of Region

New York portion outside New York City

[a] Region here excludes Fairfield County, Connecticut, for lack of data.

Note: Expenditures include current and capital outlays, assistance and subsidies, and interest on debt for the general governments of all local jurisdictions as well as for special districts and municipally owned utilities. However, state outlays in local jurisdictions and the expenditures of the Port of New York Authority are not included. Sources explained in Appendix A.

Meanwhile the Region's governments pushed their employment to higher and higher levels. By the late 1950's they had on their payrolls the equivalent of more than 400,000 full-time employees—something like 6 per cent of the Region's total working force.

Yet, grand as the dollar and employment totals may appear, they are only pale symbols of the bustle of activities which now engage the local governments. For New York City alone, the 828 school buildings now represent an investment of more than one billion dollars; its housing, redevelopment, and renewal programs are underwritten in the amount of another billion. During the building boom between the mid-forties and mid-fifties, private business investment of one billion dollars in new construction was surpassed by almost two billion dollars in capital expenditure by the City for new schools, port facilities, hospitals, parks, bridges, libraries, and other facilities.[15]

A large proportion of this investment and of the current expenditures required to maintain the plant is devoted to carrying out long-established public functions, which have swelled as the City's population has grown and congestion increased. For example, over five thousands miles of pipes, tunnels, and mains bring more than a trillion gallons of water to City residents every day; there are 34,000 acres of parks and playgrounds, 28 City hospitals, 24,000 policemen and 13,000 firemen; there are 120,000 City prisoners to be fed and guarded, thousands of miles of streets to be cleaned, 3,000,000 tons of refuse to be disposed of each year, 46,000 elevators to be inspected, and 300,000 welfare recipients to be aided. And this says nothing of teachers, ambulances, clerks, and other people and facilities that have to be maintained.

Besides these traditional functions, the City provides a wide array of relatively new or unusual services. The municipal school program maintains special classes for handicapped children, provides clinics, and offers hospital care. The municipal colleges have an enrollment of 78,000. Adult education classes benefit 40,000 more. Research is carried on in geriatrics, cancer, and mental health. Efforts to control juvenile delinquents include street clubs and free psychiatric sessions. There are voluntary clinics for emotionally disturbed adults. In the parks, children attend puppet shows and grown-ups attend Shakespeare workshops. There is a program to reduce air pollution. One and three-quarter million fares are paid in the public transit system every day, three times the number reported by all the Class I railroads in the United States. And, as safe and healthful residential accommodations at moderate rents become increasingly scarce, more and more families find space in public housing projects.

The City does not stand alone within the Region in the growth of the volume of its operations and the extension of its range of public services. It remains the focal point of governmental activity, for its annual budget is over one-half of the Region's local public expenditures, its debt-service outlays are twice those of governments elsewhere in the Region, and the number of its permanent employees is more than twice theirs. Yet, in varying degrees, and for varying specific reasons, the other jurisdictions are caught up in a process of expansion, and their activities, in proportion to the territory they encompass and the population they serve, are no less impressive.

On the New Jersey side of the Hudson River, the older cities such as Newark, Jersey City, Hoboken, and Paterson face many of the same public problems which afflict New York City. Obsolescence and blight, congestion, fire and health hazards, and shortages of space for middle-income residences have increased public expenditures and have set loose demands for new public programs.

In certain other jurisdictions of the Region, the public programs are of a different order—rapidly expanding because of population growth. Nassau, advertised as the fastest-growing county in the United States, epitomizes postwar suburban growing pains. Here, problems of supplying water, sewers, and roads have loomed large, and the public schools, operating through 59 separate school districts, have expanded so fast that capital investments during the years 1950–1954 exceeded $234 million—about 25 per cent of school construction expenditures in the whole state, including New York

City. The "get-going" costs of Nassau suburban growth are well illustrated by Hempstead, "America's largest township," where the early 1950's saw the construction of 15,000 new housing units a year.[16]

Toward the fringes of the Region, governmental activity takes on still a different character. Here expenditures have not risen so rapidly; here the range of services is not so broad nor the manner of their execution so professional. But the residents of outlying districts seem to pay increasing attention to land-use controls; they have observed the different experiences of the jurisdictions closer in—Westchester County, for example, where growth has been carefully controlled in contrast to the almost unrestrained surge of population in some other areas. In remote Monmouth, Suffolk, and Rockland Counties, recently established planning boards are laboring to set more rigid subdivision controls and to mark out industrial parks, sometimes with a realistic knowledge of the jurisdiction's economic potential, sometimes expressing the fantasies of the boosters' psychology. And quiet residential islands in Fairfield, Middlesex, and Putnam Counties upgrade already high standards of development in an effort to insure their isolation from the metropolis.[17]

The very scope of public activity in the New York Metropolitan Region, then, impels analysis. And, despite the ferment of change, analysis does not seem impossible. Certainly, it appears more feasible than it was a generation ago, for basic questions of programs, organization, and structure that were unsettled in the 1930's seem answered today. Whether government will be an important user of resources and dispenser of services is no longer an issue: the important emergency measures introduced in times of crisis have become reasonably permanent fixtures on the American scene. Neither is there much question where the major public decisions in the Region will be made. The ordeals of depression and war did not shatter the system of local government nor alter structurally the grant-in-aid pattern by which the federal government and the states bolster local activities. With administrative and financial adjustments, the same basic structure that characterized the formal government pattern of 1900 continues in effect. Even issues of the scope and nature of public programs appear to have become essentially questions of degree. Breakthroughs for specific fields, such as urban redevelopment, may be on the horizon. But, for the time being at least, the continuity in the basic domestic responsibilities of local government seems just as clear as the fact that the market mechanism and the profit motive continue to characterize the economic system.

Thus, in contrast to the tiny public sector of 1910 or the uncertain government of the thirties, the Service State has settled in. The businessman can expect local taxes to be a significant, if not a major, cost of operations. The household will continue to look to government to provide major essentials of life—more highways, utilities, schools, and welfare services. How high taxes will rise, how much service is provided, how stringent land controls may be are still open issues. But the continued involvement of government in the Region's growth seems assured for at least the next twenty-five years.

EXIT THE MARKETPLACE

If the effects of governmental activities on Regional economic affairs now seem substantial—and destined to remain so—an important corollary follows from the fact. The *process* by which expenditures are authorized and programs carried out requires exploration before we can understand the functioning of the political economy. When we move from the private to the public sector we pass, in Harold Lasswell's words, from a set of interactions typically labeled "transactions" to one in which the concept of "decisions" is central.[18] We could make no greater mistake than to suppose that the ways in which these political decisions are made parallels the behavior of firms and households.

One way to underscore the importance of process per se is to reflect on the difficulty of distinguishing between the public and private sectors in terms of the activities they carry out. Few public activities in the New York Region appear to be inherently "public" in the sense that the conduct of foreign affairs or the maintenance of national defense are public. The necessaries of modern urban life—for instance, water, electricity, gas, shelter—are supplied both by public agencies and private corporations. The responsibility for moving people and goods is shared by government and business. A large number of the Region's children are educated in private schools, and important relief activities are carried out by private charities. In some jurisdictions, the collection of refuse is a public responsibility; in many others, a private one. In some areas, public health officers provide treatment that elsewhere is provided only by the family doctor. Even the creation or enforcement of law is not an exclusive governmental prerogative; private police forces are found throughout the Region and private residential covenants often operate with more force than public legislation. So it is the distinction between the processes, not between the functions, which is critical to our analysis.

The central distinguishing feature of the governmental process is, of course, its monopoly on the lawful means of physical violence, its possession of power—not just on a parcel of private property, but everywhere in the political jurisdiction. This quality, in and of itself, sets the political economy apart, and endows it with a purpose quite separate from that of the private sector. Not only do governments have the means to compel compliance with their policies—in the provision of education, the acquisition of water reservoirs, the construction of highways—but the control over these means becomes a paramount objective of different groups within the Region's population struggling for influence and authority. Public programs are authorized for purposes other than the satisfaction of the material wants of all the residents or even of a majority. They are devices whereby political organizations survive. Taxes and public expenditures represent not just "costs" and "products" but "votes" and "influence." Political stability as much as economic prosperity is involved in the goals of a political economy.

Given this general characteristic of the governmental process, we should acknowledge three specific differences between the political economy and the private economy in the way resources are used and activities undertaken. First, in the political economy the basic unit of decision-making is not the individual producer or consumer; it is the group, formally or informally organized. Second, the mechanism through which resources are obtained and expenditures made is not the price mechanism of the marketplace, but the budgetary process. Finally, the "products" provided by government are public products; that is, theoretically they are always indivisible among persons, and practically, they are frequently so.

The significance of the group, not the individual, as the basic unit of governmental process is of course that resources are not allocated to the public sector by the invisible hand of thousands upon thousands of individual choices exercised constantly without explicit recognition of the preferences of the other participants in the marketplace. The allocation is, rather, the function of a relatively few persons presuming to speak for the voters in the name of the "public interest" and the "general will." The periodic limited expression of popular opinion in the voting booths and the occasional articulation of public preferences and expectations in opinion surveys are rarely interpreted as an aggregation of individual attitudes. Instead these expressions are analyzed in terms of ethnic blocks, silk-stocking districts, neighborhood attitudes, and common outlooks presumed to be held by persons of similar income, occupation, or racial types. And institutions—the church, the *New York Times,* the banks, business associations and labor—become significant as entities in themselves, exercising influence because they sway the preferences of citizens. Thus the aspirations of groups and leaders of groups, more than the opinions of the members themselves, become the critical elements in the process of determining what the political systems decide.

With the individual voter-consumer-citizen removed from the arena of decision-making, notions of marginal costs and prices, of income and wants are replaced by the vaguer concept of the budget. The literature of public budgeting is replete with efforts to find a substitute for the price mechanism, to devise a common unit for comparing relative benefits among different services at the margin. In actuality, however, the process of allocating public moneys among competing needs still proceeds on a basis far removed from the price mechanism—on a system of preferences filtered through group representation.

So New York City's Board of Estimate calculates the outcries likely to arise from taxpayers' associations when the tax rate is increased, weighs such protests against the influence of recipients of public education or medical services, interjects a healthy dose of personal preferences, and, in a series of sustained and sometimes frenzied discussions, cuts or expands the estimates of professional budget-makers in the course of a few short days. Outside the City, even this institutional focal point for considering competing claims is lacking. Counties, towns, boroughs, cities, villages, special districts, existing side by side or overlying the same geographic territory, proceed in jurisdictional isolation to consider small segments of the Region's aggregate local expenditures and arrive at separate judgments of group needs and group influences. Political philosophy and estimates of political strength—operating through collective mechanisms—become the key factors in distributing the Region's public resources among different purposes.

Moreover, even if the individual had a mechanism by which he could make his preferences known, each and every citizen would not be satisfied. So long as a number of alternative courses of action were available, no "optimum" solution would result—even for the majority.[19] Choices become too complicated for optimum solutions; what happens (as every politician knows) is a compromise. In the public sector, the individual citizen neither gets what he pays for nor pays a common price for what he gets. In the New York Region as elsewhere, he buys schools though he may have no children, roadways though he may not own an automobile, museums he may never visit, and hospitals he may not require. Nor does he pay for the services he receives on a basis equal to that of his fellows, but according to his presumed capacity to pay, crudely expressed in a politically constructed revenue system.

All this is justified of course in a concept of common purposes, a "public interest" or "the general welfare." But as real as the general welfare may be, the notion lacks the sharp distinction that exists between buyer and seller in the private economy, where each man knows his role in a transaction. In its place is the schizophrenic figure of the taxpayer, acutely conscious of what he pays to the government, but understandably suspicious of the "civilization" he receives in return. In the last analysis, his dissatisfaction with particular public products can be expressed in only a general way: a massive reversal in electoral behavior, a condemnation of those responsible for the general budget, or, more fundamentally, a revolt against the system.

Even public institutions expressly designed to "look and function" like private enterprises are understood best in terms of the calculus of power and the interplay of group influence. The great public corporations of the Region and the hundreds of special districts are established to provide particular services at the option of the individual. They depend on income derived from individual purchases of their services, and they are created with the explicit objectives of "keeping their programs out of politics." Yet the most businesslike of these agencies faces the reality that it exists only so long as influential political interests support, or at least tolerate, its existence. It suffers the indignities of living in a goldfish bowl in order to gain general, often inarticulate, support from the public at large and it faces always the danger of sporadic attacks by other envious agencies. And its officials, unlike those of a private corporation, expect with some confidence that dissolution will not result if, by some perilous circumstance, costs exceed revenue. Other sources of revenue will ultimately be found.

In explaining the behavior of the Region's political economy, then, we must do what some writers on municipal affairs have not done—abandon the assumptions of the Age of Reason. One cannot show how governments in fact behave by assuming the existence of the conscientious citizen rationally striving to do his duty, or the divisibility of public goods and services on a unit basis, or full knowledge on the part of each citizen of the character of his government's expenditures and receipts. The guidelines are in fact not very precise nor easily quantifiable.

So at rockbottom the significance of the Service State becomes this: as more and more resources pass from the private sector to the public sector, the process which determines their use changes from that of the marketplace to the uncertain world of politics.

SERVICE STATES AND SERVICE STATES

Decisions in the public sector, then, are made by groups that compromise to obtain benefits which are not equally enjoyed by all. The groups do not interact haphazardly, however, nor are their compromises accidental flashes of the moment. Instead, preferences are collected, budgets processed, and services allocated by systematic contacts and calculated agreements.

Participant groups engaging recurrently in these relations can be thought of as "systems." And "systems" making public decisions in the New York Metropolitan Region are diverse and countless. Some of them are internal in nature, existing within every group, institution, or political jurisdiction. So Wallace Sayre and Herbert Kaufman describe the municipality of New York City as a struggle among contestants in the population of the city, in its parties, and in its bureaucracy for prizes which government alone can offer.[20] Other systems are largely external in character—the shifting alliances among the Region's elite groups which Norton Long has characterized as a series of games in which "the players in one game make use of the players in another, and are, in turn, made use of by them." [21] Still other systems find expression in the battles waged between the City and the Port of New York Authority over respective responsibilities in port development, and in the jostling among the agencies concerned with the planning and construction of the Region's transportation network.

Systems can be informal in the sense that they involve groups and institutions which make no open declarations of political objectives but take part, for example, in the negotiations associated with a municipal bond issue or the acquisition of land destined to be a shopping center. But some systems are conducted by the most stylized rules and procedures, such as the procedures leading to zoning ordinances, or the procedures under which a municipality applies for a federal grant. And when the panorama of Regional politics and governments is unfolded, all sorts and kinds of systems come into view, each explicable in its own terms and each contributing to an explanation of the behavior of the Region's policy.

For our purposes, the two great systems we identified earlier are most relevant: the "local governments" and the "Regional enterprises." For any given program the Regional enterprises can be fairly quickly listed. In transportation, for example, the central actors are the Port of New York Authority, the Triborough Bridge and Tunnel Authority, the New York Transit Authority, the three state highway departments, and the U.S. Bureau of Public Roads.* But the "local government" system is a far more varied and complicated apparatus for decision-making.[22]

At the center of the "local" system is New York City, which swallows up five counties.** To the east and north are the seven suburban counties of New York, including by Census count 801 governmental units within their borders, and the 55 local units of Fairfield County, Connecticut. To the west and south are the 606 local units of the nine New Jersey counties.

By legal standards the New York portion of the Region is undoubtedly the most complex. New York City encompasses the broadest array of legal responsibilities within a single formal structure. Though the five counties have judicial functions and the of-

---

* Actually the Triborough and Transit Authorities are agencies of New York City, and their expenditures are often lumped into the municipal total; but they are semi-autonomous, highly specialized, and far-ranging in their effects, and therefore are best analyzed as "Regional enterprises" along with the bi-state Port of New York Authority.

** New York County (borough of Manhattan), Bronx County (borough of the Bronx), Queens County (borough of Queens), Kings County (borough of Brooklyn), and Richmond County (borough of Richmond), which is better known as Staten Island.

fices of the five borough presidents supervise street paving and certain other activities, the municipality itself is the predominant government for local affairs, operating even the schools as a municipal department.

In New York State outside New York City, responsibilities for public functions are divided among counties, cities, towns, villages, school districts, and other special districts. Generally speaking the counties have major responsibilities with respect to tax assessment and collection, highways, courts, public works, welfare, and planning. In Westchester, Nassau, and most recently Suffolk, special county charters have streamlined the structure of the Board of Supervisors, established a county executive, and placed increasing responsibilities in the county rather than the smaller units. But where cities exist within county borders—for example, Yonkers and White Plains in Westchester County—almost every local function is likely to be carried out by the municipality. Towns have important duties in licensing, zoning, property records, parks and playgrounds, and streets. Depending on the circumstances, villages may assume town functions or concentrate on particular slices of town functions—for example, traffic control, recreation, some aspects of zoning and planning, and limited welfare activities. Special districts are primarily engaged in operating schools and in public utility and protection services—water, light, sewage, garbage, and fire-fighting, though they may also undertake recreational and parking activities.

But no hard and fast rules exist with respect to the divisions of functions among New York governments. To illustrate, the relations between town and village are individually tailored. Some towns have no villages at all; in others the boundary lines of town and village are coterminous; and in still others the town is simply a federation of villages which embrace the entire area of the town. Some counties abound with special districts of all shapes and sizes. Others assign the same services to the more general units of government.

In New Jersey, though the official names of local units are as numerous as in New York State, the allocation of duties is far more regular. With variations according to population size, the boroughs, villages, towns, townships, and cities to the west and south of Manhattan all carry out roughly the same array of public services. School districts are apt to be coterminous with municipal boundaries. Other special districts are scarcer than in New York State, averaging less than five a county. County governments are not as active. Multiplicity in New Jersey is a function of geography; the territorial jurisdictions are much smaller, reaching their extreme in Bergen County where 246 square miles of land are divided among 70 units of government.

Fairfield County introduces still another pattern for the formal assignment of public responsibilities. Here, outside the city limits of the six largest municipalities, the New England heritage has established the town as the central instrument of government. The Connecticut town is far more important than its New York counterpart. Its activities are usually more cohesively organized and are directed by a much smaller governing board. Its legal responsibilities extend even to public education—though the school committees in New England have a tradition of *de facto* if not legal independence. The number of special districts is proportionately far less than elsewhere in the Region, and the square mileage of single jurisdictions is greater.*

Besides variations in the way local governments are legally organized, differences in philosophies between the state governments separate the performance of New Jersey and New York local governments. New Jersey has been traditionally a "no new tax" state, one of the three in the nation with neither a personal income tax, a general sales tax, nor a gross receipts tax, and this attitude affects the character of its local public sector. Dedicated "to the goal of disproving the widely held belief that property taxes are more easily replaced than repaired," New Jersey pro-

* But alas, Fairfield is not greater in the usefulness of its government statistics. The difficulty of obtaining comparable figures on expenditures has forced us to omit Fairfield from much of the analysis in this book.

ceeds—according to a state commission as recently as 1958—with
"no clearly defined fiscal policy . . . no basic fiscal philosophy . . .
the most regressive of all tax bases . . . and a mass of inequities that
are almost unbelievable as the basis for the support of public services in a modern industrial state." [23] New Jersey's tax pattern reflects a reliance upon local units of government to carry out major
service activities. Its state grant-in-aid programs down to the present time have been relatively modest; it has shown a disinclination to experiment with new local governmental structures; and
it has sanctioned public salaries and public services at considerably lower levels than in the neighboring states.

In contrast, New York State has displayed a far greater disposition toward innovation at the local level and toward buttressing
local resources with state revenues. "Over the past several years,"
the State Fiscal Study Commission of 1955 observed, "New York
has taken a number of significant steps to fortify local government finances against fluctuations in the economy." The state has
abandoned almost entirely the practice of aiding municipalities
by giving them a cut of specific taxes which rise and fall sharply,
"and has evolved a system of grants geared partly to compensating for economic inequalities, partly to matching expenditures,
and partly to counter cyclical protection." [24] And, in the words of
the New York State–New York City Fiscal Relations Committee, "the enveloping governmental relations" between state and
localities "have changed and are changing." The national, state,
and local governments "are participating simultaneously in several great functional fields." The committee "commends the twin
concepts of interdependence and decentralization as the pillars of
a new system of governmental relations." [25] Thus, consistently,
New York has established more comprehensive and more liberal
grant programs to support local activities, and has shown a disposition to revamp county organizational structures within the
Metropolitan Region and to establish new agencies and districts
as special needs arise.

Still another kind of variety marks the local governments of the

New York Metropolitan Region—wide differences in the amounts of taxes and expenditures. In 1955, one municipality spent $4.30 per capita for current operations while another was spending $351.20. One jurisdiction was levying $24.60 per capita in local real property taxes; another, $376.89. The New York municipalities outside New York City spent considerably more than New Jersey municipalities, on the average. And the range of spending differences among the New York governments was much wider than the range among the New Jersey ones.

Finally, the different sub-areas of the Region exhibit its different political styles. In New York City, municipal elections are partisan in nature, with the preponderant Democratic majority often sharply limited in its actions by internal factional divisions and by the watchdog posture of the Liberal Party, which sometimes participates in Democratic affairs and sometimes joins forces with the Republican minority. In the City, too, important policy decisions are the responsibility of a highly organized and generally professional bureaucracy, possessing independent bases of political support in specific programs. At the center of the stage, mediating among party factions, pressure groups, and the main centers of bureaucratic power (such as the Park Commissioner and the Police Commissioner) is the Office of the Mayor. As a result of the 1938 City Charter and the interpretation of that instrument, notably by La Guardia, the Mayoralty and the Board of Estimate together represent a focus of power rarely found in American local government.[26]

Outside the City, other styles abound. Impressionistically, one may identify a spirit of professionalism in public service, often associated with Westchester County.[27] One may trace the atrophy of old-style machine organization, once dominant in Hudson County, where, as one observer has said, a transition is underway from "a one-party county with a rather rigid hierarchy and an undisputed leader" to a "two-party situation in which the nonorganization voter is becoming at least as important as the organization voter," "each party has at least two important factions," and "a relative decline in the effectiveness of the ward and political clubs has occurred." [28]

Alternatively, the style may be representative of courthouse cliques which survived the transformation of their jurisdiction from rural to suburban. The *Bergen Evening Record,* in analyzing Bergen problems, has characterized political activity in some of the small governments as "the vested interest in the status quo." [29] Again, local political behavior may be a function of the different attitudes and objectives of old residents versus newcomers, or stay-at-homes against commuters. It may be characterized by the amateur dabbling in which part-time public officials assume local office in the same spirit in which they direct the Community Chest Drive. But by whatever indices are available—by party strength, voter participation, sources of political leadership, or predominance of career employees—the Region offers an assortment of brands unparalleled in any other section of the nation.

Given such differences in formal powers, structure, area, taxing and spending levels, and political habits, it is not surprising that the local government system does not produce common policies and decisions for the Region as a whole. Nor is it surprising that municipalities apparently inhabited by the same type of people, in roughly the same stage of development, have acquired individual public sectors all their own. To some observers, the surprising thing is that conditions of political stability and economic development are maintained at all. For the local system is hundreds and hundreds of decision-centers, represented by individual governments. Each is bent on maintaining its autonomy and each fashions its own responses to the insistent public pressures that are generated as the nation's largest metropolitan area becomes even larger and rearranges itself on the landscape. Yet the responses to the pressures are not altogether arbitrary and individualistic. The responses are sometimes even predictable—once we identify the pressures.

2

Pressures on the Public Sector

A FOREST FROM THE TREES

No one will mistake the Cook's tour of the Region's political economy we have just completed for a systematic explanation of its substance or the behavior pattern of its 1400 managers. So far we have scarcely dipped below the surface of random observation to tackle the really difficult questions about its links with the private sector. What are the main forces behind the rise of the Service State? What accounts for the wild variety in spending and tax patterns? How much is "economic" and "social"—and how much is "political"?

Our first assumption is the hardly novel one that there *is* a strong and explicable association between the community environment and governmental behavior. The very nature of municipal services—schools, streets, utilities, fire and police forces—suggests a close tie. One may expect a national military budget to shift abruptly up and down as a Khrushchev smiles or rages, or expenditures for veterans to be more a function of the political vigor of veterans' organizations than of the absolute number of veterans. But the municipal "bundle of services" should, one suspects, behave more predictably. At any point of time, we can feel sure that, where there are children, there are also schools; where there are houses, there are also utilities; where there are things of value, there are also policemen. And these relations can also be expected to hold up over time. When children increase, schools must increase.

But it is not simply a matter of enlarging programs already in full swing. As farms are turned into subdivisions, as population density increases, as traffic volumes grow, more and more activities once performed privately become, quite understandably, public in nature. Public water systems replace wells; public welfare programs supplement private charities; fire departments replace volunteer brigades.

These shifts in activities from private to public auspices occasion shifts in the allocation of resources.[1] So ever since Adolph Wagner and Henry C. Adams formulated their "laws" of increasing governmental activities a half-century ago, it has been axiomatic in the annals of public finance that the more "urbanized" a society becomes, the greater the share of income devoted to public activities.[2] Or, in the contemporary language of Solomon Fabricant, the increased importance of public expenditures comes about as a result of a "concomitance of economic growth . . . population change—its absolute growth, density, shifts in composition, ceaseless movements—advancing technology, giving rise to increased income, urbanization, industrialization, the resulting change in the climate of opinion."[3] And the growth process, of course, unfolds continually in new directions, one generation building compact, congested cities, the next generation disgorging the residents and businesses back upon the hinterland.

Of course, to recognize in a general way that the government-environment link in the Region is strong is not to specify the nature of this relation. Granted that an urban environment imposes greater demands on a government than a rural environment and that a "concomitance of economic growth" is a handy twenty-five-words-or-less explanation for changes in government expenditures, these notions do not get us very far. The urban "concomitance" is a catch-all. It includes ubiquitous influences, affecting the operations of local governments throughout the Region, and indeed the United States. Thus, rises in municipal budgets are often due to inflation; and policy decisions of the federal government have general effects—decisions, for example, to guarantee home mortgages, to raise the interest rate, to assume welfare responsibilities. The catch-all includes at the same time phenomena with highly local effects. The number of residents served by a government, their age distribution, occupations, income, fixed assets, and pattern of physical settlement can vary widely from place to place and time to time, and each of these characteristics can have important effects on the scope and nature of public activity. Finally, the urbanization pattern in any particular jurisdiction may be powerfully influenced by the way the political boundary lines have been drawn— a kind of environmental gerrymandering which may disrupt the "natural" sequence of neighborhood development and distort the links between the private and the public sectors which might ordinarily be expected. Our task in this chapter is to sort out these influences to see if we can distinguish those which most affect the public sector.

As we begin our analysis, a few words are in order about problems in evidence and inference. First off, we will rely largely on expenditure and revenue figures to reflect the scope and character of government operations. These figures have their limitations—for some purposes, public employment figures or program descriptions are better—but they represent the most comprehensive and reliable data that can be compared with what we know about the social and economic characteristics of the environment. Second, even our expenditure and revenue information is not all we would wish. We have no comprehensive financial statistics tracing long-term trends in government experiences, nor for that matter time-series for some of the environmental factors we suspect are important. Even for the short run, there is a dearth of data in some respects: Connecticut financial statistics in the detail we require are not available on a comparable basis with those of New York and New Jersey, and in some respects our information on municipalities in the outlying counties of the Region is sketchy.

These deficiencies mean that we can observe the environmental forces in action only imperfectly and that we can rarely isolate their development over time as the process of urbanization goes on.

What we can do is to borrow a method from our economist colleagues as they described the process of neighborhood evolution in the first volume of the New York Metropolitan Region Study.[4] In that analysis, the sequential stages of neighborhood growth and change were traced by making a cross-section of the present structure of the Region and assuming that the present condition of a number of different neighborhoods was a rough indication of the cycle that a single neighborhood goes through over a long period of time. Here, with modifications appropriate for our purposes, we undertake the same approach: we study the environmental forces currently at work in various combinations in different communities, and then we examine the current patterns of governmental expenditures in the same communities. The result, we believe, throws some light on the underlying forces that are tending to increase the size and substance of the Region's political economy from one decade to the next.

PEOPLE, PROPERTY, AND PUBLIC SPENDING

In our most ambitious attempt to relate community characteristics to community expenditures, we selected a sample of 64 middle-sized municipalities in the five New Jersey counties closest to the center of the Region. More specifically, the sample consists of all places with populations between 10,000 and 85,000 in the counties of Hudson, Essex, Union, Bergen, and Passaic. About a dozen of them are cities, the rest townships and boroughs, but for our purposes the distinction is unimportant, for they do not overlap in territory and they all have municipal governments which provide a full range of services. The four largest cities in the New Jersey portion of the Region—namely, Newark, Jersey City, Elizabeth, and Paterson—are too populous to gain admittance to our sample, but the group does contain some other old cities, such as Hoboken and Bayonne, as well as newer communities like Fairlawn and Saddle Brook. The 64 municipalities are shown in the accompanying map (Chart 2).

Choosing a sample of community *characteristics* was a more for-

Chart 2
Sample of 64 Middle-Sized New Jersey Municipalities

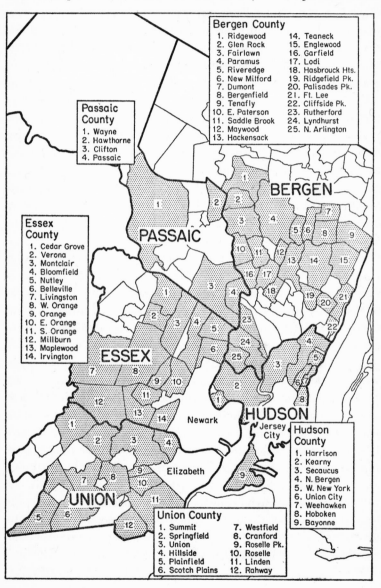

Bergen County
1. Ridgewood
2. Glen Rock
3. Fairlawn
4. Paramus
5. Riveredge
6. New Milford
7. Dumont
8. Bergenfield
9. Tenafly
10. E. Paterson
11. Saddle Brook
12. Maywood
13. Hackensack
14. Teaneck
15. Englewood
16. Garfield
17. Lodi
18. Hasbrouck Hts.
19. Ridgefield Pk.
20. Palisades Pk.
21. Ft. Lee
22. Cliffside Pk.
23. Rutherford
24. Lyndhurst
25. N. Arlington

Passaic County
1. Wayne
2. Hawthorne
3. Clifton
4. Passaic

Essex County
1. Cedar Grove
2. Verona
3. Montclair
4. Bloomfield
5. Nutley
6. Belleville
7. Livingston
8. W. Orange
9. Orange
10. E. Orange
11. S. Orange
12. Millburn
13. Maplewood
14. Irvington

Hudson County
1. Harrison
2. Kearny
3. Secaucus
4. N. Bergen
5. W. New York
6. Union City
7. Weehawken
8. Hoboken
9. Bayonne

Union County
1. Summit
2. Springfield
3. Union
4. Hillside
5. Plainfield
6. Scotch Plains
7. Westfield
8. Cranford
9. Roselle Pk.
10. Roselle
11. Linden
12. Rahway

midable task than choosing the communities themselves. We have
, seen that the very notion of urbanization implies a host of conditions and forces. As Fabricant has emphasized, the forces are
closely interrelated and their properties are not always clear. Density, income, employment, manufacturing, commerce all coexist to
make urbanization meaningful. Thus, the effect of a single element
of urbanization on variations in government activity may be difficult to isolate. Suppose, for example, we describe every community
according to indices signifying the number of persons per acre, the
proportion of persons over 65, and the proportion of land used for
industrial activities. Then suppose we find that two communities
of the same size rank high in all three indices—and also rank high
in government expenditures. Which characteristic is the most important in accounting for the high spending? Is it the density of
population, the age distribution, or the degree of industrialization?
Or is the question a barren one because the three characteristics so
often rise and fall together that a reference to one may be a reference to all? And still a further complication—quite familiar to
statisticians—is that one dare not assert dogmatically that any or all
of the characteristics "causes" the high spending, because in some
degree the high spending may "cause" the characteristic. We can
and must draw inferences about cause and effect, but all we can
prove is whether there is a faithful correlation or association between certain characteristics and certain spending levels.

The instrument by which we can begin to disentangle the snarl
is the mathematical technique called factor analysis. The technique does not solve the problem of cause and effect, but in measur-
ing the degree of association between community characteristics and
public expenditures, it makes impressive headway. The technical
reader will find in Appendix B a further description of what we did.
Briefly, the task was to boil down a large number of community characteristics—many of them very similar to one another in their relations to expenditure levels—into a small number of community characteristics that are independent of one another and therefore can be

accurately compared in importance. We took twenty measures that are customarily used to characterize the environment and reduced them mathematically to seven indices. In doing this, we did not simply sort the twenty characteristics into seven groups, each containing a certain number of characteristics *in toto*, for it would be impossible to arrive at mutually independent factors in that crude manner. On the contrary, each factor gathers together community characteristics only to the degree that they are correlated with one another—that is, only to the degree that they rise and fall together as one looks from one community to another.

Following are our seven factors. The names affixed to them should be understood for what they are—identification tags, not complete descriptions of the contents. (In factor analysis the labor of giving birth is often easier than naming the baby.)

COMMUNITY SIZE. This conspicuous but nebulous factor goes beyond nose-counting of inhabitants. It also leans heavily on the number of pupils enrolled in the schools, the value of property, and the amount of state aid to the municipality. And it includes lighter dashes of the other community characteristics—each one according to the degree in which it varies with the rest. COMMUNITY SIZE is the most prominent index of all, bearing a closer relation to governmental expenditures than all other factors combined. In another way, however, it is surely the least interesting, because it reflects the perfectly obvious fact that the more persons and property a municipality services, the larger are its expenditures. Indeed, COMMUNITY SIZE is so faithful a bedfellow to public spending that one of our aims must be to lift it out of the way—hold it constant, so to speak—in order to measure whatever other factors are underneath.

INDUSTRIALIZATION reflects primarily the proportion of land devoted to industrial purposes, secondarily the value of business and industrial property (and of course other community characteristics to the degree they are correlated).

HOUSING DENSITY. This factor, like all the others, includes traces of many characteristics, but mainly it reflects the number of dwelling units per acre of residentially developed land and the proportion of residential land devoted to multifamily structures.

AGE. Here is an index that is pulled upward by a large proportion of people over 65 years old, and downward by a large proportion under 14. Strictly, the factor pertains to age distribution of residents only, but observation suggests that, in our 64-community sample at least, a high AGE factor is usually accompanied by aged housing and public facilities.

LOW-INCOME PREVALENCE points to communities with an especially high incidence of incomes under $2,000—even after the low incomes of people over 65 have been allowed for.

RESIDENTIAL AFFLUENCE reflects not only the residents' income and educational attainments but also is highly suggestive of the character of the neighborhoods they live in.

LAND RESERVE. This is quite unrelated to HOUSING DENSITY, for it has nothing to do with how crowded the present residential areas are. It signifies, instead, the residential "potential"—the proportion of suitable residential land that is undeveloped.

In Chart 3 we summarize the relation between these factors and the operating expenditures of our 64 middle-sized New Jersey municipalities. The average total operating expenditures of the municipalities was a little over $3 million in 1955. In the chart the total variance around this average is expressed as 100 per cent. All but 4 per cent can be associated with our seven factors. About 83 per cent of the variance is associated with COMMUNITY SIZE. When this dominant factor is held to one side, the rest of the variance is associated principally with INDUSTRIALIZATION, HOUSING DENSITY, and AGE, in that order.

But we need not stop with operating expenditures in the aggregate. In Chart 4 we apply the same technique to twelve types of operating expenditures—for schools, police, fire protection, and so on. Here, too, COMMUNITY SIZE is the dominant factor, but the degree of its dominance ranges from 92 per cent in the case of "schools, except debt service" down to little more than 50 per cent in the case of health, welfare, and recreation, and only 37 per cent in the case of debt service. When we set COMMUNITY SIZE over to the edge of the picture, thus removing differences in size among the 64 communities, we find that INDUSTRIALIZATION again is the factor associated most prominently with most types of expenditures, especially the types involving the largest outlays. But the patterns are not by any

Chart 3

Relation between Community Characteristics and Total Operating Expenditures of 64 Middle-Sized New Jersey Municipalities, 1955

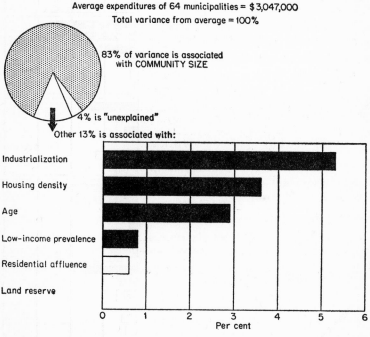

Average expenditures of 64 municipalities = $3,047,000
Total variance from average = 100%

83% of variance is associated with COMMUNITY SIZE

4% is "unexplained"

Other 13% is associated with:

Industrialization
Housing density
Age
Low-income prevalence
Residential affluence
Land reserve

Per cent

Notes: LAND RESERVE bears no measurable relation to total expenditures, though it is related to particular types of spending (see Chart 4). White bar signifies that RESIDENTIAL AFFLUENCE—when other factors are held constant—is associated with low total expenditures rather than high ones. The 64 municipalities are shown in map (Chart 2). Sources of data and further explanation of technique will be found in Appendix B.

Chart 4 Relation between Community Characteristics and Particular

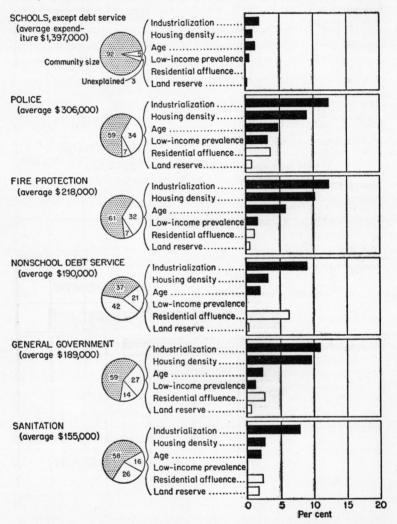

SCHOOLS, except debt service
(average expenditure $1,397,000)

Community size 92
Unexplained 3

Industrialization ....
Housing density ....
Age ....
Low-income prevalence
Residential affluence...
Land reserve ....

POLICE
(average $306,000)

59   34
7

Industrialization ....
Housing density ....
Age ....
Low-income prevalence
Residential affluence...
Land reserve...........

FIRE PROTECTION
(average $218,000)

61   32
7

Industrialization ....
Housing density ....
Age ....
Low-income prevalence
Residential affluence...
Land reserve ....

NONSCHOOL DEBT SERVICE
(average $190,000)

37   21
42

Industrialization ....
Housing density ....
Age ....
Low-income prevalence
Residential affluence...
Land reserve ....

GENERAL GOVERNMENT
(average $189,000)

59   27
14

Industrialization ....
Housing density ....
Age ....
Low-income prevalence
Residential affluence...
Land reserve ....

SANITATION
(average $155,000)

58   16
26

Industrialization ....
Housing density ....
Age ....
Low-income prevalence
Residential affluence...
Land reserve ....

0   5   10   15   20
Per cent

Notes: For each type of expenditure, total variance from 64-community average = 100 per cent; pie chart shows percentages associated with COMMUNITY SIZE and "unexplained"; bars show how much is associated with six other factors. Absence of a bar means there is no measurable relation. A white bar signifies that in this instance the factor—when other factors are held con-

Types of Operating Expenditures of 64 New Jersey Municipalities, 1955

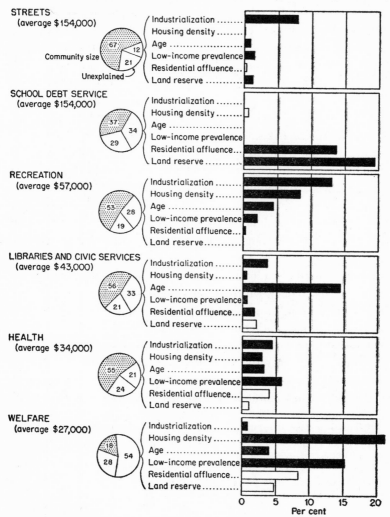

stant—is associated with low expenditures rather than high ones. The 64 municipalities are shown in map (Chart 2). "Libraries and civic services" is the same as the category which the New Jersey government calls "Educational (exclusive of school districts)." Sources of data and further explanation of technique will be found in Appendix B.

means alike in all spending categories. Welfare expenditures, for example, bear a strong relation to HOUSING DENSITY and LOW-INCOME PREVALENCE, and hardly any to INDUSTRIALIZATION. Payments on school debt appear to be especially high in communities where there is a big potential for residential development and where the residents are affluent. On the other hand, RESIDENTIAL AFFLUENCE seems generally associated with a *lower* level of spending for health, welfare, police, nonschool debt service, general government, and sanitation.

The technique of factor analysis, by drawing our attention to industrialization, confirms a very common interpretation of the relation between economic development and local government. A highly industrialized community suggests the presence of business property which, per square foot of land, yields assessed valuations higher than any alternative kind of land use, and these can be readily and lucratively tapped through the existing tax system. Business property typically pays more to a government than it absorbs in service.* In these circumstances, a local political system has the happy prospect of spending tax money which is not directly extracted from the residents and which, from industry's point of view, is not a heavy burden compared with other taxes and costs of other kinds.

Lest we give a one-sided picture, we must recognize too that an industrial area not only engenders revenues but in some circumstances—and for some public programs—may require higher expenditures than a nonindustrial area. But at least our analysis has

---

* This is a general argument widely shared by both the practitioners and theorists of public finance. It finds support in the findings of a recent study of the impact of industrial development on the tax structure and local government services on Long Island. In Nassau County, for instance, the wealth densities (assessed value per square foot of land) of industrial land and of commercial property have been found to be, respectively, 130 per cent and 250 per cent upwards of residential property. Similarly, commerce and industry paid upwards of 270 per cent of the cost of services extended to them, while the corresponding figure for residential taxpayers was only 83.6 per cent. See W. N. Leonard and W. F. Clarke, *Does Industry Pay Its Way?* (The Long Island Industrial Survey, Vol. 2; Hempstead, L. I.: Hofstra College Bureau of Business and Community Research, 1956).

done nothing to demolish the rule of thumb of the practicing public official that the "perfect" town is an industrial park run by automation.

Housing density and the prevalence of older people, however, present more sobering dimensions of the environment, for they clearly intimate government spending not from a sense of opulence but from obvious and articulated needs. Tightly packed settlements make the provision of established municipal services more complicated and they require a larger number of services: full-fledged fire and police protection, more elaborate traffic controls, more inspections to ensure the public's health and safety, formal governmental action to provide recreational activity. And the prevalence of older people bespeaks not only the service requirements of the aged but also, more generally, situations in which schools and other capital facilities are likely to be both obsolete and oversized, where in effect, the entrenched municipal establishment is bigger and more costly than the population requires. In short, the New Jersey sample suggests that the critical forces at work may have the character of both supply and demand. Generally speaking, it reports that "them that has, spends," but "having" the sources of revenue brings responsibilities which also increase the tendency to spend.

We can supplement this first survey with evidence drawn from other municipalities of the Region, though in these instances neither our data nor our techniques are so elegant. For 65 smaller New Jersey communities, with populations of 1,000 to 10,000, we calculated differences—as of the mid-1950's—in (1) population, (2) the number of dwelling units per acre of residentially developed land, (3) residential property valuations, and (4) business property valuations. (The property values were adjusted to eliminate differences due merely to different assessment practices.) Then we determined which of these four measures—separately or in combination—would have served as the best "predictors" of nonschool municipal expenditures of that same time. By far the most important measure turned out to be business property valuations. Residential property valuations and population carried some weight, while dwelling-unit density was not at all significant as a "predictor." *

In New York State much the same situation exists, at least on the basis of the evidence available to us. Chart 5, for example, makes a report concerning the 82 New York places having the status of towns —for example, Hempstead, Smithtown, Eastchester, and Greenburgh. The chart relates property values to local government expenditures, using per capita figures as a device for controlling variations in population. Though industrial property cannot here be separated from other property, the bars do depict a strong association between expenditures and valuations.

Wherever we can make test-borings to compare local public expenditures with specific environmental characteristics, then, property values bear a close relation to expenditures. A high level of expenditures occurs most frequently when relatively ample industrial assets exist, particularly when these are amenable to appropriation by the existing tax system. Beyond the industrialization effect, however, other dimensions intrude to complicate the analysis. Housing density represents a different kind of impetus to spending, for people living close together create needs which have to be met if minimum conditions of political stability are to be satisfied. Frequently this characteristic is supplemented by other demand-oriented ones, such as prevalence of older people and low-income families. In the case of schools, residential affluence takes on special relevance. And in all instances, there is a substantial residue of differences which remain unrelated to any index we have concocted. Nonetheless, our first excur-

---

* The technique used here was that of multiple regression.

The estimating equation for 1955 nonschool operating expenditures (Y):
$$Y = 21.9 + 0.0138X_1 + 4.47X_2 + 6.27X_3 + 3.12X_4,$$
where X_1 stands for 1955 population (mean 4,799, standard deviation 2,345), X_2 for 1955 residential property valuation (mean \$16.7 million, standard deviation \$8.4 million), X_3 for 1955 business property valuation (mean \$9.7 million, standard deviation \$13.2 million), and X_4 for dwelling-unit density (mean 5.36 dwelling units per residential acre, standard deviation 3.56). When adjusted for the differing dispersions of the several variables, the regression coefficients ("beta coefficients") indicate the relative weight of each variable in estimating expenditures. These coefficients were 0.260, 0.309, 0.660, and 0.089 respectively.

Chart 5

Relation between Per Capita Market Value of Property and Per Capita Total Expenditures of Local Government Units in New York Towns of New York Metropolitan Region, 1955

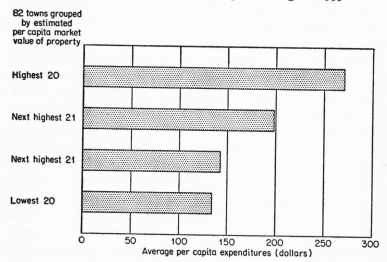

Notes: Expenditures include both operating and capital outlays made by governments of towns, by the villages and special districts within the towns, and by county governments as allocated by towns. Source of data: New York State Comptroller, *Special Report on Municipal Affairs—1955.*

sions do arm us with a notion of the three or four environmental characteristics whose variations among communities at a given point in time are most intimately related to variations in expenditures.

STAGES OF GROWTH

But how do these forces operate over time and in what combinations? Since historical comparisons between environmental characteristics and expenditures are not available, the answer must be sought by studying present-day communities in different stages of development. The pressures on government in the new Levittowns and the pressures in the five boroughs of New York City obviously differ—and we must say how they differ and with what results.

In a broad-brush fashion, one can expect that as the process of urbanization goes on, public expenditures rise absolutely and also in relation to private spending. The oldest parts of the Region can be expected to have highest expenditures, for here the greatest concentration of industrialization, population—indeed all the pressures for public spending—are amassed in largest quantity. This is true even when the obvious factor of population is removed from consideration by the use of per capita figures. The pattern is manifest in Chart 6, which shows per capita operating expenditures—as defined in the United States Census—by major zones of the Region and by counties. The New York City figure of $233 is the highest in the Region, and as the eye moves outward across the counties in almost any direction, the spending per inhabitant diminishes. It does not diminish at uniform rates in all directions; for example, the "New York Inner" counties of Nassau and Westchester spend more per capita than "New Jersey Inner" counties in similar stages of development—a discrepancy which we have already ascribed to political differences. Nevertheless the link between centrality and per capita governmental spending is unmistakable, particularly in the figures for zones.

What the map reflects is the different stages of evolution which now exist in the Region. At the fringes, the neighborhoods are mostly at the frontier of new development, the stage of single-family residential construction. Closer in, there are communities of advanced urban development with sizable amounts of land devoted to industry and commerce, large middle-class neighborhoods of apartments and row houses, and heavy residential densities. In New York City and the old cities nearby, there are neighborhoods that have gone over the hill and are in the process of decline, wrestling increasingly with conditions of obsolescence and congestion. These words express more than difficulty in movement or access; they signify an absence of open space, a large proportion of old apartments and three-deckers, and many families crammed into houses intended for single occupancies. Interspersed across the Region are areas where a young and growing population inhabits mass residential developments with their inevitable shopping centers, or where the land is almost exclusively devoted to homes of the wealthy.

Chart 6

Per Capita Operating Expenditures of Local Governments in Zones and Counties of New York Metropolitan Region, 1957

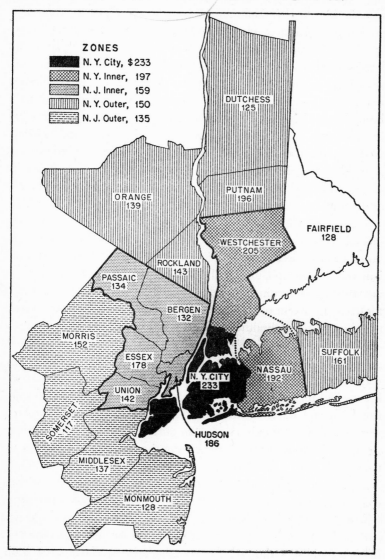

ZONES
- N. Y. City, $233
- N. Y. Inner, 197
- N. J. Inner, 159
- N. Y. Outer, 150
- N. J. Outer, 135

DUTCHESS 125

ORANGE 139

PUTNAM 196

FAIRFIELD 128

WESTCHESTER 205

ROCKLAND 143

PASSAIC 134

BERGEN 132

MORRIS 152

ESSEX 178

SUFFOLK 161

N. Y. CITY 233

NASSAU 192

UNION 142

SOMERSET 117

HUDSON 186

MIDDLESEX 137

MONMOUTH 128

Sources: Expenditure data from U. S. *1957 Census of Governments* (also see Appendix A); population data estimated on basis of various state reports. Expenditures of Port of New York Authority are not included.

These different neighborhoods, in different periods of evolution, call forth distinct types of governmental activity. The environmental factors—industrialization, density, and the rest—do not simply proceed hand-in-hand as farm acreage is put to urban purposes. Instead, one characteristic or another comes to predominate, and each has its special implication for the public sector. New York City's steadily increasing budget is not a function of increasing population, nor of increasing density, for in recent years the opposite trends have been apparent. Nassau's spectacular postwar rise in public spending is closely correlated to the population's changing age composition as well as its greater number. The seashore communities in Monmouth, actually within the New York Metropolitan Region only by grace of a geographical definition, are reputed to be high spenders because of the impact of their resort activities on property values.

We can gain one kind of insight into the variations in governmental activity as they are associated with different subregional environments by examining current budgets. New York City, with half the Region's population, had over 60 per cent of the Region's governmental operating expenditures in 1957. But the City accounted for over 70 per cent of the Region's current spending for public welfare, hospitals, and health, and lesser proportions for other purposes —all the way down to 38 per cent for sewer maintenance. Chart 7 gives the picture. The closest ring of counties around New York City—that is, the two zones we call New York Inner and New Jersey Inner—had unusually large shares of the Region's expenditures for education and sewer maintenance. The outermost counties, which were responsible for only 11 per cent of total operating expenditures, stretched this to well over 20 per cent in the case of highway maintenance.

More directly we can observe the evolution of public activities in different stages of the growth process by tracing the expenditure pattern of five groups, each consisting of seven or eight communities and each typifying a particular environmental characteristic. The five characteristics thus typified are: high INDUSTRIALIZATION, high HOUSING DENSITY, high RESIDENTIAL AFFLUENCE, low RESIDENTIAL AF-

Chart 7

Local Governments' Major Operating Expenditures,[a] Distributed by Zones [b] of New York Metropolitan Region, 1957

(Region total = 100 per cent)

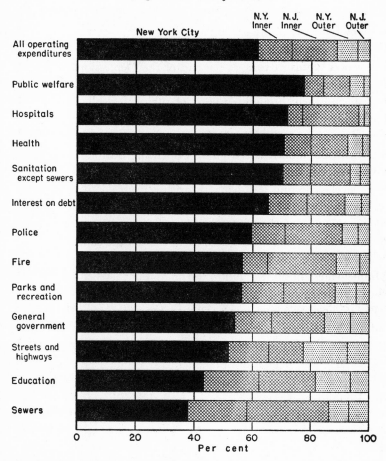

[a] The chart excludes capital outlays for highways, schools, sewers, and hospitals, but small capital outlays of other kinds did creep into the "operating" figures and could not be separated. Expenditures of Port of New York Authority are not included.

[b] The zones are mapped in Chart 6. But in the present instance we threw Fairfield County, Connecticut, into "New York Outer" for statistical convenience.

Source: U. S. *1957 Census of Governments.*

FLUENCE, and rapid population growth between 1945 and 1955.* The next two charts compare the five groups of communities with respect to their per capita operating expenditures during recent years. The amounts have been reduced to constant dollars in order to eliminate the influence of price changes.

Chart 8 traces municipal spending for purposes other than schools. The period begins in 1940, at the end of the Depression when few municipalities were well off; it goes through the "cocoon" period of the war and then through ten years of suburban explosion to 1955. The highly industrialized communities and the ones with dense residential areas operate at the highest per capita municipal expenditures, with the industrialized group evidencing a strong capacity to increase expenditures after 1950. The affluent communities are at a lower level, reflecting less demands arising from population needs; but they are somewhat similar to the industrialized group in their comparative rate of change—suggesting their capacity to withstand the budgetary erosion of inflation. Significantly, the communities of rapid population growth, embroiled in the get-going costs of creating a municipal establishment, fall to the bottom as they begin the process of transformation from rural to urban status.

School expenditures, shown in Chart 9 for a somewhat shorter period, tell a different story—and a less reliable one since capital outlays cannot be separated from operating expenditures. The settled residential municipalities are highest in per capita school spending and have increased their lead over other communities, for their nonschool public needs are not extreme and the backgrounds of their residents indicate a propensity to emphasize education. Industrialized communities with ample resources and less obvious needs follow second. Rapid-growth communities, though they have not matched their more established neighbors, have *had* to respond to the pressures of young and large families. They therefore ranked third at the end of the period, instead of fifth as they did for municipal

---

* The first four of these are calculated by means of factor analysis as before; the rapidity of population growth is a simpler measure. All the communities are drawn from the sample of 64 middle-sized New Jersey communities referred to earlier in the chapter and mapped in Chart 2.

Chart 8

Per Capita Municipal Operating Expenditures, in Constant Dollars, by Five Groups of Middle-Sized New Jersey Municipalities, 1940–1955

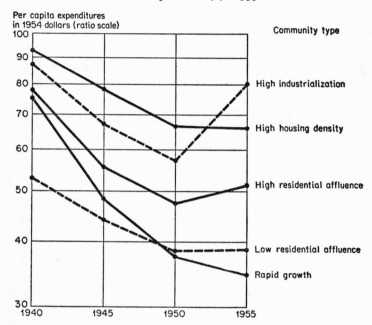

Sources: Expenditure data from New Jersey Department of the Treasury. Figures were changed to constant dollars by means of price deflators for local government purchases of goods and services in U. S. Department of Commerce, *U. S. Income and Output, a Supplement to the Survey of Current Business* (1959). Population data for 1940 and 1950 from U. S. Census; for 1945 and 1955 estimated.

expenditures. High-density and low-status communities bring up the rear.

The evidence at hand, then, shows that the New York Metropolitan Region encompasses a spectrum of environments, each influencing the relative volume and elaborateness of public activities. Older cities, dormitory towns, affluent suburbs, settlements abuilding have quite different public problems and work out their destinies in quite different ways. Although industrialization and housing density are

Chart 9
Per Capita School Expenditures (Operating and Capital), in Constant Dollars, by Five Groups of Middle-Sized New Jersey Municipalities, 1945–1955

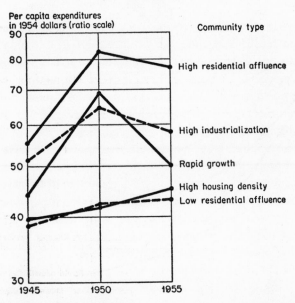

Sources: Same as Chart 8.

hallmarks of areas with well-developed public sectors and although they go far in explaining why expenditures mount, there is plenty of room for deviation, as the chart on school expenditures demonstrates. The sheer magnitude of the Region and the different stages of evolution it encompasses become a first explanation of the variety of experience we have observed.

THE METROPOLITAN MOSAIC: THE SEGREGATION OF RESOURCES AND NEEDS

So far, the explanation of the size and substance of the Region's public sector and the variations within it has been given largely in terms of "natural" evolution. The forces we have identified, the effects they have had on governmental activity, have arisen out of the urban environment, and have been arranged according to what appears to be different stages of development. In effect, we have been single-mindedly tracing the consequences of urban growth on government.

Between the growth process and the political economy, however, there is a feedback relation which introduces an "unnatural" element into our considerations. As Chapter 1 emphasized, the New York Region is more than an urban area—it is a metropolitan area. It is metropolitan in the sense that its five hundred autonomous general governments and almost one thousand other governments with various legal and functional prerogatives share responsibility over the urban complex. Thus, though the separate forces represented by industrial property, density, and the like are inseparably intertwined in the economic and population aspects of this complex, the political and sometimes social identities within the Region are quite distinct. Political boundary lines criss-cross the entire area and interject a number of additional complications into the interaction between economic development and governmental behavior.

Thus, some jurisdictions receive a lion's share of business and industrial wealth; others accept major deposits of population. Some, situated in sparsely settled portions of the Region, face the problems of installing new community facilities and at the same time can hope for a tax windfall from a new plant in a space-hungry industry. Others are little more than clusters of neighborhoods afflicted with the liabilities of old age, and their governments are plagued with problems of blight. The political fact of separateness pulls apart the concomitance of factors which, if taken together, constitute an urban economy. Thus on top of the complications introduced by the different stages of neighborhoods represented in the Region is the further complication that these neighborhoods are something more than collections of peoples. They are municipalities or school districts or villages—legal entities—and this fact, in and of itself, bequeaths a particular identity.

Perhaps the most obvious effect of present governmental arrange-

Chart 10

Distribution of Municipal Operating Expenditures in Two
Hypothetical Communities Differing Only in Size

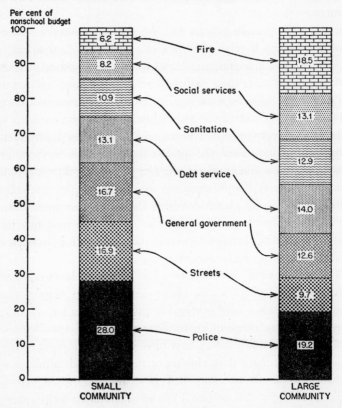

Note: Calculations are based upon the data collected for the 64 middle-sized
New Jersey municipalities mapped in Chart 2. "Social services" include health,
welfare, recreation, and libraries and civic services.

ments is that they are responsible for extreme variation in size
among the jurisdictions—and this fact alone is of some consequence
for our expenditure analysis. The size of the community has a significant bearing upon the relative scope and variety of its major public
programs. Chart 10 depicts, for the sample of 64 middle-sized New

Jersey municipalities, the association of size with the pattern of expenditure allocations of the municipal budget while holding constant every other environmental characteristic.* With variations in these characteristics controlled, the smaller governments appear to concentrate their nonschool budgets on police protection and street maintenance, and to require a larger administrative overhead to do so. The larger ones allocate their money more evenly across the array of services and give relatively more emphasis to other programs—notably fire protection, sanitation, and social services.

By other calculations we concluded that there seems to be a critical threshold in the size of a jurisdiction—somewhere around 10,000 population—below which differences in expenditure levels appear primarily a function of the availability of revenue rather than of needs and pressures. Holding constant the value of residential and business property, we found that dwelling-unit density, which is symbolic among the 64 middle-sized New Jersey municipalities of a particular cluster of service requirements, exerted no significant impact upon expenditure levels among the 65 smaller jurisdictions co-existing in the same counties.**

The middle-sized New Jersey municipalities then are not just the

* What we have done here is to assume initially that two hypothetical communities, exactly alike, have exactly average endowments of the seven community characteristics we identified earlier in the chapter. Being located at "dead center," these "absolutely average" communities could be expected to allocate proportions of the total nonschool operating budget to the various functions exactly equal to the mean proportions we have empirically ascertained for this sample. Chart 10 illustrates what would happen to the distribution of expenditures in the two municipalities if we made them different—and extremely so—only in respect to COMMUNITY SIZE. Technically speaking, we have moved one community two standard deviations above the mean and the other two standard deviations below the mean.

** Looking into the possibility that the apparent lack of a significant relation between density and expenditures among the small municipalities may be a reflection of the fact that about half of the small communities are located in upper Bergen County (where dwelling-unit densities are generally low and may fail to attain certain critical values), we have selected two samples of municipalities for closer study. One was made up of 35 municipalities under 10,000 in the New Jersey Inner counties *excluding* municipalities in upper Bergen County. The second sample consisted of 32 municipalities with popu-

small municipalities "writ large." They respond differently to a similar mix of environmental circumstances; they serve up different "packages" of public programs. The casualness of a small suburb, even when as densely populated as the Bronx, may allow its residents to avoid installing curbs and sidewalks and to rely on volunteers instead of a professional fire department. New York City, at the other extreme, has to support not only fire stations but Shakespeare festivals, public baths, official quarters for distinguished visitors, parades and concerts. Apparently there is a different level of expectations and capacities, and a different political process for registering public needs.

Beyond bequeathing an assortment of public sectors across the Region so that similar environments have different programs, the metropolitan governmental structure has another effect. It pulls apart the forces which, over a large enough territory, coexist. If, on a flight of fancy, for example, one conceived of a single local government embracing the entire Region, that government would comprehend both the demand-oriented factors that go along with population concentrations and the supply-oriented factor of industrialization. The question of government spending would boil down pretty much to

---

lation between 10,000 and 21,000 in the same area. Average dwelling-unit density was about the same in both samples, and so was their dispersion about this average. Average density in the small municipalities was 6.55 (standard deviation 4.32) dwelling units per residential acre, while in the larger ones density was 6.56 (standard deviation 5.10). Regression equations for per capita nonschool operating expenditures (Y) were computed for both samples, using population (X_1), per capita residential valuation (X_2), per capita business valuation (X_3) and dwelling unit density (X_4). For the larger communities, the equation, expressed in terms of beta coefficients (with their standard errors in parentheses) read

$$Y = -0.061X_1 + 0.585X_2 + 0.605X_3 + 0.705X_4,$$
$$(0.066) \quad (0.089) \quad (0.082) \quad (0.106)$$

while the corresponding equation for smaller communities gave no weight at all to dwelling-unit density:

$$Y = -0.045X_1 + 0.459X_2 + 0.653X_3 + 0.137X_4.$$
$$(0.142) \quad (0.183) \quad (0.151) \quad (0.179)$$

an issue of how much resources the politically effective residents decided to divert from private spending.

Given the present boundary lines in the Region, however, all the forces of urbanization do not necessarily go hand in hand. Instead, the now familiar pattern of some municipalities wrestling with urgent public needs and others serenely accepting the tax bounty of "light industry" appears. In Middlesex County, for example, where the predominant occupational concentrations are craftsmen, operatives, and laborers, many municipalities have relatively high residential densities without having many industrial plants within their borders. For those governments the estimated cost of providing public services in 1958 was $600 per family. But with an average value per residence of about $15,000, they had no resources base commensurate with their obligations. The 1955 tax rate was $9 per $1,000 of assessed valuation and that valuation was set at 22 per cent of market value; thus the tax levy was $297 per family—or half the municipal service cost. Without state aid or industrial windfalls, the only fiscal alternatives are deficit financing or sharply increased tax efforts. By contrast, in Greenwich, Connecticut, where exurbanites abound, the average value of a new house in 1956 was $31,250. With such a base, the town's ratio of assessed to true market value of property had fallen by 25 per cent in the last seven years, and all capital improvements were being financed on a pay-as-you-go basis.[5]

Extremes such as these can be found within a single county. In Bergen, the municipalities of Teaneck and Teterboro are near each other physically but far apart in other ways:

Population—Teaneck 39,616, Teterboro 28.

School enrollment—Teaneck 7,700, Teterboro 2.

Taxes paid by industry and business—Teaneck 16 per cent of total budget, Teterboro 99 per cent.

Assessed valuation per school child—Teaneck $33,000, Teterboro $5,500,000.[6]

These variations, moreover, are not just random in character, at least not for those municipalities we have been able to study. In our New Jersey sample of 64 middle-sized municipalities, there is a fairly

Chart 11

Relation between Housing density [a] and Per Capita Market Value
of Residential and Business Property in 64 Middle-Sized
New Jersey Municipalities, 1955

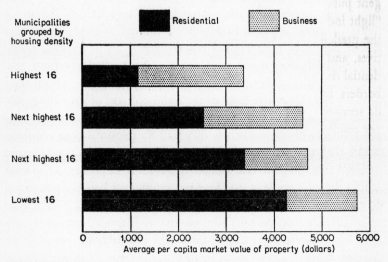

[a] As computed by factor analysis and described on pp. 35–36, and as used
in Charts 3 and 4.

strong tendency for the density and wealth characteristics to be politically divided. Chart 11 shows the 1955 relation between Housing
density and the per capita market value of residential and business
taxable property. The chart confirms the thesis advanced in *Anatomy
of a Metropolis,* the first volume of the New York Metropolitan Region Study, that higher-income families tend to trade ease of access
for space and privacy. It also points up the tendency of higher per
capita business valuations to be found in high-density localities.

From our viewpoint, however, a significant relation is suggested
by the decreasing *total* wealth per capita as communities become
more dense. The higher business property valuations in dense communities fail first of all to compensate for the contracted residential
tax base—relative to the populations to be serviced. Even more im-

pressive, the average *total* wealth per capita in the sixteen communities highest in residential density falls considerably short of the mean per capita value of residential property *alone* in the communities ranking lowest. Thus, in this part of the Region at least, the communities under the heaviest density pressures to spend have a tendency to be poorly equipped to meet these pressures.

The consequences of this segregation of resources and needs may be seen when the environmental differences among the New Jersey communities are related not to expenditures but to "tax effort"—the ratio between total local taxes raised in a given year and the estimated full market value of taxable property. As Chart 12 shows, density is controlling. Thus, though industrialization is highly important in setting the level of *total* local expenditures, density is characteristic of those localities allocating the greatest amount of their taxable resources to public purposes. In this way, the pattern of governmental arrangements, by creating different mixes of environmental forces, imposes unequal burdens and provides unequal resources.

FROM PRESSURES TO POLICIES

So far we have tried to make three main points about the relation between the process of urban growth in the Region and the extent and substance of its public programs. First, by various devices, we have pinpointed the environmental forces which seem the most significant determinants of public activity in the Region. Second, we have tried to indicate their changing influence over time according to broad stages of development. Third, we have tried to trace the simultaneous influence of the structure of government organization as a separate influence channeling environmental pressures. Can we go further and report the aggregate effect of all these properties taken together?

It should be immediately clear, of course, that no simple answer is forthcoming, given the complex relations and cross-currents of influence we have been describing. Because the final expenditure pattern in relation to environment is a function of both supply-oriented and demand-oriented forces, existing in different shapes and combi-

Chart 12

Relation between Community Characteristics and "Tax Effort" in 64 Middle-Sized New Jersey Municipalities, 1955

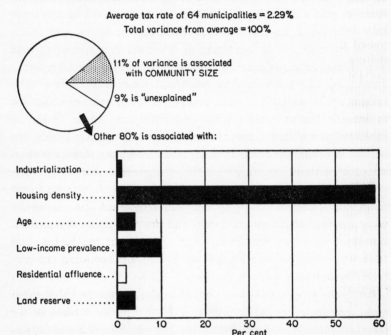

Average tax rate of 64 municipalities = 2.29%
Total variance from average = 100%

11% of variance is associated with COMMUNITY SIZE

9% is "unexplained"

Other 80% is associated with:

Notes: In this chart the "tax effort" is the ratio of local property taxes (county, school, and municipal) to the estimated market value of taxable property. White bar signifies that RESIDENTIAL AFFLUENCE—when other factors are held constant—is associated with a low tax effort rather than a high one. The 64 municipalities are mapped in Chart 2, early in this chapter. Sources of data and further explanation of technique will be found in Appendix B.

nations at different times, it is not easy to arrive at common "types" of municipal public sectors. Communities may spend because they have to for reasons of population pressures; they may spend because, being large, they acquire a special bundle of public services, or being new they require heavy capital investment. Nothing can be riskier than to assume a simple "have and have-not" explanation of the Region's public sector or to infer that high spending means high-quality public sectors.

In the inner suburban areas, both Hudson and Westchester Counties between 1945 and 1955 have levied roughly the same amount of local property taxes on a per capita basis, $75 and $85 respectively at the beginning of the decade and $134 and $133 at the end. Yet Hudson is the most densely populated of the inner belt of counties and Westchester the least. Hudson has the lowest median income, Westchester the highest. In the outer counties, Orange and Somerset have similarly had the same revenue experience, an increase of about $30 to $70 over the ten years, and they ranked next to each other by measures of residential density. But the median income of Orange in 1955 was $1628, while that of Somerset was $2309, the highest of the outer counties.

We can get a further sense of this complexity if we go back to the sample of 64 middle-sized New Jersey municipalities and look at the environmental endowments of communities resembling one another closely in per capita spending. Table 1 shows the ten highest and ten lowest communities with respect to per capita operating expenditures (nonschool).

Among the high spenders—the upper group—almost all of them rank high in INDUSTRIALIZATION, as indicated by the figures in the last column, and most of them rank high in AGE. But that comes close to exhausting the similarities. Montclair is large; Weehawken is small. Harrison has very little potential residential space; Linden has a great deal. Summit is noted for its affluence; Kearny is not. Hoboken's residential areas are densely occupied; Hackensack's are sparsely occupied. And in all those characteristics the ten communities are fairly well scattered in the rankings.

The differences in pressures bespeak quite different financial situations among the high spenders. Some have considerable leeway in their public budgets and some are spending much more on "essential" services. Weehawken seems clearly a representative of the hard-pressed. With an average of twenty dwelling units per acre of residential land, and a tax rate of 35 mills to the dollar, it spent only 7 per cent of its total nonschool budget on the "optional" or "luxury" services of recreation and adult education. Summit, in contrast, with less than four dwellings per residential acre, and a tax rate one-half of Weehawken's, allocated twice as large a portion of its budget to those services. It is clearly impossible to tell from per capita expenditures alone what sort of environment a government has within its boundaries or what services it concentrates on.

Among the low spenders in Table 1, too, there are differences, notably with respect to the degree of RESIDENTIAL AFFLUENCE against a common experience of small SIZE, low AGE, and low INDUSTRIALIZATION. Generally speaking, we do not think of these communities as particularly hard pressed because their expenditure levels are low. Rather, their financial pattern seems a result of their stage of urbanization—their low per capita spending dictated partly because their rudimentary programs require less and partly because they have not achieved heavy industrial endowments. With a low demand for those services that are typically associated with urbanization, they place the major emphasis in their budgets on schools. On the average, for these municipalities, school expenditures account for almost two-thirds of total expenditures, in contrast to an allocation of about two-fifths in the more urbanized areas. Still, there appear to be some circumstances of duress or choice. Some of the low-spending group tend to be young and affluent; others tend to be peopled by lower-status occupational groups where the per capita residential tax base is smaller.

Emerging from a study of all the possible combinations in the environment-government relations, one is impressed most of all by the distorting influence of governmental structure. The longer one examines the jurisdictions' expenditure patterns at the present time, the more apparent it becomes that historical caprice, in the form of ancient boundary lines, disrupts the pattern of regularity which the forces themselves display. Thus, especially in New Jersey where the jurisdiction is small and where the county does not carry out the broad range of functions assigned to its New York counterpart, the location of a single industrial plant, the decision of a developer to

Table 1 Profiles of High and Low Spenders among 64 Middle-Sized New Jersey Municipalities, 1955

		Quintile rankings [a] on community characteristics [b]				
	Expenditures	COMMUNITY SIZE	LAND RESERVE	AGE	RESIDENTIAL AFFLUENCE	HOUSING DENSITY	INDUSTRIALIZATION

	Expenditures	COMMUNITY SIZE	LAND RESERVE	AGE	RESIDENTIAL AFFLUENCE	HOUSING DENSITY	INDUSTRIALIZATION
Ten municipalities highest in per capita municipal operating expenditures							
Harrison	$124.4	5	5	3	5	1	1
Linden	84.1	1	1	5	4	5	1
Hoboken	83.3	2	4	2	4	1	1
Hackensack	77.3	2	3	1	4	5	2
Bayonne	73.5	1	3	4	3	2	1
Weehawken	73.3	5	3	1	3	1	2
Montclair	73.2	1	4	1	1	5	5
Englewood	71.9	3	2	1	2	5	2
Kearny	71.3	1	2	4	4	2	1
Summit	68.4	3	2	1	1	3	2
Ten municipalities lowest in per capita municipal operating expenditures							
Lyndhurst	34.8	3	3	4	5	4	5
East Paterson ...	34.2	3	2	5	4	3	4
River Edge	33.4	4	5	5	1	2	4
Scotch Plains ...	33.2	4	1	5	2	1	4
Roselle Park	33.2	4	5	4	4	4	3
Cedar Grove	29.0	5	2	4	1	1	4
Palisades Park ..	28.8	5	3	3	4	2	4
Saddle Brook ...	26.6	5	2	5	1	1	4
New Milford ...	24.2	3	4	5	3	2	5
Wayne	24.1	4	1	4	5	1	5

[a] For example, the figure 1 means that the community ranks in the top 13, the figure 2 that it ranks in the second 13, the figure 3 that it ranks in the next 12, the figure 4 that it ranks in the next 13, and the figure 5 that it ranks in the bottom 13. For map of the 64 communities see Chart 2.

[b] Only six of our seven community characteristics are used in this table. The seventh, LOW-INCOME PREVALENCE, could not be used because the values could not be accurately estimated for the present purpose.

build one hundred homes, the construction of one express highway—insignificant elements in the total urban complex of the Region—drastically affect the public fortunes of the jurisdiction. In any jurisdiction the character of public needs and the resources available to meet needs are almost certain to be sharply different not only from its neighbors but also from the Region's at large. It may not be too far-fetched—though it is certainly an oversimplification—to think of local governments as players at a roulette wheel, waiting to see what number will come up as a result of decisions beyond their direct control.

The larger a municipality is, of course, the more chance it may have to encompass a balanced blend of expenditure-inducing factors. Hence the less vulnerable it becomes to decisions made in the private sector—the choice of individual industrial locations or the consequences of population settlement pursued in a general search for space and status. New York City appears in command of a large enough territory to comprehend almost all the elements of urbanization. The close to $10 billion of taxable real estate in Manhattan, almost half of the entire City's valuation, provides a base from which the six million inhabitants in the other more residential boroughs may be supported. The public sectors of Westchester and Nassau Counties, by virtue of the pre-eminent role of county government, also have access to industrial and commercial valuations for many programs on a reasonably broad geographical basis.

Yet, even these larger units are likely to have a mix of forces which is quite different from that of the Region at large. Certainly, New York City and Newark have a disproportionate share of the special expenditure-inducing factors. Being the first home of immigrants and almost the only home for some minority groups, they have the largest number of hardship cases within their borders. As old cities, they are pressed more heavily by conditions of age and obsolescence. As we shall have occasion to observe again later, such conditions plus the absence of open space for future developments frequently provoke a set of public problems as serious in their financial implications as those of densely populated residential communities which lack compensating industrial resources.

Thus the existence of as many different types of public sectors as there are combinations of the components of urbanization forbids any one-shot generalization on the public financial patterns of the Region. In place of a broad interpretation which views the over-all Region's political economy as a result of a coincidence of demand and supply components, the total public sector is revealed as the sum of many small compartmentalized and quite different sectors. Within this complex, a high level of expenditures is not, by and of itself, indicative of any single component or any single combination. It may be the result of an ample supply of taxable wealth; it may arise from a reasonable supply of wealth plus a predominant civic preference for "quality" public product; it may occur through the compulsion of high density. By the same token, low levels of expenditure may not express conditions of fiscal struggling; they may be a function of the absence of many obvious needs for public service or a consciously conservative disposition on the part of the jurisdiction's inhabitants. Out of this diversity of experiences, one municipality may find itself so insulated from the pressures of urban growth that it has real choices about the level and extent of its public services. Another may be a captive of its environment—with little industrial property and with low-value residences, yet with a population which requires large expenditures simply to provide minimal services and meet the urgent needs of the moment.

Paradoxically, however, as various and haphazard as these municipal public sectors appear to be, they yield a common interpretation for the behavior of the 1400 managers, a backdrop for understanding the process of political decision-making and behavior as it relates to economic development. When we understand how different components of urbanization work in quite different ways to force up the level of public expenditures and to distribute the burdens of cost, the moves and countermoves among the factions within a local citizenry do not appear as senseless controversy, born of misunderstanding and misinformation. Rather, they emerge as the actions of highly sensible people who realize that the outcome of political battles on tax rates, assessed valuations, and budgets bestow unequal penalties and unequal benefits. Environmental circumstances combined with an established revenue system make particular strategies and particular controversies almost certain.

In the same way, when we recognize the roulette-wheel aspect of municipal finance, combined with the predominant influence of industrial wealth on expenditures and of density on tax effort, we come to understand the policies adopted by local public officials. In this context, their contentious squabbles with their neighbors, their insularity, their persistent claim to self-identity, the protective devices they employ—all these are not the products of whim or a failure to recognize reality. On the contrary, with an intuitive grasp of the political implications of urbanization, these officials shape policies adapted to the given situation. By whatever way they proceed, they are reaching toward an accommodation to the forces spawned by urbanization. The pattern of their response provides an additional explanation for the substance of the public sector today and feeds back on the process of urbanization itself. That explanation and the examination of the feedback are the subjects of the next chapter.

3

Responses of the Local Governments

ENTER POLITICS

What responses can the Region's local governments effectively make to the urban environment which surrounds them? Essentially, three main lines of action are open.

First, within a given municipality's borders, the politically active element of a constituency can strive to avoid the effects of urbanization and metropolitan growth. That is, by purely political strategy and policy, a dominant group can redefine economic resources and population needs to mean something quite different from the environmental forces we have studied. We shall say more on this presently.

Second, instead of relying on political redefinitions, the group may use public powers and prerogatives to modify the environmental circumstances under which it operates. Timely measures to guide growth can sometimes avoid unpalatable by-products of the Region's steady increase in population; efforts to attract industry can sometimes bolster sagging tax bases.

Third, in concert with other localities, a municipality can break out of the formal strait jacket of metropolitan organization. It can work to persuade the higher echelons in the American federal system to take up local burdens it cannot alone sustain.

Of course not all local strategies and policies have their origins in the financial implications of the economy. The Region's citizenry is no assembly of rational economic men, lightning calculators of marginal costs and benefits. A new industry in town often solves a revenue problem but creates an aesthetic one. An influx of newcomers adds disproportionately to public costs, but sometimes it improves a politician's election chances. Planning may be rejected as an appropriate instrument of public policy because it offends ideological rather than economic standards. Many factors outside the realm of public finance go into the shaping of municipal policy, and their influence is not to be discounted.

But to the extent that financial considerations are important, the three main avenues of maneuver are as described above. Depending on the particular alternative chosen—or combination of alternatives —expenditure levels and tax efforts can be adjusted in ways other than those which environmental forces might otherwise indicate. As time goes on, the alternative first adopted tends to become a governmental tradition, a political style, and even may crystallize into law. So New York communities in the Region at about the same stage of development as some of their New Jersey neighbors consistently have higher per capita expenditures and offer more public services. So New Jersey as a state has been far slower to widen its tax base than New York or Connecticut. The state and local political processes of the Region arrive at dissimilar responses to similar experiences, and political forces enter to explain our "unexplained" statistical residuals of the last chapter.

We will be concerned in this chapter with exploring the different kinds of response to the growth process which the Region's governments have adopted. On a Regionwide basis, we will go more deeply into those responses—into the nature of the "definitions" game within the local governments; into the kinds of strategies which cope with residential and industrial movements; and into municipal efforts to tap resources existing outside the Region proper through political means. Then we will outline the combinations of particular policies and practices which have come to characterize the separate parts of the Region. The upshot of both inquiries will be to give some sense of how the many and separate independent units of government deal with the pressures generated by the larger and expanding economic systems—and how in doing so they affect the economic system itself.

STRATEGIES OF ADJUSTMENT: (1) VIEWING ECONOMICS THROUGH POLITICAL-COLORED GLASSES

Our line of departure for describing the political response to economic change lies with the internal politics of the Region's localities. More properly it lies with one kind of local politics, the kind that has to do with money matters—how budgets are approved, how tax rates are set, and when decisions to issue bonds for new schools are made. It is here that the political tampering with economic circumstances takes place, a process which pits different factions of a locality's constituency against one another. In the fixing of assessments, the management of public debt, the authorization of new revenue sources, and the establishment of new units, governments make their peace with urbanization—and maintain simultaneously some manner of political stability.

It is the distinction between the environment as it is and the environment as the governments choose to define it which we wish to emphasize. For the public sector is a peculiar sort of artifact, capable of subtle definition and redefinition. And depending how its managers choose to view it, different consequences fall upon the "real" world of households, industry, and commerce.

Perhaps the most obvious possibility for adjustment is found in the legally established local revenue system, in particular the method by which real property taxes are levied. Throughout the Region, the amount of the property tax is a function of a tax *rate*, set by the town fathers and subject to state limitation, and an assessed *valuation*, typically established by experts in the local bureaucracies. Since the assessed valuations are generally set considerably below full market value, the revenues resulting from any given rate are usually less than those which a municipality could extract if it chose to raise the assessments. Hence, the political elite in any locality has the continuing option to expand the tax revenue at a given moment, almost regardless of economic developments. Alternatively, it can reduce the size of its yield by a local ordinance or bureaucratic decision. Finally, it may squeeze through loopholes of state law to impose differential burdens on different types of property—and thereby shift the incidence of taxation.

Manipulating the assessments provides the most obvious opportunity for controlling the supply of revenue and thus reshaping the environmental pressures. To the traditional "taxpayers association" whose members pay the largest share of a municipality's bill and are convinced that public programs provide them few direct benefits, this manipulating has logical appeal. Regardless of motive, it is administratively difficult to keep assessed valuations in a constant proportion to market values, especially in times of rapid economic growth. Whether through conscious policy or administrative lag, a wide disparity between assessed and market value acts as an ultimate deterrent to increasing expenditures. Tax rates climb, of course, but sooner or later they bump against ceilings imposed either legally by the state or politically by local indignation. Thus a municipality can exhaust its legal revenue capacities without any increases whatever in the tax burden relative to the market value of the property. It can also generate psychological panic among residents untutored in municipal finance. These good citizens, watching the rates spiral and not realizing that the assessments lag behind the market value, may believe that taxes are climbing astronomically, and may organize crusades against "excessive spending."

We have considerable evidence that there has indeed been a lag in assessed valuations. Taken together, the Region's local governments entered the period after World War II with their assessed valuations pegged at considerably less than one-half of market value. Ten years later, despite the new demands for public services, the steady economic growth, and the unparalleled investment in housing and industrial facilities, the gap was even larger.

In New Jersey, the statewide ratio of assessed to market value declined between 1951 and 1957 from 34 per cent to 28 per cent. Decreases of between one percentage point and eight percentage points were registered in the nine New Jersey counties of the Region, as indicated in Table 2. By 1957, in six out of the nine counties, assessed value was less than one-third of full value.[1]

Table 2   Change in Average Municipal Assessment Ratios,
New Jersey Metropolitan Counties

(assessed valuation as percentage of estimated market value)

	1951	1957	Change
Bergen	26	22	—4
Essex	48	41	—7
Hudson	56	55	—1
Middlesex	24	22	—2
Monmouth	22	19	—3
Morris	22	18	—4
Passaic	43	35	—8
Somerset	20	16	—4
Union	37	30	—7

Source: State of New Jersey, Commission on State Tax Policy, *Ninth Report* (Trenton, 1958).

In New York, the same pattern of disparity between assessed and market value exists, although this time we do not have a direct comparison of valuations over time. We can make much the same point, however, by examining the change in the ratio between total property taxes and estimated full property value. For the 82 New York towns outside New York City there was an average decrease in this ratio between 1945 and 1955 of 30.3 per cent, ranging from 3.7 to 71.9.[2] In only two instances did taxes command a larger share of full value at the end of the decade than they did in the beginning.

It is not only *total* assessed valuations that are manipulated. The administrative process of assessment also offers opportunities to impose different burdens on different classes of property. New Jersey localities, for example, have long been notorious for "tax-lightning" —a sudden raising of the assessment on a particular item of property. In this respect, New Jersey municipalities have established so noticeable a pattern of assessment discrimination against business firms that the New Jersey Commission on State Tax Policy has officially incorporated "tax-lightning" into the vocabulary of public finance.[3]

Yet it is not just business property which is discriminated against in the Garden State. In its 1953 investigations, the Commission found that, in a sample of 21,275 properties, "low value" business and residential property was assessed at higher than average ratios. Specifically, business and residential properties with market values between $2,000 and $4,000 had assessed valuations averaging 41 per

Table 3 Property Versus Nonproperty Revenues [a] of Local Governments,[b] New York Metropolitan Region, 1945–1955

	1945		1950		1955		Per cent rise in revenues, 1945–1955
	Millions of dollars	Per cent of total	Millions of dollars	Per cent of total	Millions of dollars	Per cent of total	
The Region [c]							
Property	418.3	62.3	520.8	56.2	724.4	54.2	73.1
Nonproperty ..	253.0	37.7	405.2	43.8	611.3	45.8	141.6
New York City							
Property	299.5	60.2	330.6	49.7	478.9	48.6	59.8
Nonproperty ..	197.4	39.7	334.1	50.3	506.0	51.4	156.3
New York Inner							
Property	29.2	73.2	38.0	73.2	52.2	69.4	75.1
Nonproperty ..	10.9	26.8	13.9	26.8	23.0	30.6	111.1
New Jersey Inner							
Property	69.9	67.2	122.0	74.7	147.3	72.1	110.7
Nonproperty ..	34.0	32.8	41.2	25.3	56.9	27.9	67.4
New York Outer							
Property	9.5	72.5	14.4	75.3	23.0	76.9	142.1
Nonproperty ..	3.6	27.5	4.7	24.7	6.9	23.1	91.6
New Jersey Outer							
Property	9.6	57.4	15.8	58.3	23.0	55.4	139.5
Nonproperty ..	7.1	42.6	11.3	41.7	18.5	44.6	160.5

[a] Not including revenues for schools, borrowed funds, or state or federal aid.

[b] Not including school districts.

[c] Not including Fairfield County, Connecticut.

Source: Estimates by New York Metropolitan Region Study, calculated as explained in Appendix A.

cent of market value. Properties between $8,000 and $10,000 showed an average of 29 per cent.[4] The Commission also found that one-family houses were more lightly assessed than multifamily dwellings or business and industrial properties; that built-up blocks, old neighborhoods, and accommodations in the process of rehabilitation carried higher-than-average assessments; and that the ratio of assessed to market value of undeveloped land was almost twice the ratio for residential buildings. These variations reflect, of course, a general sensitivity of town fathers to the political strengths of different classes of property owners. For our purposes, they also mark a further refinement in distinctions between what constitutes taxable resources and what does not, by identifying the resources "most available" politically for public purposes.

Changes in legal definitions of property valuations are not the only ways in which potential resources can be differentiated from existing resources and tax burdens shifted. A second alternative is to restructure the entire local revenue system, pre-empting more resources by legislative declaration. The search for new types of local revenue has, in fact, been evident in all parts of the Region since World War II, although no single other tax has yet approached the property levy in importance. The changing role of the property tax for the Region's local governments is shown in Table 3. This table covers nonschool revenues during the postwar decade 1945–1955. It emphasizes the dwindling dependence of most jurisdictions on the traditional property tax. As seen in the upper right-hand corner of the table, property revenue increased only 73 per cent while other revenue—not including borrowed funds or state or federal aid—was increasing by 142 per cent. The table also shows, however, that not all parts of the Region followed the general trend. In the "New Jersey Inner" and "New York Outer" counties * the local governments increased their property revenue faster than their nonproperty revenue.

Still another way by which local governments can tamper with

* For map of zones see Chart 6 on page 45.

their financial arrangements is to persuade the state government to change the legal limitations on tax rates and borrowings. Alternatively, they can ignore unwelcome limitations and persuade the state to accept interpretations which, to say the least, are flexible. In New Jersey, where the limitations take the form of maximum debt allowances expressed as a proportion of assessed valuation, this latter course often appears to have prevailed. In 1956, 236 out of the 585 municipalities in the whole state had debts exceeding their legal limits. These debts, totaling $360 million against legal limits amounting to $229 million, attested to the ability of municipalities to break through their ceilings by extensions of credit and other special arrangements.[5]

In New York State, where limits are applied to the local tax rate, a more formal amendment procedure must be followed to bring about adjustments. Until 1949, these limits were calculated relative to assessed valuations. In that year a constitutional amendment expressed them relative to market value in a jurisdiction, estimated by the state and calculated on the basis of the last five years' valuations. This change greatly increased the leeway that communities had in increasing tax rates, but the leeway was least in jurisdictions where assessments were already closest to market value. Surveying the revised situation in 1954, the Temporary Commission on the Fiscal Affairs of State Government reported, "While New York City has not gained sufficient additional property taxing power to solve its revenue problem and a few other cities still occupy a marginal situation, the great majority of the cities and apparently most of the villages have secured a taxing potential that exceeds their immediate needs—in some instances, the excess is large." [6] The Commission went on to note that the expansion of the revenue base had caused concern among local officials and "more concern among real estate groups." [7]

Buttressing the strategies of financial adjustment and manipulation is a fourth device—the outright creation of new governments. Essentially, this amounts to a double-tapping of the same revenue base by simply establishing another governmental layer. The usual form is the special district established to provide a single public service, and the revenue source may either be property taxation or a user charge. Except in New York City, this alternative is applied uniformly in the Region for the provision of schools, and it is also in vogue with respect to sundry other services. Whatever the purpose and however financed, the special district has the effect of establishing another channel to the wealth of a local constituency without either affecting the tax rates of the traditional government or introducing new kinds of taxes.

In the New York portion of the Region there are some 300 school districts, generally within the borders of the towns, occasionally extending across town or even county lines. In the New Jersey portion there are about 240 school districts, for the most part coterminous with municipal boundaries but with a tendency to consolidate on a larger basis.[8] In each state, separate levies on the general tax base are authorized for schools, and special limitations on the tax rate or debt volume are set for school purposes. The expenditures of these districts constitute the largest single activity of the Region's local governments, and the pattern of school financing differs sharply from that of the municipalities of general jurisdiction.

That the patterns differ sharply was evident in the last chapter; differences in environmental characteristics such as industrialization, housing density, and age "explain" a much smaller part of the variations in school expenditures than they do in general expenditures. Underlying this relative insensitivity of school expenditures to environmental factors other than community size is the fact that the separate local school taxes, already big, are powerfully supplemented by state grants, which for the Region as a whole are larger for schools than for all other local purposes combined. Moreover, state aid constitutes 25 per cent of total school revenue compared to only 12 per cent of revenue for other purposes. Thus, outside New York City, the school districts of the Region raised $313 million in 1955 from the local property tax in comparison with $245 million raised by governments of general jurisdiction from the same source. But, in addition to these funds, the school districts could count on over

$90 million in state aid, while the general jurisdictions were getting only $21 million. Even including New York City, 47 per cent of all state aid in the New York and New Jersey portions of the Region went for school purposes. For the New Jersey counties of the Region, the figure was 75 per cent. For the New York counties outside New York City, it was 52 per cent. By contrast, in New York City, where no independent school districts exist, it was only 40 per cent.[9]

But it is not just for the school function that the New York Metropolitan Region has come to turn increasingly to the special district. Particularly on the New York State side of the Region, the special district becomes the principal means by which the suburban governments meet the new needs which arise in the transition from rural to urban communities. In the New York counties, the number of special districts other than school districts increased more than 20 per cent during the first postwar decade. At latest count the entire Region had 289 such units, if we go by the definition of "substantial autonomy" employed by the U.S. Census Bureau. According to the definition applied by the New York State government, Nassau County alone had 259 nonschool special districts in 1956 and all the New York counties combined had more than a thousand.[10]

There is still another dimension of flexibility in the district device. By creating special districts, the governments of more general jurisdictions are able to pinpoint areas of growth and to assure that costs in these areas are borne by their residents alone. In addition to this geographical segregation of responsibility, there is functional segregation, in that the expenses of a single public program can be paid for by the actual users. In some cases, the services provided on a district basis are mundane: sewage disposal, street lighting, fire protection, water supply, and refuse collection. In other cases, the district is a flexible instrument to meet essentially modern needs. Parking authorities, park districts, and housing authorities are obvious examples. However based in law and for whatever object established, the district presents an organizational solution to a financial problem.

Moreover, the special district, it should be noted, often serves as a meeting ground for competing political factions within a locality. For groups prone toward more public spending, the capacity of the districts to develop new lines of access to state coffers and to tax property again and again provides a convenient way to avoid head-on budgetary and reassessment battles. For property owners, the judicious design of special districts offers a way of placing upon the newcomers in the community the burden of the additional costs they either want or require. Indeed, if a district is laid out carefully enough, a further discrimination among types of property can result, this time according to geographical location.

In the last analysis, as ingenious as the four principal strategies of redefining the environment are, there is a limit to their effectiveness. Even if a municipality is dominated by a taxpayers' bloc intent on reliving pastoral days, certain modern expenditures are necessary. Even if the majority in a jurisdiction is devoted to quality services, they cannot spend revenues they do not possess. The tax rates for any given revenue source ultimately have their limits, and the development of new tax sources depends on the existence of some sort of taxable economic activity within a jurisdiction's boundaries. The creation of special districts cannot be extended indefinitely, tapping and retapping the same revenue sources to the point of confiscation.

In several ways we can trace the dwindling amount of "elbow room" left for political maneuver and the redefinition of needs and resources in the most-urbanized sections of the Region. One test is to examine the relation between assessed and market value for particular types of municipalities in the Region. It will be recalled that Table 2 revealed a growing gap between these values in the New Jersey counties, but those county ratios did not show the wide range of differences among municipalities. In 1953 the ratios for municipalities varied from 15 per cent to 41 per cent throughout New Jersey and from 27 per cent to 61 per cent throughout New York State. Where the most advanced stages of urbanization were present, and densities highest, the ratio was highest. Uniformly the New Jersey Commission on State Tax Policy found that large, densely-populated municipalities had a strong tendency to assess at higher than the statewide average.[11] It is in these municipalities, the Commission reported, that tax rates rise and the search for new tax sources intensifies as basic requirements for public programs become more costly and less easily avoidable.

There are not only economic but also political limitations to intramunicipal infighting. Highly discriminatory property assessments invite court intervention. In New Jersey the courts, in 1957, mandated equalized assessment in such clear terms as to bring about comprehensive changes in law and administrative practice for property taxation. Quite apart from the violence done to ethical standards, extreme examples of manipulation can provoke bitter controversy and make uncertain the outcome of political conflict. No local official welcomes a position on the top of a powder keg, and most work strenuously to avoid such situations. In these circumstances, then, as urbanization proceeds the Region's political elites turn more and more to different methods. Rather than redefining the environment, they seek to shape directly the processes of urbanization.

STRATEGIES OF ADJUSTMENT: (2) CONDITIONING THE GROWTH FACTORS

The politics of guiding growth—zoning, planning, and industrial promotion policies—involve a different time perspective and result in different payoffs from the strategies of fiscal manipulation we have just traced. The use or nonuse of these policies is important, however, often explaining why islands of high-value residential neighborhoods are surrounded by industrial sections, or why enclaves of industrial activity persist in areas apparently economically unsuitable for their location. But there is a sizable time lag, usually measured in years, before the consequences of these types of political action show up in the distribution of population and economic activity. The politician relying on them reconciles himself to less dramatic results, which will not be apparent overnight. This evolutionary quality may account for the fairly rudimentary state of these measures in the Region in comparison to alternative strategies.

By far the most universal of the policies employed to guide growth in the Region is the control of land use; and by far the most popular control device is zoning. In 1956, the Regional Plan Association reported that zoning laws were in effect in 465 municipalities within the Region. Within the five boroughs of New York City and the four counties of Bergen, Essex, Nassau, and Westchester, all land use was at least technically governed by zoning regulations. Only 85 municipalities in the Region had no provision for zoning in that year; and all but a few of these jurisdictions lay in the outer counties. Indeed, 43 of them were in two counties alone: 23 in Orange and 20 in Dutchess.[12] Even such "unprotected" communities had the benefit of county planning boards, and public attention to the public control of growth was increasing. Throughout the Region, zoning is now recognized as a device by which densities can be regulated, land use apportioned between "net-revenue-producing" and "net-revenue-using" property, and an individual municipality's fiscal position brought into tolerable balance.

But it is not only the geographical extent of zoning that is significant in the Region's development. Less recognized but perhaps more significant for the future are the changes which have recently taken place in the techniques and practice of zoning. Originally, ordinances governing land use consisted of little more than the designation of broad areas as residential, industrial, or commercial districts, and their principal objective was to exclude industrial activity from better residential neighborhoods. Now, more and more of the Region's municipalities use zoning with precision and sophistication.

Thus the residential, industrial, and commercial categories of land use are today often subdivided according to specific types of residential, commercial, and industrial activities. Further, modern planning doctrine goes beyond simply excluding manufacturing and commerce from residential zones. The practice of also excluding residences from manufacturing and commercial zones (the essence of what planners call "noncumulative districting") has increased in popularity. New techniques for classifying land have appeared: for example, "performance ratings," which measure the intensity of noise, smoke, or odor produced by a plant to determine the appropriateness of industrial activity at a given site. Architectural and design standards are now incorporated in many zoning laws, reflecting an increased concern with aesthetics. Governments now frequently exercise the authority to regulate both the time at which new development is permitted and the phases of its construction. In short, zoning as a control measure is now a much more influential instrument in guiding population and economic patterns than it was before World War II.

Coincidentally with the development of zoning, policies of municipal mercantilism—"beggar-thy-neighbor" policies—have emerged within the Region. With technical and professional advisory staffs paid for by federal and state grants, most of the county governments and many of the small units within the Region are embarked on formal programs to attract what, in their constituency's view, is desirable industrial and commercial development. Sometimes, these activities take the form of special commissions and research projects which review existing public policies for their effect on private locational decisions. Examples are the New Jersey Commission to Study Laws Affecting Industrial Development; the Long Island industrial survey carried out by a bureau of Hofstra College; and the studies sponsored by the New York State Department of Commerce.[13]

More frequently, the drive for industry becomes a major objective of county or local planning boards. Under their direction, land is set aside for future industrial development, transportation plans are made with a view to enhancing the area's industrial potential, and the private acquisition and improvement of land for business purposes are facilitated by public action. In all these endeavors, the governments are often closely associated with business and civic groups. Influential citizens are designated as "economic ambassadors." Special tours for outside industrialists are arranged to emphasize both the natural and political advantages of a given jurisdiction.

Not infrequently, these activities engender hostility among a municipality's neighbors, with accusations of "pirating" of industry or social irresponsibility. It was, for example, the promotional and zoning activities of Fairlawn, New Jersey, which led the Deputy City Administrator of New York in July 1959 to charge that the community which "had been luring industries out of New York is refusing to house workers from the city." In reply, New Jersey spokesmen stoutly denied any special concessions to industry. They did concede, however, that New Jersey's tax levels might be considered "assets" by a company on the move and that workers might find difficulty in buying homes in developments where "look alike" housing is not permitted and where the new homes being built were in the $20,000-and-up range.[14]

The application of zoning powers and promotional techniques varies substantially in different parts of the Region, and some of the instruments are far more effective than others. Quite frequently, comprehensive zoning regulations appear only after the pattern of development in a jurisdiction has been set, and the opportunities for controlling growth are thus reduced to fairly narrow limits. As for the mercantilist policies, there is little solid evidence that promotional efforts to attract new industry are effective counterweights to limitations imposed by geography or market considerations. Counterbalancing the Fairlawn story are studies in Long Island and Middlesex County, which report that special tax and service arrangements for new industry are often regarded with suspicion by a firm, and that it takes a fairly long time for a government to establish a reputation for a "favorable business climate."[15]

Nonetheless, planning, zoning, and promotion do represent ways by which all local units of general jurisdiction can keep "undesirables" out and encourage "desirables" to come in, if they choose. And of course the definition of desirables and undesirables varies from place to place. No common policy toward the control of land or the encouragement of economic development exists within the Region. Instead, land-use controls are applied in an atmosphere of intergovernmental jostling, and the ensuing pattern of population and industrial distribution is often determined according to the respective political capacities of the municipalities involved.

STRATEGIES OF ADJUSTMENT: (3) THE APPEAL
UPSTAIRS

The policies and strategies we have summarized so far have all been largely the province of local governments. As such they are "Region-bound"—restricted in application to economic activities within the 22 counties and as varied in effectiveness as are the number and types of government. In these circumstances, a final estimate of their significance must await the later area-by-area survey, in which their effects can be localized.

The governments possess one more alternative, however, which is less dependent on their own particular mix of urbanization forces. By drawing on revenues from outside the Region, by turning to state and federal governments for support, the local units can to a considerable degree escape their environment. Indeed, they can find assistance of such dimensions as to dwarf the effects of their individual efforts to come to terms with urbanization. At least in terms of the additional sources of revenues, this avenue is of critical importance in accounting for the size and substance of the public sector.

For the Region as a whole, outside financial assistance is now second only to the property tax as a source of revenue. For several services, they are the prime support. In schools, welfare, health, highways, and redevelopment, outside contributions typically outweigh total local contributions for the respective services. Thus, in 1957, state aid was 20 per cent of the total revenue of New York City, 24 per cent of the total revenue of the local governments in the rest of the New York part of the Region, and 11 per cent for the New Jersey side. Broken down by type of government in 1955, the Region's general-purpose municipal governments except for New York City received over $21 million from state sources, compared to the $246 million raised by local property taxation. The county governments received more than $31 million compared to property revenue of $109 million. The school districts received $91 million as against $313 million in property levies.[16]

The experience of the New York and New Jersey sections of the Region and the experience of inner and outer counties within each state differ sharply in the patterns of grants-in-aid. Both in absolute and per capita terms, New York State has displayed a far greater disposition to put its funds at the disposal of its localities. Thus, in 1955, New York State aid to municipalities in the Region (again excepting New York City) was almost six times as great as that of New Jersey, while the total amount raised by property taxes in the New Jersey portion of the Region was twice that of the New York portion. In the period 1950–1955, the New York grants increased 34 per cent compared to a 9 per cent increase in New Jersey. On a per capita basis in 1955, state assistance to general governments below the county level amounted to 65 cents in the "New Jersey Inner" portion of the Region and $6.65 in "New York Inner." * In the outer counties, the New Jersey units received grants averaging $1.24 per capita in contrast to the "New York Outer" average of $7.15.[17]

The numbers and types of assistance programs, as well as the size of the grants, serve as a further contrast between the two states. In New York, the array of state grants includes not only those primarily stimulated by the federal government in welfare, highways, and public health but also a series of programs supported almost entirely by the state. New York pioneered, for example, in the postwar development of general-purpose grants to municipalities— which for the whole state exceeded $108 million in 1956. Its educational assistance program is both sophisticated and comprehensive, covering some 22 special programs in addition to the basic "minimum foundation" grant which is aimed at establishing a floor for school expenditures across the state. Assistance is also offered in such varied fields as public works planning, service to veterans, conservation, probation, and delinquency. So large have the programs become that in 1956 state aid constituted over half of the state's annual operating expenditures.[18]

New Jersey takes a far more conservative posture. Statewide, four out of every five assistance dollars are earmarked for school pur-

* For map of zones see Chart 6 on page 45.

poses in New Jersey, and the bulk of the remaining allocations falls
in programs strongly supported by the federal government. In 1958,
state assistance to all school districts totaled $150.8 million. By con-
trast, the second largest grant program, welfare, amounted to $18.4
million, followed by highways at the $16.9 million mark; police and
fire pensions, $4.4 million; and beach and waterways, $1.3 million.
Allocations for all other programs totaled only $2.2 million—less
than New York was assigning to Youth Service Bureaus. Perhaps
even more significant is the comparatively sluggish trend in New
Jersey grants over the past few years. Between 1953 and 1958, grants
for welfare increased $4.4 million, highways $1 million, and fire and
police pensions $3.4 million; beach and waterways declined $0.5 million; and all others increased $0.8 million. In vivid contrast, school
assistance rose from $40.8 million to $107.6 million, an increase of
158 per cent. Indeed, between 1956 and 1958, school aid accounted
for more than 90 per cent of the rise in all grant programs.[19]

The state-aid differences between New York and New Jersey emphasize—but by no means explain—the extraordinarily complex effect of the grant programs on the Region's political economy. One
significant result of those differences is that New Jersey and New
York municipalities equally endowed in economic resources and
equally beset by public demands will be in quite unequal positions
so far as their total resource base is concerned. Even more important, the formulas for allocating funds differ according to the legal
status of the local governments involved, and therefore different
volumes of support are found within the same state. In New York,
the existence or nonexistence of a village within a town, the decision of a community to seek incorporation as a city, the kind of
charter a county adopts—all affect the amount of state revenue available, quite apart from the number of residents or the assessed valuation within a given area.[20]

The total of federal and state money channeled into the New
York Metropolitan Region is not, then, a reliable indicator of the
contributions available in any given sector. Small jurisdictions share
better proportionally than large; one kind of public function receives

funds and another does not; two types of school district find their allocations calculated on the basis of quite different criteria. Though grants expand the tolerance limits in which local governments maneuver, these consequences are by no means uniform. Certainly, they do not have an equalizing influence on levels of expenditures.

The differential impact of the grant programs thus expands rather than reduces the range of political alternatives available to any single jurisdiction in coming to terms with its environment. Like the purely local strategies, grant programs provide further options for adjustment and additional revenues for the maintenance of the present system of metropolitan government. Since their effect cannot be estimated on an across-the-board basis, the grants become subsumed as one of the array of weapons each jurisdiction has at its disposal.

Over time, then, each part of the Region has come to rely on a special combination of the strategies available and to fashion its particular style of adaptation. If we are to understand how the policies are actually applied—in contrast to what opportunities exist—we will have to abandon a general survey. In the next sections, we will build up piece-by-piece a knowledge of how each part of the Region has fashioned its policies of response: what room for maneuver exists, what the respective odds are for modifying or escaping the forces of urbanization, and how intense the infighting has become among local factions.

COMBINATIONS: (1) NEW YORK CITY—
EVERYTHING GOES

By far the most sophisticated municipal strategist within the Region is the City of New York, although paradoxically its policies have few prospects for real payoffs. At the center of the Region, with the pressures of size, density, and age playing full force upon it, the City must run fast to stay in the same place. It has at once a powerful motivation for manipulating its environment and awesome obstacles in this pursuit. Necessarily, then, it has developed the available strategies in their most elaborate and advanced form.

We have already given some indication of the magnitude of New

York City's environmental challenge. One quick way to summarize its position is to note simply that even while the suburban areas have undergone their explosive growth the City has nonetheless maintained approximately the same share of the Region's local governmental expenditures throughout the postwar period. In 1945 it accounted for 68 per cent; in 1955 its share hovered at the 65 per cent mark; and in 1957, at 66 per cent.[21]

It is true that these years have witnessed an extraordinary emphasis on capital replacement and expansion and that some of the major construction programs would not be duplicated in the near future. It is also true that where suburbs felt the impact of rapid population growth most strongly, as in Nassau, the rate of increase in spending has been fastest. But certainly there has been no perceptible reduction of the expenditure-generating forces within the City's boundaries: high density, an aged population, physical obsolescence, and the prevalence of low-income families.

The most obvious effect of those pressures is sharply reduced room for maneuver in the traditional game of defining taxable resources. The assessed valuation of New York City is now officially estimated at 89 per cent of market value, the highest in the Region, and unofficial estimates of the ratio rarely dip below 80 per cent.[22] The City is also the only major jurisdiction on the New York side of the Hudson where tax rates have consistently touched constitutionally established limits. Regularly, in the last fifteen years, expert observers and special study commissions have predicted "gaps" between revenues and expenditures ranging from $200 million to over $500 million annually. Regularly, the annual balancing of the budget has been portrayed by the press more as a feat of magic than as a rational process of financial management. No government has less elbow room in the age-old game of adjusting tax base and tax rate than the City.

In New York, unlike some of its neighbors, the legal squeeze implied by high assessed valuations and tax rates at the constitutional limit has real significance. There are few informal, "practical" ways to circumvent the law. On the contrary, in the long tradition of City-

State antagonism and suspicion, Albany treats the downstream gargantua in a different way from other municipalities. Albany applies special tax limits, special debt limits, and other unique requirements and restrictions to the City's fiscal management.

Moreover, New York City does not enjoy the privilege of the cumulative tax limits which operate where village, town, special district, and county are superimposed one on the other. The City has, for example, operating responsibilities for functions that elsewhere are carried out by school districts and counties, but it is not granted the additional rates of between 1.25 and 2 per cent authorized for these functions when school districts or counties perform them. Thus its tax limit of 2.5 per cent of full value must be compared to limitations in other places permitting a combined rate as high as 6 per cent—and suburban towns are not subject to direct tax limits at all. Similarly, New York City's debt limit is fixed at 10 per cent of assessed valuation, whereas in the other New York portions of the Region the combined debt limit is much higher—from 16 to 19 per cent depending on the particular combination of towns, villages, and school districts.[23]

Finally, as pointed out earlier, the City also has not benefited as much as other governments in New York State from the extensive 1949 revisions in property tax administration. Because the City's assessed valuation was already much closer to market value than in most other localities, the "equalization" formulas introduced at that time did not expand the City's tax base proportionally. Subsequent legislation intensified this disadvantage. Between 1954 and 1959, when the full effect of the new program was still to be realized, the state legislature adjusted the City's taxing power in such a way that the effective limit was at 2.25 per cent at the end of the period— pegged below the constitutional provision.

Restrained in its capacity for internal maneuver by property tax limitations and state regulations, the City is also limited in its exercise of planning and zoning prerogatives. True, its government possesses a full array of techniques in this field—and it is probably more actively engaged in efforts to change the physical environment of the

community than any other of the Region's governments. Its 1951 and
1959 proposals for rezoning the City represent detailed programs of
development and would apply advanced techniques of control. Indeed, so far as individual structures are concerned, the City's zoning regulations already have an important impact on private development. In the regulation of building design, for example, the
City ordinances are frequently felt to be so specific and rigid that as
late as 1958 the Regional Plan Association reported ruefully that
"the most able architects in New York City have been baffled by its
iron laws of zoning for more than a generation." [24]

Despite the detail and complexity of the City's controls, the very
magnitude of the job involved in changing the land use in any comprehensive way makes the effectiveness of even the most sophisticated of efforts questionable. One major handicap, of course, is the
scarcity of vacant land within the borders of the five boroughs—a
characteristic which sharply restrains the alternatives for new development. Thus, only Richmond and portions of Queens presently offer sizable areas where development can start from scratch. The
main pattern of the City was established before zoning programs
were legally recognized, let alone brought into effective application. Although the Department of Commerce and Public Events
has as its major objective the expansion of industry and commerce,
the available means to carry out this aim are comparatively few.
The Department can sponsor trade fairs, provide information,
smooth the path of small business by offering assistance in fulfilling
legal requirements and meeting governmental standards, try to persuade big business not to relocate outside the City's borders, and
arrange receptions, luncheons, and parades.[25] But it can offer little
in the way of tangible inducements to businesses that are in search
of space and special transport facilities, and it lacks the capacity to
mold in any major way the total industrial or residential composition of the City. With the pattern of development well established,
the City perforce rides the main streams of economic development—
the expansion of office construction, the drift of large industries outward—with only a few opportunities to exercise calculated control.

A corollary which follows from the relative completeness of the City's physical development is that any fundamental change in the character of its land use must be, in the exact sense of the word, re-development. Thus, the City's efforts to change its environment are focused at a minimum toward rehabilitation of existing buildings and at a maximum toward their destruction and clearance prior to rebuilding. As we shall have occasion to observe later in more detail, New York's record in this respect is impressive, compared to other localities in the Region, or to the central cities of other metropolitan areas. New York City's percentage share of the nation's federally-aided public housing apartment units is considerably larger than its percentage share of the nation's population.[26] In terms of the size of the job of physical renewal which the City faces, however, the over-all effort appears in quite a different light. When *all* projects contracted for, planned, under study, or simply identified as future possibilities are totaled, under present redevelopment and housing programs, they involve about 1000 acres. Yet the total acreage which the City's Committee on Slum Clearance considered suitable for redevelopment is over 5000 acres.[27]

Limited in most of the strategies it can devise on its own, New York City is also limited in its opportunity to shift financial burdens to higher levels of government. As already seen, the City does not participate in the grant-in-aid program on the same basis as other local governments in New York State. Although the bulk of state revenue comes from the City's residents, in grant program after grant program, special arrangements—and, from the perspective of City officials, financially disadvantageous ones—are made for the metropolis. In education, highways, and health allocations, separate formulas apply to the City, and occasionally, as in the case of highways, the City is excluded entirely. Especially in the general-purpose grants, where flat per capita allotments are made to different classes of government without respect to estimates of need or effort— $6.75 in the case of cities, $3.55 for towns, and $3.00 for villages—the City's unified structure appears to place it at a comparative disadvantage.[28] For a given suburban area, where a village exists within a given town, the cumulative general-purpose grant of $6.55 can approximate the City's grant; yet there is no assurance that the localities in question operate under the same pressures of density or have smaller per capita resources at their command. On the contrary, there is assurance that quite frequently these units have both smaller densities and larger per capita resources. And thus, the almost equal grants are applied to localities with widely different needs and resources.

The effect of these special arrangements for the City shows up in the per capita over-all support received by the City in comparison to the suburban New York counties. In 1956, state aid for all purposes to the City amounted to $34.92 per capita in comparison to $42.05 for the other local governments in the New York portion of the Region. Between 1953 and 1956, state aid to the City increased 12.9 per cent, but in the suburban governments taken together the increase was almost twice as much—24.9 per cent.[29] And in 1957, officials pointed out that New York City and Westchester County received approximately the same school aid per pupil, $154 for the City and $155 for the county, whereas market value of taxable property per pupil was $25,519 in the City and $31,480 in Westchester.[30]

These comparisons have added significance when the special population characteristics of the City's constituency in relation to its revenues are taken into account. The present grant formula is essentially based on head-counting and only indirectly related to more sophisticated measures of needs or to such factors as revenue availability and tax effort. In a comparative study of ten counties and eighteen cities in New York State, the New York State–New York City Fiscal Relations Committee placed the counties within New York City as first among the ten counties in "need" (as defined by the Committee) and last in the amount of state assistance received. Among the eighteen cities, New York ranked second in tax effort but eighteenth in assistance. Among cities within the Region it placed first in ratio of expenditures to property value, and last in aid.[31]

Given the limited effectiveness of land-use controls and the disadvantageous position with respect to property taxation and grants-in-aid, the City's strategy boils down primarily to a search for other sources of revenue. In the postwar period the City government has developed a number of special taxes which provide a steadily increasing share of its total revenue. New York City levies every tax imposed by any other locality in the New York part of the Region and five other taxes that were allowed no other jurisdiction. In its fiscal year 1956–57, some $400 million, or 22 per cent of its total budget, was financed by a combination of twelve nonproperty taxes.[32] Over one-half of the $400 million came from a retail sales tax of 3 per cent, and another one-quarter was received from a general business and financial tax. Taxes or user charges were also applied to cigarettes, utilities, motor vehicles, amusements, hotel rooms, parimutuel pools, horse race admissions, retail liquor licenses, overnight parking, and payrolls. As a proportion of total revenue, the municipality's reliance on nonproperty taxes is twice that of the large upstate cities of New York State. Between 1945 and 1955, the share of total revenue received from these taxes more than doubled, and consistently over the last few years the City has petitioned the governor and legislature to authorize still more new tax sources.

The City has also adopted less obvious financial policies to bolster its revenue base. In its capital outlay program, now sizable because of a backlog of construction requirements postponed throughout the depression and war years, or necessary to accommodate the rapid shifts in population going on among the boroughs, the City has sought to escape the flat 10 per cent debt limitation by a series of special contrivances. Wherever capital outlay needs could be plausibly related to programs which might be self-supporting, constitutional exemptions from debt regulations have been sought and on occasion obtained. Bond issues to finance transit and dock improvements have been the favorite subjects of this type of exemption despite the fact that these enterprises do not always meet their costs from their own revenues. Certain school and housing debts have likewise been exempted, as has debt incurred for "recreational and other facilities incidental or appurtenant to" the construction of low-rent housing, thus placing the cost of some additional playgrounds and school buildings outside the general limitation. Further, since 1951, the City has been authorized to exclude some of the *partially* self-supporting programs in proportion to the degree to which these activities actually pay their own way.[33]

The policies of applying new local taxes and juggling debt limitations have not appeared to relieve substantially the City's financial pressures. Since World War II, the City has been forced to adopt still another approach: the transfer of certain major programs to other public agencies. Typically, these transfers have been in the field of transportation and cultural activities, and the recipients have been the independent authorities which operate partially or wholly within the City's boundaries.

Thus, although Mayor La Guardia was in large measure responsible for the initial development of the City's airport facilities, the investment in Idlewild proved too much for the City to handle.[34] Consequently this facility, though ultimately scheduled to be self-supporting, was transferred to the Port of New York Authority for final development. Similarly, in 1953, when recurring deficits in rapid transit appeared to make a fare increase financially inevitable despite its political unpopularity, a complex series of negotiations and skirmishes between the City and the State finally resulted in the establishment of the New York Transit Authority.[35] Since the City is still responsible for the transit debt, its financial relief in this instance has been by no means complete, but at least the operating losses were excluded from the City's budget. More recently, transfers have been made to the Triborough Bridge and Tunnel Authority. This agency, using surplus revenue received from bridge and tunnel tolls, has been able to venture into more speculative activities —the construction of the Coliseum and the East Side Airlines Terminal—and has undertaken major highway construction within the City in order to improve access to its river crossings.[36]

In the long run, such transfers of responsibility can work to the financial disadvantage of the City. The prognosis for the airports, for example, is that they will be sizable money-makers in the future. But the conditions of fiscal stringency under which the City operates often force it to sacrifice long-run profits for short-run savings. A larger and larger proportion of its budget in recent years consists of tax-supported programs rather than programs paid for by user charges—charges which in some cases yield handsome surpluses.

The major elements of New York City's fiscal policies consist, then, of a search for new sources of local revenue; intricate schemes to make maximum use of existing tax and borrowing powers; and the sometimes willing, sometimes reluctant abdication of program responsibilities. It would be a mistake, however, to interpret these strategies as the product of a carefully conceived and comprehensive design. On the contrary, the conclusions of the expert study commissions which repeatedly survey the state of City finance is that present conditions make rational financial planning difficult, if not impossible.[37]

A number of factors have combined to preclude any comprehensive approach. A recurrent one is the sensitivity of various groups of taxpayers within the City to changes in the revenue structure. Another is the upstate conviction that real economy measures have rarely been undertaken in the state's largest local government. The comparative lack of sympathy of the legislature toward what City officials believe are urgent and pressing needs acts as a further drag. The present financial structure does not reflect a discernible philosophy of regressivity, progressivity, equity, or calculated exploitation of a particular source. Rather it is a reflection of individual pressures cumulating over a long period of time. It is the end-product of a series of compromises between a mayor and a governor or state legislature to meet immediate demands in the least unpalatable way. Though uniquely endowed in the volume and variety of its tax sources, the City is also burdened with the most complex pattern of public demands in the Region, and it is consequently unique in the atmosphere of agitation and crisis which surrounds its budgetary process.

Over the long haul these *ad hoc* solutions add up to a kind of unpremeditated policy solution—a pattern of progressive exploitation of the politically most available resources according to the state's definition of availability. As assessments approach market value, and sales taxes appear to jeopardize retail activity, there is a tendency to shift to another, less vulnerable tax base. So proposals are made to tax activities for which a central-city location appears a necessity: the stock exchange, off-track betting, and taxicabs. And as particularly acute demands build up, like the demand for better transportation, they are assigned to other governments, apparently capable of nursing the program along to financial solvency.

Yet these policies remain incipient, never committing the City to one philosophy or another. Business enterprises, taxpayers associations, interest groups find political means to restrain the municipality's capacity to exploit any particular inflexibility they may have in geographical location. Political considerations and personality factors handicap the City in establishing close working relations with the Authorities within their borders. Pressing demands for public services, stemming from characteristics of density and obsolescence, lead to new and expanded programs whenever it seems possible to scrape together the necessary funds.

Thus, no City administration in recent years has found a workable strategy which will remove the paradox that the property-richest part of the Region regularly experiences the most persistent crisis in public finance. No politically acceptable policy has been discovered to counteract the fact that effective public demands are disproportionate to available tax revenues and are rising at a rapid rate—while the economic base for taxation, measured in either income or employment, has been declining relative to the rest of the Region. The resulting fiscal squeeze makes the position of budget-maker in the City the least-enviable political spot in the Region. In the interplay of politics and economics, he is no careful calculator of costs and benefits, of priorities among demands and of relative tax burdens among constituents. He is, to borrow a phrase previously appropriated to political analysis, a cat on a hot tin roof.

COMBINATIONS: (2) THE NEW YORK SUBURBS— MULTIPLICATION AND DIVISION

In contrast to the City of New York, where officials appear prone to use whatever expedient lies at hand, the local governments in the seven New York counties outside the City still seem in a position to be selective in their strategies. To be sure, they are not free from financial problems; in some cases they are beset with difficulties perhaps exceeding that of the central city. But they have been in a better position to choose one or another major strategy with some promise of success.

For the longest-settled suburban communities, the strategy has been principally one of land-use control. Sometimes at the last moment before the bulldozers appear, sometimes with exceptional foresight, the residents of these suburbs have decided to resist the outward migration of people and business. In carrying out these policies, they have been assisted by the size and legal structure of their local governments. New York governments of general jurisdiction embrace far more geographical territory per unit than those in New Jersey. The county, in particular, has proved capable of centralizing many powers and programs of the kinds that, in New Jersey, are still in the hands of municipalities. The combination of large territory and power has permitted New York counties and towns a much broader and much more systematic use of planning and zoning powers than in New Jersey.

The outstanding example is, of course, Westchester County—and most particularly northern Westchester. At least since World War I, Westchester has been stereotyped as a refuge of upper-income families from the City who settle in "quality" neighborhoods and consequently enjoy high-quality public services with relatively low "tax effort." During the same period, the county's political leadership has devoted most of its energies to public policies which support the pattern of low densities which topography originally encouraged. Though exceptions exist among its municipalities, Westchester remains, as someone has quipped, dedicated "to zoning against 'Bronxification.' " The stand against "Bronxification" consists fundamentally of policies designed to maintain reasonably low levels of density; to exclude developments of a character likely to result in more public expenditures than they return in revenue; and to discourage the construction of major state highways wherever possible and, when not possible, to prevent unsightly commercial developments on through highways. More recently, the expansion of "Westchester-type" industry has been encouraged; outsiders have been excluded from the county's well-developed park system; and considerable attention has been paid to keeping out what has been termed "the undesirable element." In one expert's view "the exclusion policy will no doubt stick. There is only one state park in this county, Mohansic, and Westchesterians don't particularly want any more. . . . They do hope, of course, that Bob Moses will build lots of state parks elsewhere to draw off the pressure." [38]

The clear, if somewhat negatively expressed, image of what Westchester should be, supported by a tradition of political leadership which has enabled the county to stimulate timely municipal action, reveals itself in the sophisticated state of zoning and planning within the county. A check of eleven of the county's sixteen towns by the staff of the Regional Plan Association in 1958 revealed that in seven of them over 80 per cent of all residentially zoned property was zoned at one acre or more. Of the remaining four towns, one had 75 per cent zoned this way, and the others had approximately 50 per cent. Nor is it only the spaciously zoned communities which apply land-use controls. All 46 municipalities in Westchester had zoning ordinances in 1957—most of them operative for over a quarter of a century and four-fifths of them revised or newly adopted since 1945. The entire county's population is served by planning boards; over 90 per cent of the population live in areas where subdivision regulations apply and official maps are in existence; over 60 per cent are in jurisdictions where master plans have been adopted. A majority of the jurisdictions have retained planning consultants to carry on new planning, revise zoning ordinances, develop master plans, and advise on redevelopment projects. [39]

One result of the unflagging efforts to shape the county according to the vision of the first migrants from the City is the relative ease with which the county supports high-cost public services. Although Westchester in 1955 was third in total per capita expenditures among the seventeen counties of the Region outside New York City and had the highest expenditures among counties of about the same densities, its per capita increase in total property taxes between 1945 and 1955 was the lowest of all. In that period, its municipalities experienced an absolute decline in per capita payments for debt service—a record approached only by outlying Dutchess County.

In contrast, the other New York counties outside the City had increases ranging from 85 per cent to 228 per cent. Though revenue from nonproperty sources rose 68 per cent in Westchester, this trend too is below the Region's average when New York City is excluded. In short, while maintaining a high level of expenditures and providing services generally rated by professional observers as among the highest quality in the Region, the county units kept their public financial affairs in good order, and the proportion of their resources devoted to public purposes, whether measured in terms of income or market value of property, was below the average for the New York portion of the Region.[40]

Other local governments in the New York State portion of the Region, outside New York City, also rely on land-use policies to maintain a favorable political economy, though in no other county have such policies been so consistently and comprehensively applied. In Oyster Bay Township, Nassau County, eleven of the fifteen villages have zoned all land set aside for residential purposes at one acre or more. Here and there in North Hempstead there are municipal islands with similar regulations—Kings Point, North Hills, and Roslyn Harbor, for example. In these communities, the tradition of spacious life is so politically strong that their governments have turned aside the postwar wave of mass development which only a few miles south changed farmland into Levittowns. There are also hints that in counties yet to feel the full impact of the urban exodus —Rockland, Putnam, and possibly Suffolk and Orange—the Westchester lesson is being taken to heart. In the last ten years, planning boards have been activated, master plans adopted, and zoning laws enacted in an effort to produce "balanced" communities.[41]

Nevertheless, in none of the other New York counties has Westchester's zoning record been approached, and some have adopted altogether different strategies. In Nassau, for example, the fairly primitive land-use regulations existing at the end of World War II proved inadequate to stem the influx of new population in the center and south of the county. The rush eastward in search of vacant land set the stage for mass residential development, spurred on, in Robert Moses' acid words, by "the estate owner who is surrounded, can't pay higher taxes and has lost interest in his home and the community; the truck farmer who wants to retire or head east to cheaper open land; the speculator who aims to cut up real estate into as many postage stamp lots as weak zoning resolutions and weaker officials will permit." Reflecting on the recent past, Moses offered the judgment that "if intelligent forethought had forced larger lots and higher restrictions in recent subdivisions, the future overpopulation would have been controlled and most of the evils which flew out of that Pandora box would have been kept tightly under cover." Looking to the future, he could predict in blunt terms, "If lying or exaggerated real estate advertisements mean more to you than decent standards, if your surviving country squires continue to sell to developers for the most they can get and leave to jackals what they claimed to prize, if the small owner is so stupid that he permits cheap promoters to repeat the mistakes of the city, you are going to have suburban slums as sure as God made little apples." [42]

Mr. Moses' verdict on Long Island's possible future may be somewhat overdrawn—he himself has proclaimed that the joke is on the pessimist. Yet certainly in the decisive stage of its suburban settlement, Nassau's governments were not prepared to guide growth in the Westchesterian manner. On the contrary, its principal response has been to adapt the governmental structure to the new environment rather than to shape the character of the environment itself. One major modification has taken place in the county government:

Nassau was the first New York county to adopt a "strong executive" plan. Its government has also assumed increasing responsibilities in the fields of highways, health, sewage construction, water supply, and welfare, and it has exercised a centralizing influence in tax assessment and collection. A countervailing structural development which has occurred, as population growth in specific parts of the county has generated specific pressures, has been the establishment of more and more special districts to handle specific public programs.

On balance, these latter forces have tended to predominate. While the number of villages in Nassau has remained at 63 since 1933 and the number of school districts has decreased from 65 to 62, a steady growth in other special districts has occurred. Between 1945 and 1955, their number rose from 173 to 268, providing such diverse functions as fire protection, street lighting, parking, parks, police, garbage disposal, sanitary regulation, sewage facilities, water, and drainage.[43] It would be a mistake to regard the districts as totally unrelated to other governmental units, for they are created under town law, their tax and assessment policies are reviewed by the County Board of Supervisors, and their activities are knit together by informal political ties among their officials. What the districts do represent, however, is a device for gaining access to tax revenue which under state limitations might otherwise be foreclosed and for assigning particular tax bills to particular classes of inhabitants.

Thus the resident of Nassau County receives his services from, and pays his taxes to, a number of governments. They provide him with a plethora of opportunities to enjoy the benefits of home rule, but they also bring a considerable layering of tax bills and a considerable differential in taxes depending on residential location. As Samuel F. Thomas has pointed out, a property owner in one unincorporated area in the Town of Hempstead received in 1955 a consolidated town tax bill of $3.63 per $100 of assessed valuation representing the charges of ten separate districts, to which was added a second bill of $4.26 per $100 for schools, or a total of $7.89. By contrast, a property owner in an incorporated area received a consolidated town bill of $1.50 per $100 representing the charges of the county and town for general purposes and of the county sewer district, a school tax bill of $2.78, and a village tax bill of $1.79. Thus, his total tax bill was $6.07 per $100, almost $2 per $100 less than the resident in the unincorporated area. Although the standards of services were not necessarily the same, it is doubtful that services in the unincorporated area were greater in number or higher in professional quality. More likely, the reverse condition was true.[44]

It is not only at the town and village level that the principle of multiplication is applied in Nassau County. For the county and indeed for all of Long Island, special authorities and state commissions play an important role. Thus the Nassau County Bridge Authority was created in 1945 to acquire the privately owned Atlantic Beach Bridge and to construct a new span. Both the Jones Beach State Parkway Authority and the Bethpage Park Authority have important responsibilities in the construction of the county's highway network and the provision of recreation facilities. Tied to the Long Island State Park Commission by identical membership on their governing boards, these three authorities provide another means of relieving the general government of responsibilities and costs.

The result of the strategy of fragmentation in Nassau is a public sector exceeded by no other in the Region in the resources diverted from the private sector. Nassau not only experienced by far the fastest growth in expenditures after the war—some 160 per cent between 1945 and 1955—but its per capita total expenditure in 1955 was $244 compared to the City's $226 and Westchester's $227. As the Commission on New York City–State Relations has pointed out, Nassau's total expenditures in 1954 amounted to 6.7 per cent of personal income, compared to 6.5 per cent and 5.6 per cent for New York City and Westchester respectively.[45]

Comparisons between expenditures and income give a sense of the magnitude of Nassau's public programs; they do not, however, indicate who pays the bills. It is especially important to realize that one out of every four residents is a child. Therefore the major local expenditure for Nassau is for public schools. And schools are more heavily supported by state aid than any other activity. In terms of property taxes per capita, for example, the amount collected in Nassau in 1955 was $128 in contrast to Westchester's $133.[46] In short, Nassau's high spending record is not necessarily accompanied by an equivalent drain on local resources. Its governments have managed to live with the consequences of expansion—although few of them may consider it gracious living.

The remainder of the New York counties do not present the sharp delineation in choice of weapons which distinguishes Westchester and Nassau. Suffolk, for example, has experienced the effects of the suburban migration only in its western areas and to date has behaved in its political response like a house divided. Its five western townships, within commuter range of the City, have increasingly sought to adopt some of Westchester's and Nassau's techniques. Its five eastern townships, as yet largely unaffected by the course of the Region's development, have continued on accustomed ways. The result, as described by Long Island's *Newsday,* is a "case of governmental rickets . . . brought about by a split personality between the rising suburban areas which need a strong county government . . . and political thinking in the east end which generally rejects the need for a county government any more modern than 1900."[47]

Whatever the root causes of the east-west split, Suffolk's bifurcated politics has meant—at least until recently—that the county's response to the problems of growth has been more reflex than calculated. As development has proceeded, Suffolk has relied on either surplus funds husbanded from the past or large increases in assessed valuations of residential property. The efficacy of this policy seemed dubious in 1957 when "county officials became aware of a startling fact. Building was beginning to fall off. The county's assessed valuation appeared to be nearing a static point—leveled off by industry's unwillingness to establish itself in a county which has little to offer in the way of tax abatement programs, good roads, or a good labor pool. In the meantime, the county had obligated itself for more than $12,000,000 worth of new projects." To meet this situation, "the county board authorized a $50,000 special census. By proving a substantial rise in population, the county was able to claim an additional $1,000,000 in state aid." [48]

The pattern of instinctive reaction has varied widely among the Suffolk townships. Each of the ten towns until 1958 made its own assessments, with resulting variations from 23 to 43 per cent in the ratio of assessed to market value. Each had its own planning and zoning philosophy. According to *Newsday,* "four east end towns do not even have zoning ordinances and there is nothing to prevent the building of a glue factory next to someone's home. . . . Only one township has what is considered a proper allowance for industrial growth. . . . In Huntington, recently, complicated zoning requirements set off a legal tussle when the zoning board was haled into court by the town board. . . . In case after case, Suffolk towns, operating under 20-year zoning ordinances, have failed to stay ahead of or even keep up with fast-changing conditions. Suffolk zoning remains a hodge-podge of inconsistencies." [49]

There are signs that Suffolk is girding itself for the adoption of a more consistent policy toward growth. After two false starts, the county has adopted a new charter modeled after the Westchester and Nassau ones and providing for an elected county executive to begin unifying the county, administratively and psychologically. Even earlier the Suffolk County Planning Board had been revitalized and town planning and zoning activities speeded up. Inherent in this process of reorganization is a philosophy becoming more and more explicit, that Suffolk must rely on industrial development to provide the basis for its political economy. Thus Babylon has set aside 8 per cent of its land area for industrial use; Islip has undertaken to rezone 4000 acres; Huntington is planning to make industrial sites available along the new Long Island Expressway to Riverhead. Similarly, Greenport has offered an existing two-story building free to an acceptable business; Brookhaven has established a Town Industrial Advisory Committee; and Port Jefferson has been opened as a deep-sea port after a "three year battle against civic and boating groups." [50]

Economically, of course, one can question the feasibility of Suffolk's plans for industrial expansion. In comparison with other parts of the Region, this distant county continues at a disadvantage in transportation costs. Nevertheless, to the degree that a conscious strategy is emerging, this strategy aims at attracting business.

While this general policy is being fashioned, the comparatively moderate rate of Suffolk's growth relative to Nassau's, and the large amount of land still available, keep its public financial problems in manageable proportions. Suffolk's population doubled from 276,000 to 528,000 between 1950 and 1957. But, in per capita expenditures in 1955, it was fourth among the seven New York counties outside New York City. In the rate of growth in per capita expenditures between 1945 and 1955, it was fourth, and in the ratio of real estate taxes to income it was still fourth.[51]

Political strategies in the Region's other New York counties, Rockland, Putnam, Orange, and Dutchess, present a more muddled picture. In all of these counties, assessment ratios still provide ample room for maneuverability. In all of them, particularly Rockland, planning and zoning programs are being actively developed. Nonetheless all but six of the New York municipalities without zoning in 1957 were in these counties, and agitation for cooperative planning and uniformity of policy do not at this time seem as intense as in Suffolk. The northern counties have much lower densities than those prevailing in the other parts of the Region and much more vacant land. Their search for additional sources of revenue is not as evident, and their impetus toward expansion of services and facilities is more muted.

But the more isolated position of these four counties does not necessarily mean lower public expenditures on a per capita basis. On the contrary, Putnam in 1955 ranked first in this respect among the seven New York counties outside New York City, in contrast to Rockland, Orange, and Dutchess, which fell at the bottom of the New York list. In rate of change from 1945 to 1955, Putnam was second only to Nassau, and Rockland followed in third position.[52]

Putnam's high expenditure level appears to be in part a function of sparsity of settlement, for extremely low densities like extremely high densities make for high per capita expenditures. Undoubtedly, a second influence is the number of high-income families that have migrated there, purportedly to re-establish the Westchester of the twenties. Thus, the county seems presently to have the public services typical of rural areas, supported by the higher incomes of its newer residents. Rockland seems much more a part of the metropolitan area. It has a low density, to be sure, but its growth has passed beyond the break-point between rural and urban living, and the "get going" process of modern public programs has now appeared.

The same comparative ranking of these four northern counties exists so far as local taxes are concerned. Putnam was first again among the seven New York counties outside New York City in per capita local property taxes in 1955 while the other three bring up the rear—separated from the nearest county by a substantial $20 per capita.[53] This ranking bespeaks the mixed situation of peripheral counties where the array of public services need not be as elaborate as that in more urbanized areas, but where either a decision for high-quality services or the "diseconomies" of a rural environment may call forth heavy per capita public spending.

At this stage of incipient development, then, it is not surprising that the policies of the counties have not yet crystallized. Rockland, faced with the most immediate prospect of heavy immigration, is characterized, in the rueful language of a nameless developer, by "the politics of the mau-maus"—residents attached to rural bliss who descend from the hills to fight at the first hint of large-scale development.[54] Orange has not yet experienced the political battles of the Rockland variety. Dutchess is oriented as much to Poughkeepsie as to the center of the New York Metropolitan Region. Putnam has a mix of farmers and exurbanites living in an uneasy political peace.

If there is a single instrument on which these governments rely, it is the beneficence offered by the state through grant programs which are designed to favor their semirural status. In nonschool grants to municipalities in 1955, calculated on a per capita basis, the municipalities of Orange, Dutchess, and Putnam ranked first, second, and third among all the counties of the Region, and Rockland ranked fifth. In the five years between 1950 and 1955, the increase in such grants exceeded 20 per cent in Putnam and Rockland, and was 16 per cent in Orange. Dutchess experienced a moderate rise of 4 per cent. In the same period, Nassau experienced a *decrease* of 17 per cent, while she underwent her most rapid period of growth.[55]

When one reviews the experience of each New York county, then, a sequence of governmental policy-making appears, corresponding to the stages of urbanization in which the jurisdictions find themselves. In the first onrush of urban settlement, a government may choose to face the mounting tide of population primarily by catering to the public needs of the new residents. If so, it may be compelled to expand its tax base, either by closing the gap between assessed and true property valuation or by seeking new revenue sources. Or it may create new institutions which have the legal right to call upon the wealth and income of the constituency a second or third time, or even more. Alternatively, a jurisdiction may anticipate the forces poised to enter its boundary lines and by timely planning or zoning divert the pressures of growth. It may even try to assure by promotional activities, land-use measures, and tax policy that population increases are accompanied by additions to the industrial base of the community.

Depending on which decision is made in the beginning, a basis is laid for new strategies at the more mature stage of development. Governments which have relied upon zoning and planning tend to adopt policies akin to "holding actions" and take on more and more the appearance of islands amid the surge of growth around them. Governments which have permitted their land to become densely populated intensify their search for new funds and may become immersed in technical maneuvers to expand debt limits and tax yields. As obsolescence sets in, the need for renewal becomes increasingly apparent and as the cost of renewal becomes recognized, appeals for new revenue sources or more grants-in-aid are mounted with growing intensity—though customarily they receive a cool reception at the capitol.

This pattern may not continue. Though Nassau and Westchester provide contrasting object lessons and the counties farther out have displayed in the 1950's an increasing awareness of the implications of growth, their decisions are not yet firm. Zoning and planning techniques which served Westchester well are not as applicable today. The real probability in the suburbs of the future is not one-acre lots of the relatively well-to-do, or the Levittowns of Nassau, but instead fairly compact developments interspersed with open spaces and industrial parks in the new style of Sterling Forest, in Orange County. Since a planning philosophy directed to that end is still in the process of formulation, one can doubt its application in advance of the migration itself.

COMBINATIONS: (3) THE NEW JERSEY SUBURBS— FIGHTING ECONOMICS WITH IDEOLOGY

In a way, the New Jersey portion of the Region is even less susceptible to broad generalizations than the New York portion. In another way, it exhibits a remarkable uniformity. On the one hand, the much smaller size of New Jersey's local municipal governments and the more restricted role of the counties suggest a picture of variety rampant. On the other hand, a universality of ideology and tradition appears to pervade the governments of the Garden State, and many of the same policies have been independently adopted by the majority of the local units.

The most striking demonstration of variety occurs in the field of zoning and planning. Here the presence of a large number of governmental units presiding over small areas, combined with the comparatively limited role of the county governments, produces a potpourri of planning programs. Although New Jersey has had enabling legislation since 1935 for the establishment of county and even multicounty planning boards to supplement local actions, most measures for land-use control are still applied at the municipal levels. The county boards rely principally on voluntary municipal cooperation to effect their plans, and most of them have functioned actively only since the end of World War II. Multicounty planning programs, designed to coordinate land-use policy over the entire New Jersey portion of the metropolitan area, have begun even more recently. The impact of both of these broader efforts, in the language of the Commission to Study Laws Affecting Industrial Development, has been limited by "the natural disinclination of municipalities to surrender any of their sovereignty." Meantime, local planning and zoning agencies have multiplied at a rapid rate in the state as a whole—from 120 in 1945 to 356 at the end of 1956 and 389 one year later. As of 1957, 124 master plans had been completed and 86 had been officially adopted.[56]

For the New Jersey side of the Region, then, the proliferation of local zoning ordinances and land-use plans attests to an assortment of specific municipal approaches to development. Although the municipalities of the inner counties tend to have more detailed requirements and regulations than those farther out, each county exhibits a number of exceptions, and each municipality demonstrates an inclination to fashion its own response. Among the nine counties, for example, jurisdictions in Morris and Passaic have made considerable progress in the development of industrial performance standards, while those in Bergen County appear to have pushed ahead in establishing time limits for nonconforming uses. Minimum lot sizes vary throughout the counties from less than 5,000 square feet to over 45,000. Five municipalities have established three separate industrial zones apiece while 42 have none at all. The number of residential zones within a single jurisdiction varies from one to nine. In short, like Noah's Ark, New Jersey seems to feature at least two of every land-use control device known to the planning profession. Yet, next door to the government with elaborate master plans and complex subdivision controls may be a jurisdiction whose constituency fiercely resists any effort to restrict the private builder. Coexistence of extremes in planning philosophy is a fact of the state's political life.[57]

Two results of this variety of attitudes and approaches to land-use policies are a continuing display of intergovernmental hostilities and an occasional exaggerated sense of local power. Head-on collisions among municipalities over the efforts of one borough to establish industrial or shopping districts adjacent to residential areas in the adjoining township are not infrequent.[58] One can admire the efforts of the planning board of the Borough of Wallington in Bergen County—with an area of less than one square mile and with only 57 acres of usable vacant land remaining—in making systematic investigations of their land-use potential. But one can also question the utility of their planning efforts. As one studies the carefully prepared planning reports of each of the New Jersey counties with their detailed summaries of land use, park needs, journey-to-work patterns, highway plans, and water supplies, the divergencies between the general forces of growth and the particularistic responses to these trends become apparent. Land-use measures appear more and more designed to attract a certain business plant, or to exclude residential houses which do not pay their way, or to capitalize on a windfall of an exclusive development which might come a municipality's way.[59]

This variety of land-use policies is paralleled, of course, by variety in municipal financial policies. We have already had occasion to emphasize the wide range in assessment practices, debt management, and tax rates among New Jersey municipalities. One set of figures, however, among those reflecting what the New Jersey Commission on State Tax Property termed a "morass of inequities," deserves attention. In a sample of 49 municipalities the Commission found that the variations in the assessments on similar types of property ranged from 17.2 per cent of market value to 50.7 per cent and the average variation for all types of property was 26 per cent. The Commission attributed these results to a "breakdown in the assessment process," and it concluded, "The principal reason for the increases in local real estate tax rates which have occurred since 1939, is the failure of the local assessors to give effect to the general increase in price level for properties that were constructed either before or after building costs were affected by inflation." [60]

Yet, if the small size and independent ways of the New Jersey municipalities produce a pattern of variation and complexity for land-use policies and external strategies, certain policies apply across the board in the Jersey section of the Region. The most obvious is New Jersey's insistence on maintaining a local revenue base that is far more limited than New York's. The heavy reliance on the property tax, the historic policy of "no new taxes," and the much smaller volume of state grants-in-aid impose more or less uniform restraints on all the municipalities. Consequently, the local governments have not possessed the array of strategies with which to handle growth problems and their response typically has been a lower level of expenditures than that of their New York neighbors.

The differences between New Jersey and New York in levels of per capita expenditures for 1955 have already been noted, and these differences have persisted throughout the postwar period. Total expenditures per capita between 1945 and 1955 increased 113 per cent for the "New York Inner" municipalities (Nassau and Westchester), but only 78 per cent for "New Jersey Inner" (Hudson, Essex, Union, Bergen, and Passaic).[61] The increases for the outer areas were 130 per cent in New York and 87 per cent in New Jersey. As another index to the differences between the two states, consistently over the last twenty years the pay schedules for teachers have been substantially lower in New Jersey. In 1935, the average salary for teachers in New Jersey's metropolitan school districts was $1,800; the comparable New York figure was $2,200. In 1958, the respective averages were $3,100 and $3,600.[62]

Not only have the local revenue sources in New Jersey been fewer in number and less susceptible to modification, but the possibilities of fiscal reform through governmental reorganization have never been seriously exploited. The Jersey portion of the Region does have its special districts and authorities but nothing like the number and variety that exist across the Hudson. Certainly the application of the device of the special district does not compare with practices in Nassau County or even in Suffolk County. By Census count in 1957 there were only 73 special districts, other than school districts, in the

New Jersey portion of the Region—mostly confined to sewage disposal and pollution control—together with a scattering of municipal housing and parking authorities.[63]

The very universality of tax and organizational policy in New Jersey, therefore, may act as a counterweight to municipal diversity. Precisely because real property has borne the brunt of public demands brought about by urbanization, per capita property tax levies have increased much more sharply in New Jersey than in New York —85 per cent in the first postwar decade, for example, in the "New Jersey Inner" municipalities, compared to 14 per cent in "New York Inner." [64] Pressures have therefore been intensified to reduce arbitrary variations in assessments on equivalent property and to authorize nonproperty taxes.

The judicial decision in *Switz v. Middletown,* requiring assessment at 100 per cent of true value until the legislature decreed otherwise, may well mark a milestone in the state's fiscal history.[65] This decree has already reduced the differentials in assessments among the municipalities—and, by making possible sharp increases in property levies, inflamed the issue of new kinds of taxes. Shortly thereafter, the state abandoned the strict application of the "no new tax" philosophy and imposed a corporation income tax. The state also enacted major new school-aid laws—first, a so-called "minimum foundation" program, which for the first time related state grants to the fiscal resources of the local community; then a crash program for school construction, with a consequent increase in school grants from $40 million in 1953 to over $107 million in 1958.[66] In these ways New Jersey moved to accommodate the underlying growth pressures by state rather than municipal action.

There is one other common strategy which applies in the New Jersey sector. Given the heavy reliance on property taxation, both the state and a majority of the localities have a special incentive to attract new industry. In many ways, of course, these activities parallel efforts in New York—the establishment of special study commissions to review tax policy and labor laws, and the inauguration of planning programs with an eye toward assuring a friendly "political climate" for business. But the promotional policy has been a special favorite among New Jersey governments, more so than in New York.

Middlesex County, for example, in 1938 established an industrial department which it calls the first in the nation. This department provides a clearing house for locational information; acts as liaison between, on the one hand, firms looking for new locations, and on the other hand, real estate brokers and local governments; and encourages local planning agencies to reserve land for future development. It has pioneered in the establishment of industrial parks. The department lays claim to the development of a "friendly community attitude" which it holds as "perhaps the most important factor in attracting industry." [67]

One can discount the crucial role which neighborliness plays in locational economics. The rapid growth in industrial activity in Middlesex is undoubtedly more influenced by its easy highway access to national markets and the availability of the Raritan Estuary for nuisance industries. Nevertheless, the Middlesex department has served as a prototype for other metropolitan counties in New Jersey, and they all undertake to trade effectively on the state's "low-tax" reputation. At least, New York counties look on these promotional activities with some envy. To them Middlesex has "found a cure for its problems in new, modern industry" and has developed "a far-sighted program . . . bringing the benefits of employment and tax contributions to help that suburban area prosper." [68]

Despite the individual variations which persist in New Jersey, the metropolitan communities of that state have always come up with somewhat common responses to deal with economic growth. The historic response has been a conservative attitude toward public expenditures and public activities, as indicated by a heavy reliance on a single tax and a resistance to experimentation in structural changes or fiscal policy. In recent years, these policies have undergone transformation, but also in uniform ways: a substantial revision in property-tax administration by state judicial decree, the application of new state taxes, the expansion of grants-in-aid. The municipalities have also been characterized by similar efforts to stimulate industrial development.

Yet the fact remains that New Jersey still spends a smaller proportion of its income or wealth for public purposes than New York, still relies on smaller units of government and narrower revenue bases which restrict the effectiveness of its policies. In short, New Jersey focuses on methods to limit the public demand, while New York searches for new resources to fulfill demands, present or anticipated, or makes more vigorous use of governmental power to guide growth.

CONSEQUENCES

What is the upshot of this complex process of move and countermove among the local governments of the Region, the net effect of the combinations of policies which the jurisdictions have adopted toward the increasing pressures of urbanization? Beyond providing an understanding of how differences in expenditure and revenue patterns arise apart from environmental circumstances, do the political maneuvers alter in any major way the underlying forces which shape the substance of the public sector? Do they have any really significant implications for the private sector?

Answers to these questions can necessarily be only conditional ones. In an estimate of the influence of the strategies, alone or in combination, in any particular part of the Region, we are in effect asking ourselves what would have occurred if the economic and population forces had operated without political intervention. What density pattern might have resulted or what would have been the revenue potential of a "natural" pattern of industrial location on the basis of its actual market value? We can simulate some of these conditions, but we can never examine them first-hand.

On the basis of the evidence which is on hand, however, certain general conclusions seem warranted. So far as the policies of redefining urban environments are concerned, these strategies, in and of themselves, have little effect on the mainstream of economic development. Their alert and timely application may save a politician's career, but as the process of urbanization wears on, the capacity for maneuver, at least on the basis of the property tax system, is sharply reduced. Municipalities also reach a limitation in the use of special districts whose effect is to increase the volume of the property revenues taken from a single geographical area. Here too the limitation of the size of the property tax base comes to apply. Thus, the focus of political attention turns, as in New York City, increasingly toward a search for new sources of revenue—a search the success of which depends on the vigor of the private sector itself.

So far as policies designed to guide land use are concerned, these can obviously be important. Westchester stands as an example of how effective political action, if applied with energy and imagination, can affect the pattern of population settlement and industrial location. And the enclaves in Nassau and parts of New Jersey similarly testify to the capacity of determined constituencies to thwart the natural pressures of expansion.

The real effectiveness of land-use policies hinges on their timing: the date when comprehensive programs are applied. In Nassau, zoning and planning measures were developed largely after the heaviest waves of migration had settled in. In New Jersey, the small size of the municipalities has precluded a comprehensive approach. In most of the Region, the economic gains promised to individual landowners by selling out their holdings have outweighed considerations of organized community development. For the future, one must conclude that in Suffolk, Rockland, Monmouth, and Middlesex, the counties most likely to receive the bulk of new growth, the issue of whether public policy will be decisive is still unclear.

As for the industrial development programs of various localities, they appear to have a Don Quixote quality of impracticability. Undoubtedly, particular firms have been influenced in their choice of sites by the discovery of a "friendly" government. But, as another volume in this series has suggested, tax levels do not appear to be prime considerations in the location of industry. Certainly the most ardent booster plan cannot compensate for a municipality's deficiencies in transportation, labor, character of terrain, and water. Even grants-in-aid from higher levels of government, the major strategy of adjustment on which the Region's governments rely for survival, do not seem substantially to affect the process of economic development. Present grant formulas are not geared to compensate decisively for differences in either demand-oriented or supply-oriented dimensions of municipal environment and they leave the relative position of the governments undisturbed. Hence their impact is to exaggerate present differences in financial status—enabling the smaller, outlying jurisdictions to rock along under their present structure of organization and finance.

Not one of these strategies, then, has important implications for the private sector of the Region taken as an entity. An industry barred from one locality can in all probability find a hospitable reception in another with equivalent economic advantages. High-income families take refuge in Westchester, southern Putnam, and Fairfield, while mass developers make breakthroughs in Nassau or Monmouth or Rockland to provide middle-class housing. With so many different constituencies, many options are open for firms and households alike, and though the process of industrial and population diffusion may occasionally be skewed, the forces are not, in general, thwarted, turned aside, or guided.

Yet, if these policies have little effect in shaping the Regional economy, they do keep the local-government system continuously agitated *about* economic affairs. Indeed, they engender a pattern of behavior more closely approximating rivalries in world economic affairs than a domestic system of government intent on aiding the processes of economic development. Because particular combinations of strategies may be effective for any one jurisdiction, there is a strong tendency for each to "go it alone" to develop appropriate protective devices to escape the expensive public by-products of the private process of development. Municipalities come to concentrate on ways and means of getting as large a slice of the existing economic pie as possible and of mitigating the effects of new residential settlement. The development of hundreds of separate policies, in various combinations, among hundreds of jurisdictions engenders a spirit of contentiousness and competition. As the possibilities of shifting burdens within a municipality diminish, as development programs fail to counteract the economic considerations which predominate in locational decisions, as urbanization goes on apace, the temptation to embark on municipal mercantilism becomes stronger. Paradoxically, the policies also become less effective, since a government's neighbors are likely to adopt comparable tax rates, make the same zoning policy, and grant equal concessions to new industries. In these circumstances, the management of the political economy goes forward in ways localized, limited, and largely negative in character.

Thus, little opportunity exists for the development of Regionwide public policy. Each government is preoccupied with its own problems, and collectively the governments are not prepared to formulate general policies for guiding economic development, or to make generalized responses to the financial pressures generated by urbanization. They are neither in a position to establish and enforce public criteria for appropriate conditions of growth nor to provide public services which the private sector requires on a Regionwide basis. By their organization, financing, and philosophy, they forswear the opportunity for the exercise of these larger powers.

Nonetheless, the Regional private sector does require public action in this larger sense. It cannot, by itself, either ensure the conditions of order and stability which are prerequisites for the transaction of private business, or control by a process of self-regulation some of the unpalatable by-products of private activities, or provide basic services essential to its effective operation. Filling the vacuum, which the local governments of the Region have themselves created, are other and quite different forms of government with objectives and policies all their own. It is these governments which have become most influential in shaping, by public action, the dimensions of the private sector, and it is to their organization and activities that we now turn.

4

The World of the Metropolitan Giants

Regional gov't's

The Region's public sector, pushed to greater size and importance by forces inherent in the Region's growth, requires more and more managing. We have divided the managers into two great systems, the "local governments" and the "Regional enterprises," and have come half-way in our examination of how these systems feed back upon the private sector. As for the local governments, rolling with the punch of urbanization, their responses have been found to be mainly defensive, unpremeditated, and parochial, and their influence upon the private sector must be considered haphazard and localized. The same cannot be said of the Regional enterprises, whose programs and behavior we now explore.

THE HELPING HAND OF GOVERNMENT

The exploration will necessarily be a selective one. A full examination of activities through which Regional enterprises play upon the private development of the Region would have to include such matters as state regulation of water and air pollution, the establishment of parks, the preservation of open spaces, and even the plans of state and federal agricultural agencies as they adjust their programs to meet suburban rather than rural problems. We would have to delve deeply into the operations of the United States Congress, and unravel complicated bureaucratic maneuverings in Washington, Trenton, Albany, and Hartford. And we would have to master the complex technical problems involved in the engineering and financing of modern highways, waterworks, and sewage treatment plants.

With such an abundance of pertinent material, our effort will be limited to clarifying how the Regional-enterprise system appears to operate in three fields of particular importance to the Region's development. In each, we will try to indicate what kinds of organizations and entities are active; what goals they pursue; what instruments they use to accomplish their objectives; and what the results are for the private sector. By such a focus, even though we do violence to the engineering aspects of the operations involved, we can perhaps throw light on how and why government participates in decisions about where jobs and people will be located.

The first and most important of the fields we have chosen for study is that of passenger transportation. Here, the arrival of the automobile has placed government in a central position of influence. As other volumes of the New York Metropolitan Region Study have made abundantly clear, the high-speed express highway has transformed the meaning of access for the business firm and the household alike; opened up parts of the Region for development which otherwise would have remained rural; by-passed other areas almost completely; changed land-values decisively; and revised distribution systems and journey-to-work patterns. Nor is it only in highways that government has the decisive word. Mass transportation facilities nominally under private management have become largely a public responsibility. The subways are under public auspices, and the future of railroad commuting now turns largely on public action. Terminal facilities for water and truck freight are a matter of public concern and are being constructed by public agencies. In every phase of passenger transportation, governmental decisions, by influencing the location of people and jobs, exert direct and profound effects on the private sector.

Our second field for investigation is water. The provision of this elemental resource in sufficient volume and purity is now more a public than a private responsibility within the Region. At a minimum, the development of future sources of supply—in contrast to the provision of distribution systems—depends on public action. And water development plans affect other government programs in recreation, land management, and flood control.

The third field we canvass is that which has come to be called physical development—the actual shaping of the Region through positive governmental action, notably renewal and redevelopment programs. For example, whatever activities are undertaken to reclaim obsolete areas within the old cities of the Region—New York City, Bridgeport, Newark, Jersey City, Elizabeth, Paterson—have to be financed and controlled by public authority. So do efforts to prevent blight from spreading or to reduce the danger of its emergence in later years.

In these three fields—transportation, water, and physical development—government intervenes much more directly in the operations of the private sector than it does when underwriting the more familiar municipal services of schools, welfare offices, police, and fire fighting. Moreover, in these three broad areas the character of the public program more heavily affects basic economic factors: the ease and efficiency in moving persons and goods, the location of jobs and homes, the stimulation of capital investment. Quite apart from the not inconsiderable share of income and manpower claimed by public programs in these fields, or the number of private industries which rely upon them for direct support, they constitute obvious and essential links in the economic system. Only public policy can decisively answer such questions as where and in what way port facilities will be developed, where housing for minorities will be available, what action will be taken to develop new reservoirs, what emphasis will be given highway expansion versus rails. Without the helping hand of government in these respects, it would be difficult to conceive of the "Region" in the sense in which we speak of it today.

THE NO-MAN'S-LAND OF REGIONAL SERVICES

In our detailed discussions of transportation, water, and physical development, we will find ourselves in quite a different political system from the one we have just explored. Up to now, our concern has been with governments which, despite their many differences, possessed the common characteristics of a definite geographical jurisdiction, a roughly similar set of revenue sources, and a pattern of expenditures which by and large dealt with much the same kinds of public needs. They also had many similarities in governmental structure, legal powers, and political practice. Each had a local constituency in a position of ultimately sanctioning the actions of the officials. Dealing with a considerable number of jurisdictions possessing these common properties, we could describe a good deal of their behavior in quantitative terms; we could almost always classify them and generalize about them.

When we deal with Regional services, however, the familiar if complex lineup of counties, cities, towns, villages, boroughs, and districts disappears. Gone, too, is the capacity to examine public activities in terms of the differing social and economic characteristics of the communities. In place of more or less fixed governmental boundaries, of formally developed public institutions, of long-established rules of procedure, of more or less clear-cut allocations of responsibilities, is a much more elusive political system. The public functions which seem most critical to the course of Regional development, and which form the most obvious underpinnings of the private sector, are carried out for the most part by unique organizational devices and *ad hoc* understandings, developed in a maze of divided responsibility and authority. The statutory basis for action is more complex; so is the involvement of different levels of government; so are the provisions with respect to financial support and the participation of the local constituencies. And the pattern of activity—the programs developed, the expenditures authorized, and the functions performed—emerges without clear relation to the characteristics of the Region's population and economic activity. The definitions of needs, of resources, and of appropriate action take on increasingly the coloration of the institutions involved.

One would go too far, of course, if he insisted there is an utterly impassable boundary between "local governments" and "Regional enterprises." There are instances where Regional or at least subregional services are carried out through cooperative agreements among the local governments. Municipalities do join hands on matters such as uniform traffic laws, common administrative procedures, and consolidated fee schedules for routine services.[1] Within a given part of the Region, several jurisdictions may agree to share fire or police equipment, garbage trucks, or other facilities. But, by and large, these cooperative arrangements are limited both in the kinds of activities involved and the extent of territory embraced. They rarely encompass the services most important to the functioning of the private sector or most significant in terms of scale of operations.

The scarcity of cooperative arrangements among the Region's local governments is not surprising. For one thing, such problems as transportation and water could not be tackled for a significant portion of the Region without involving a large number of legally autonomous municipalities. Such a combination requires highly complex and cumbersome procedures, involves protracted negotiations, and in the end demands a political and administrative finesse which the local units do not customarily possess. Moreover, "Regional" programs deal with the allocation of scarce physical resources, under circumstances which do not promise either equal benefits or equal costs for the jurisdictions involved. So hard decisions must be made among the claims of conflicting interests. In an atmosphere already charged with a competitive spirit, such decisions are not likely to come about through a cooperative process requiring unanimous consent.

Illustrations of the difficulty are easy to find. Old cities in New Jersey think twice—even thrice—before joining hands in a mass transportation plan which has the obvious intent and possible effect of attracting commerce and industry back toward New York City. A decision to build a new highway in one municipality rather than another may ensure the success of a suburban shopping center while spelling financial hardship for the downtown of an older city. The same decision may open land for development in one community while by-passing another, and it is certain to have unequal implications for the fortunes of railroads, trucking concerns, warehouses, bus companies, offices, and factories.

Similarly, when issues of water supply and purification are concerned, downstream and upstream communities have quite separate stakes in how the questions are resolved. A householder in Hunterdon County, New Jersey, does not actually want anyone in Hoboken to die of thirst, but neither does he want the Hoboken reservoir in his basement. The provision of adequate recreational space for city dwellers is a laudable objective to which most Region's residents could subscribe—except suburban residents who do not want their town transformed in character on Sunday afternoon. The creation of a forest preserve in Rockland County may preclude the development of an industrial park. In all these instances, the aims usually have to be spelled out, for most of these programs require long-range planning, sizable land-taking, and large capital outlays; and the more clearly the aims are spelled out, the more likely it is that conflicts among jurisdictions become explicit.

As the limits of spontaneous cooperation are recognized, the need for other governmental arrangements becomes correspondingly apparent. At this juncture, a new complication ensues to dictate the shape and character of Regional public institutions. In a constitutional sense, the structure of government is already complete, and awesome obstacles stand in the way of establishing a new single governmental structure to solve all major problems which the Region as an entity faces. Any new institution which possessed the usual attributes of a fixed set of boundaries, an electorate of its own, and the customary legal and financial prerequisites would constitute a direct threat to the authority of units already in being.

In this atmosphere a special system of politics has emerged and unique institutions have developed. Faced with the dilemma of having to fulfill obvious needs and still not tamper directly with established governmental structure, the Region's lawmakers have made special arrangements which do not directly impair traditional means of financial support or require local popular approval. Over the years, they have authorized a variety of special devices. One important device is the assignment of new metropolitan programs to state and federal agencies. Another is the creation of entirely new instruments of government—the public corporation and the metropolitan authority. Others include negotiated contracts for the exchange of services among governments; the establishment of *ad hoc* planning groups, half public, half private in their membership; and similar mechanisms which defy neat clarification.

Regardless of what device is used, the resulting "Regional enterprises" share the characteristic of being responsive to political pressures different from those existing within a local constituency. If the institution is a state agency, as is the case with major portions of highway development, the determination of the program, the budget, and the financing follows a complicated route through state legislative and executive branches. Along the way they may be intermittently affected by decisions in Washington, transmitted through the federal agencies working in the field.

Where the institution takes the form of a public corporation, its creation is formally designed to remove the program "from politics." Yet political pressures do arise in the informal relations that are established between the corporation's executives and other public officials, influential groups, and private individuals. In this instance, the office-holders are not seeking "votes" in the usual sense. More likely they are cultivating "public opinion" in such forms as favorable editorial comment, the assistance of a strategically placed bureaucrat, or the support of an influential civic leader. When the institution affecting the Region is an agency of the United States, following federal rather than local policy objectives, its legal or actual accountability lies outside the Region entirely—a fact which by no means makes it "nonpolitical." Whatever the diverse character of the politics involved, however, the institutions of major "Regional," as opposed to "local," impact are alike in being free from regular, formal relationships with local residents as a taxpaying ballot-casting "constituency." The arena of action is one in which executive talents, skill in negotiating, and a flair for publicity are more important than campaigning.

A second feature of the Regional institutions is that their revenue base is sharply different from that of a general government within the Region. As for the public corporations and authorities, their process of acquiring revenues closely resembles that of a private corporation. The Port of New York Authority and the Triborough Bridge and Tunnel Authority rely on user-charges, fees paid by the individual consumer of their services. The consumer's payment is not always a completely free choice, given the nature of the facilities involved, but neither is it as completely mandatory as the charges imposed by the local special districts concerned with street lighting, water distribution, public schools, and refuse collection. Whatever the consumer's position, his patronage frees the corporations from having to depend on general tax revenues. Because their activities are self-supporting, their objectives, programs, and operations are likely to be self-determined. Hence, in their behavior they are more closely akin to private enterprise than to other government agencies. As for the state and federal agencies—those concerned with highways, housing, planning, water, conservation, and the like—their programs are, of course, tax-supported. But their appropriations flow through state or federal channels; they do not depend directly on property values; and they do not require the support of the local citizens in the way the municipal governments do.

Finally, the Regional institutions have the common characteristic that none of them is in exclusive command of the activity for which it has responsibility. They share their duties with private enterprise and with other public agencies—local or Regional in status. In transportation, the responsibility for developing the highway system is the province of the public corporations, the state highway departments, and the federal government, while rail transportation remains largely in private hands. The development of air and water terminal facilities involves private companies, Regional institutions, and general-purpose governments. The same sort of combination exists with respect to recreation, housing, the supply and distribution of water, and pollution control. Nowhere within the province of major Regional public services does a clear focal point of public action appear.

The three special characteristics of the Regional institutions have resulted in a special kind of political process. The determination of public needs is not made in the marketplace, nor in the voting booth. Instead, the public needs are what the Regional organizations say they are, subject to the organizations' capacity to find financing and subject to the presence and strength of other interests in the field. As for financing, the amount of real property in the Region is not directly relevant, nor is the Regional income. What counts is the ability to persuade officials above the municipal level to approve budgets, or to get financing independently of normal revenue sources. But the attitudes of Regional colleagues and rivals are important too, for their support or enmity can influence the appropriate official and make available or foreclose a revenue source. Since no single organization stands astride its own field, each works in acute awareness of the goals and policies of others. Each calculates the effects of its moves on the programs of the others, and is affected in turn by the others' decisions.

In this interplay among the organizations, and in the scramble for their special sources of authority and revenue, a response of a sort to Regional needs takes place. People are transported to and from work; water is supplied to the housewife; impressive rehabilitation and renewal programs get underway; parks are preserved; beaches are opened. But these activities come about as a result of the particular views of particular agencies about what the situation requires. To understand the decisions which set these programs in motion, we need to know how the agencies define public needs, what financial and political capacities they possess to achieve their objectives, what opposition by other parts of the Regional political system they encounter, and what corresponding strategies they adopt.

TRANSPORTATION: THE HEYDAY OF THE
AUTOMOBILE

By far the most visible part of the Regional-enterprise system consists of the agencies concerned with passenger transportation. The facilities and services they provide are part of the everyday life of most inhabitants of the Region. To the Wall Streeter they signify, in Harrison Salisbury's words, "bumper-to-bumper traffic and the stench of exhaust fumes in the Jersey tunnels at 5 p.m.," and to the Darien, Connecticut, housewife they add up to "the 5:32—late again, too many martinis, dinner getting cold, short tempers, tears." [2] The problems and issues generated by the functioning or malfunctioning of transportation programs are also before the public eyes in news accounts of the plight of the suburban railroads, announcements of the opening of new sections of expressways, and revised regulations affecting traffic movements in downtown New York. Even the public institutions themselves are familiar parts of the metropolitan scene. The Port of New York Authority, the Long Island Railroad, the Hudson Tubes conjure up specific, if not always delightful, images in the minds of New Yorkers.

In a physical sense, the present transportation network consists of a complex mix of highways, subways, railroads, airlanes, and terminal installations designed both to support the internal functioning of the Region's economy and to assure access to the outside world. The statistics of the transportation network are available in other documents, and it is unnecessary to rattle them off here, except just enough to remind the reader that the business of moving people and goods to and fro in America's largest metropolitan area is immensely complicated. More than five thousand miles of streets criss-cross New York City alone, not to speak of the Region's other communities, and the Region is laced with hundreds of miles of fast highways designed for cross-Region and interstate travel. The Region's rivers have been conquered by seventeen major crossings at a cost of more than seven hundred million dollars. More than six thousand subway cars run on the tracks of the City's subway system. Private railroads

have over a thousand miles of rail in the Region, and, besides, one
can find twenty-odd major bus stations, four airports, and several
hundred piers. Every day nearly a million passengers enter New
York City from other parts of the Region, riding in automobiles,
trains, and buses, in that order of importance.[3]

The allocation of the Region's passengers among the various modes
of traffic is by no means a stable one. Particularly since World War
II, major shifts have taken place and are continuing. The diffusion of
homes and jobs spurs a spectacular rise in highway traffic and a decline in the number of rail and transit riders. The most pronounced
shift has occurred in daily commuter movement between the New
Jersey metropolitan counties and New York City. Between 1948 and
1958 the number of commuters moving daily by private automobile
through the Holland and Lincoln Tunnels and over the George
Washington Bridge increased from 15,500 to 33,300. The number of
bus commuters using those facilities rose from 37,200 to 56,500. At
the same time rail commuters between New Jersey and New York
City declined in number from 101,600 to 69,900. Non-rush-hour traffic in this part of the Region behaved somewhat the same: an 89 per
cent increase in automobile riders and a 30 per cent rise in bus riders, compared with a 42 per cent decline in the number of rail passengers.[4]

Elsewhere in the Region, similar though less dramatic changes
were underway. Rail commuting from the Westchester-Fairfield and
Long Island sectors to the City has increased in absolute number,
but the proportionate rise in highway travel is far greater. Meanwhile the number of riders on the City transit system fell from a
1945 peak of over two billion paid riders a year to a 1957 volume of
about one billion. New patterns of commuting, again favoring the
automobile, have developed in reverse rush-hour traffic from cities
to suburban work places and intersuburban travel. In the first instance 58 per cent of the daily rush-hour traffic volume from the City
to New Jersey moves by private auto, and in the second, the number
of auto riders among suburban counties is growing twice as rapidly
as the total movement of persons among these areas. Radical changes

have been occurring as well in the transportation of passengers to and from the City other than in rush hours. Sizable increases have been registered in automobile use for weekend and holiday travel. A similar trend is also underway in *workday* travel at other than rush hours.[5]

➤ THE PLAYERS TAKE THEIR STAND

Given such swift and massive changes in transport, even a single organization would find difficulty in developing a comprehensive and steady policy. But the Region's network is not only divided by type of facility; it is divided by type of ownership—and so a further complication is added. As traffic volumes shift from one set of facilities to another, an agency in command of a portion of a single set of facilities feels acutely the impact of the changes. Its goals, capacities, and strategies are altered. Changes come about in the nature of the services, the volume of revenues available, the agency's special form of relationship to the public, and in the end, in its institutional prospects for survival. As one agency adopts new programs, they conflict with the interests of another, and new policies and new strategies are triggered off.

We can see such conflicts emerging over control of particular types of facilities, not necessarily passenger facilities. New York City and the Port Authority, for example, have long vied with one another in port development. The City has allocated many millions to new pier and terminal construction in Manhattan and Brooklyn since World War II, and the Authority has undertaken even greater programs in Brooklyn, Hoboken, Newark, and Elizabeth. But such conflicts achieve their most dramatic—and important—form in issues arising over the future of the commuter network.

Clearly, the most unwilling participants in this larger battle of providing commuter transportation facilities are the suburban railroads. Though these are privately owned, their public role and participation in the Regional transportation arena make them, in fact if not in law, "Regional enterprises" for the purposes of this analysis. They continue to provide services mainly because they are commanded to do so by state and federal utility commissions. In recent years, the six railroads in the New Jersey sector, the two servicing Westchester, and the Long Island Railroad have all undertaken to fashion their own responses to Regional transportation developments.

They have sizable compulsions to do so. As privately financed self-supporting enterprises, they have long carried traffic as a persistent and sizable red-ink entry on their ledgers. Direct losses from this traffic approach an estimated $14 million annually. Railroad man-power is now idle 60 per cent of a working weekday and equipment is unused 80 to 90 per cent.[6] In these circumstances, railroads alter-nately experiment with new schemes for attracting commuter busi-ness, fight for permission to raise their fares, and seek to curtail or abandon commuter service. On balance, their role is one of abdica-tion and withdrawal—an effort to leave to their publicly supported rivals the major task of handling commuter traffic.

Occasionally, it is true that the railroads test out the effects of pro-viding more and better service, as the Pennsylvania did with some modest gains in volume in 1956.[7] But more frequently their actions move in the opposite direction. The ferry services operated by various railroads to 23rd Street were abandoned in 1954, as was the Christo-pher Street ferry of the Lackawanna in 1956. The New York Cen-tral, the Susquehanna, the Erie, and the Jersey Central have all re-ceived permission for the abandonment and curtailment of certain branch lines and daily services. In 1956 the Erie cut the commuter trains on its northern and Newark branches from 30 to 3, and the Jersey Central came down from 30 to 6.[8] The Hudson & Manhattan Railroad is in receivership, and the Long Island Railroad operates under semipublic auspices.

In the view of railroad management, the plight of their companies stems not so much from changing transportation technology as from the growing competition of public facilities devoted to automobile and bus movements. "The name of the Port Authority," Tom Bar-rett of the *New York Herald Tribune* reports, "is not a popular one in New Jersey railroad circles. This is because the railroads feel that the Port Authority's Hudson River crossings are mainly responsible

for the 50 per cent drop in rail passengers over the last thirty years." [9]
When the third tube of the Lincoln Tunnel opened and the Interstate Commerce Commission granted an interstate bus franchise for
a New York–New Brunswick service, the Pennsylvania Railroad
abandoned its experiment in expanded commuter service.[10] The New
Jersey railroads characterize the Port of New York Authority as "the
East India Company" and "the Port of Authority," and the Long
Island and New York Central cry alarm at the expanding domain
of the Triborough Bridge Authority.

In 1954, a New Jersey railroad president, summing up the railroad
position, declared: "During the last 30 years or so, the State of New
York and New Jersey, the City of New York, and the Federal Government have spent billions of dollars in tunnels, bridges and connecting highways and parkways leading into and out of New York
City. . . . Bus lines have not only taken away from the railroads the
larger portion of their passenger traffic, but they have taken the best
paying part, that is the shoppers, theatre-goers, etc., who travel on
round-trip tickets which pay the railroads a slight amount above the
cost of operation. The Susquehanna lost over two-thirds of its passenger traffic in ten years following the opening of the George Washington Bridge." [11]

The private railroads are not the only institutions which set down
the changing trends in passenger movements to what in their view
is the privileged position of the automobile-oriented agencies. The
New York Transit Authority, which operates the City's subways, has
troubles of its own. Reorganized in 1953 as a public corporation
within the general governmental structure of the City of New York,
but with one member of its three-man governing board appointed
by the Governor, the Transit Authority is an institutional reaffirma-
tion of the philosophy that rapid transit should be self-supporting.
The reorganization freed the system from the fixed five-cent fare,
long maintained as a political necessity, and subway fares, like railroad rates, have increased 200 per cent. The reorganization also
relieved the City from supporting operating deficits, though not capital outlays. It did not, however, substantially affect the downward

trend in transit riders evident since 1946. Traffic fell over 35 per cent between 1946 and 1956.[12] Again like the railroads, the Transit Authority has had to handle a large volume of rush-hour business, which has declined only slowly, while the profitable off-hour riding was falling sharply. In short, the system has experienced both losses in total revenues and increases in costs.

The Transit Authority has made strenuous efforts to reduce costs and to lure passengers back on the line. Some $100 million in savings was effected in the five years between 1953 and 1958, and some 8000 jobs were eliminated.[13] On the strength of a bond issue of half a billion dollars, the agency embarked on a modernization program, purchasing new subway cars and buses, and contemplating new connections among existing lines, improvements in station facilities, and additional trackage. This program, however, has yet to reverse the long-term downward trend of traffic.[14]

In contrast to the worsening financial conditions of public and private institutions responsible for mass transit, the agencies presiding over the highways, bridges, and tunnels of the Region flourish. Obtaining revenue from the toll-paying motorists and encouraging the expansion of this traffic by their construction programs, the Port of New York Authority and the Triborough Bridge and Tunnel Authority, in collaboration with state highway departments and supported by federal grants, have steadily enlarged their activities. The Port Authority owns six river crossings, four airports, four motor-vehicle terminals, and four marine terminals, representing a total investment of more than $600 million.[15] The Triborough Authority, representing a consolidation of agencies during the 1930's, now operates five bridges and two tunnels, and builds and improves parkways and highways within the City which form direct connections to these crossings.[16] Its annual income averaging over $30 million allows it to engage in such nontransportation activities as the construction of the New York Coliseum.

For many years, the two giant Authorities functioned in a relatively independent fashion, on a basis paralleling the "sphere of influence" doctrine in international relations. The Port Authority was oriented toward Hudson crossings and air and terminal developments largely outside Manhattan; the Triborough concentrated on East River developments and access highways thereto. The increase in the volume and distance of automobile movements within the whole area, together with the growing importance of state and federal highway programs, has tended to bring the two agencies into closer and closer collaboration. In 1955, they released a joint study of arterial facilities in the metropolitan area which now serves as the general basis for future construction. The objectives are "convenient arterial highway communications" among the suburban counties as well as "the rapid movement of through traffic without adding to the congestion of Manhattan streets." Major elements of the plan are the Narrows Bridge, the lower deck of the George Washington Bridge, Throgs Neck Bridge connecting the Bronx and Queens, and relevant approaches. The original estimates for these facilities was about $400 million, with connecting highways to be built with state and federal funds and calculated at $200 million.[17]

Coordination among the agencies concerned with automobile transportation is not limited to the work of these two Authorities. Systematic relations now exist between the state departments of highways and the federal Bureau of Public Roads and between those agencies and the Authorities. During the 1940's and 1950's the alliances have been cemented by the informal but highly efficient mechanism of placing various programs under the direction of a single individual. Robert Moses, as chairman of the Triborough Authority, dealt with himself—as City Construction Coordinator—in considering the relations between his Authority's activities and the development of the arterial highway network within the City. He has met himself again in negotiations relating to Long Island highway plans, for he has served as President of the Long Island State Park Commission—which has a membership identical with that of the Jones Beach State Parkway Authority, which has built and maintained Jones Beach State Parkway and the Southern State Parkway.

Moreover, Mr. Moses has often afforded, through his own personality, the opportunity not only to join together different segments of the highway network but also to relate highways with park and housing projects. He has simultaneously held the posts of president of the Bethpage Park Authority, New York City Commissioner of Parks, a City Planning Commissioner, and, on a broader horizon, chairman of the State Power Authority and of the State Council of Parks.[18] Indeed, no figure has better exemplified the special brand of "Regional-enterprise politics"—a high degree of executive and diplomatic skill blended expertly with a genius for keeping in the public eye.

Thus the "rubber-tire" agencies of the Region, relying on both formal and informal means of collaboration, steadily push forward in their programs. Since they are able to anticipate large amounts of funds from the higher echelons of government and to bank heavily on user-charges, these institutions possess the resources as well as the legal and organizational capacity to expand. The two major Authorities' combined investment in largely self-supporting enterprises is projected to exceed two billion dollars by 1965, and the institutional position of all the agencies responsible for the highway program stands in sharp contrast to the situation of those providing mass-transit services.[19] The attitude of the officials in these institutions contrasts as well. While acknowledging the present necessity of mass transit in rush-hour movements and for continued access to Manhattan, their utterances indicate a conviction that the Region's transportation future will be dominated by the automobile. Testifying in 1954, Mr. Moses said:

> Generally, with the exception of the New York City subway lines, there is little need for an expansion of railroad commuter facilities in the New York metropolitan area. . . . We have been making steady progress in the construction of an arterial system of highways, expressways and parkways in the New York metropolitan area. . . . The cooperation which has been developed between all of these different agencies in planning and constructing a coordinated system of arteries demonstrates what can be done under our democratic system.[20]

Four years later in a similar vein, the Commissioners of the Port Authority took care to point out the separateness of the problems of mass transit and highway transportation. At a New Jersey legislative hearing they emphasized their conviction that for non-rush-hour traffic and for commuting to suburban manufacturing plants, there was no real interchangeability between different modes of transportation. They said that only 5 per cent of all the automobile riders using Port Authority crossings "can be considered to be in any way even potentially divertible to the New Jersey railroads." They added, "The extent of the real competition then between commutation travel by automobile as against commuting by rail or bus is small." And, emphasizing their faith in the bus and private car, the Commissioners pointed out that, so far as the growing volume of traffic among suburbs was concerned, "Most of such trips by rail could only be accomplished, if at all, with extreme inconvenience and awkwardness. As long as the motorist has his car at his disposal to use when he wants to for this type of travel, and is not forced by some overpowering government ukase to use the railroad for such journeys, he will not do so." [21]

✓ THE RELATIVITY OF TRANSPORTATION NEEDS

The wide disparities between the rail and auto agencies with respect to financial resources, organizational arrangements, legal responsibility, and attitudes are at the heart of the Region's transportation politics. These disparities dictate sharply contrasting definitions of transportation "needs" and sharply contrasting philosophies of "the public interest." Each agency becomes convinced that its own program best promotes the general welfare, and the stage is set for controversy. Unceasingly the promotion of alternative plans and programs, each with a ring of persuasive logic, goes on without any single, clear, or final point at which the controversy may be formally resolved. On the contrary, the political process which responds to the transportation pressures generated by the Region's expansion is one in which the authority of a general electorate does not exist.

Conceivably, a disinterested observer might determine the optimum combination of rail and highway facilities required to move the greatest number of people with maximum ease and comfort at the lowest cost. But the transportation agencies themselves can rarely afford the luxury of detached analysis. Engaged understandably enough in an effort to ensure their institutional survival, able to develop and propose their own goals without direct mandate from the Region's residents, the agencies take the contrary positions that their own facilities most closely serve the public interest. Given these positions, it is only a short step to advocating policies which will expand their programs and then emphasizing to the public the beneficial effects on the total transportation network.

Essentially, two major competing definitions of the "best" transportation network are involved in the political process at the present time. The rail and transit agencies, and the interest groups clamoring for mass transportation, proceed from the postulate that the best transportation network is the one which moves the greatest number of people most rapidly in the shortest period of time. Hence, they emphasize the engineering fact that one highway lane normally carries 2,200 persons per hour and that each automobile requires between 200 and 350 square feet of parking area at the end of its trip. In contrast, buses operating in reserved lanes carry 9,000 persons per hour and a single rail or rapid transit line carries between 45,000 and 50,000 passengers per hour—the equivalent of 20 lanes of highways.[22] From these figures the rail advocates argue that the public interest is best served by extending and renovating the transit and railroad facilities, with feeder links provided by buses. In their view, such a program would maximize the "superior" capacity of rail facilities to handle large volumes of passengers, would reduce the load of expenditures for major highway extensions and parking facilities, and on balance would require a smaller outlay of public funds.

Thus the rail-transit agencies' estimate of "real" transportation needs contemplate a continued expansion of their present facilities. The Transit Authority, for example, estimates its rehabilitation and extension needs at $2 billion. In recent years it has sought $50 million to improve and extend bus service within New York City, and $18 million a year to replace old subway cars. The railroads, with an increasing air of desperation, seek public subsidies and tax relief from federal, state, or local governments to ensure that existing services are maintained.[23]

The automobile-oriented agencies, on the other hand, begin with quite a different set of postulates. They define transportation needs in terms of what it takes to satisfy the preferences of the individual highway user. So these agencies calculate the trend in increased automobile registration through the Region, determine the lanes of highway required to move these vehicles rapidly, and estimate cost accordingly. By their rationale, the task of a highway network is to assure that the automobile may be used for every transportation task which physical circumstances permit. Thus, future highway requirements are calculated to accommodate holiday, non-rush-hour, and intersuburban traffic at their largest estimated volumes.[24]

On these assumptions, the Region's transportation requirements are very different from those outlined by rail and transit agencies. The highway program for the Region as a whole, through 1970, is envisaged to cost $2 billion to $5 billion. Another and more detailed estimate for the City alone, including 480 miles of express highway, places the cost between $3.4 billion and $4.3 billion.[25] The Port of New York Authority has a present over-all capital improvement program in the neighborhood of $600 million.[26] The Triborough investment in the two bridges alone—Throgs Neck and Narrows —exceeds $300 million.[27] The future plans for off-street parking facilities in the City call for an additional $66 million.[28] And there are more expansive estimates, looking toward the achievement of ideal engineering standards of expressway construction, which would push expenditures for all highway and parking facilities within the City over $6 billion in the 1960's.[29]

It is not beyond the realm of possibility to reconcile these conflicting philosophies of transportation requirements; indeed, proposals for unified transportation management flow regularly from the desks of students of the Region. But the actual resolution of the divergent points of view takes place in the political interplay among the agencies involved. What matters is not a determination of which set of assumptions is "right" according to the criterion of some outside party. What matters is which agencies possess the financial and political capacity to translate their own goals into operating programs. The present pattern of transportation facilities is a historical reflection of the relative capacity of one agency or another to act, the ability it has demonstrated to carry out the philosophies it has adopted. Similarly, the future character of the transportation network is most likely to be the result of the power position of the metropolitan giants in the field—the resources they possess, the freedom they exhibit to determine their own programs in their own lights, their skill in political maneuver against their competitors.

✔ THE SYSTEM AT WORK

Institutional differences, then, beget different definitions of public requirements, and these definitions in turn beget conflict. There remains the tracing out of political strategy and tactics: to identify the means by which influence is brought to bear in critical places of authority, to understand how plans are turned into programs, how one part of the transportation network is extended, and how development is thwarted elsewhere.

The arenas for combat in Regional transportation are many: the hearing rooms of public regulatory commissions, the columns of the press, the legislative halls of the state capitols, the offices of the state governors. Moves are made in the full glare of public controversy but they are also made in quiet, informal negotiations with local officials or federal administrators. The planning of strategy and the application of tactics go on every day, each agency now turning one way and now another to seek its goals. The railroad companies appeal to the City of New York or the states for tax relief. The Port Authority and the City dispute over who will construct new piers—and where. The Port Authority battles the Greyhound Bus Company on the issue of consolidated bus terminals.[30]

The showcase most relevant to a comprehensive understanding of the Regional-enterprise system at work, and having the most implications for the future shape of the transportation network in the Region, is one in which all of the principal players are engaged at once, preferably over an issue concerned not with the location of a single facility but with the design of a major segment of the network. In the 1950's that showcase was the activities of the Metropolitan Rapid Transit Commission (MRTC), a special research agency established jointly by New York and New Jersey to "study present and prospective rapid transit needs of the New York–New Jersey Metropolitan area and develop, recommend, and report as soon as possible the measures for meeting such needs."[31] By its mandate, the Commission has tried to find a common basis for reconciling the transit and auto definitions of need. In the history of its efforts can be discerned the ways by which each party sought to protect its interest and to assemble forces of sufficient political power to win its objectives.*

At the outset, the Commission took at face value its obligation to develop a single transportation philosophy. It declared in its first interim report in 1955 that "the problem of mass transportation of people and merchandise is inevitably intermingled with that of automobile and truck transportation," and it announced its intention of developing a "new and over-all approach . . . whole-heartedly pursued, adequately financed and on an Area-wide scale." Moreover, the Commission then adjudged that the solution of the problem lay in a reemphasis on mass transportation facilities, pointing out that "all prominently announced traffic proposals for the Metropolitan Area, however worthy in themselves, call for the further expenditure of many hundreds of dollars of public funds in the further creation of tax-exempt arteries for the very motorized traffic which is creating the very spiral of congestion." It pledged itself therefore to a "comprehensive study by the best available, wholly neutral and nonpolitical engineering and scientific organization." It promised "a resultant comprehensive plan, not only for the present but for the next twenty-five years at least," and it spoke of the necessity for courage "as big as the problem and the need."[32]

* We acknowledge a special debt to Jamieson Doig of the Department of Politics, Princeton University, who supplied valuable data from his own investigations.

Yet even as the Commission formally announced its objectives, circumstances had already been working for their substantial revision. The state government of neither New York nor New Jersey stood ready to finance an investigation on the scale the Commission deemed necessary for a satisfactory analysis. MRTC negotiations with the commuting railroads for their support were "barren of results," and while business organizations promised "wholehearted support" and technical assistance, no major funds were forthcoming. Consequently, the Commission turned to the Port of New York Authority, and in January 1955 negotiated an agreement whereby the Authority provided $800,000 for studies of the transit problems in the northern New Jersey–Manhattan area.[33]

This agreement solved the Commission's financial difficulties to a major extent, but it also brought a new emphasis to the inquiry. In its memorandum of agreement with the Authority, the MRTC recognized explicitly that "there is no conflict between the effort to maintain adequate rail transportation and to provide new by-pass arteries for highway traffic." It also acknowledged the exclusive revenue franchise of the rubber-oriented agencies in the section which stated: "The two agencies give full recognition to the framework within which the Port Authority is able to undertake transportation and terminal facilities which can be financed by revenue bonds only if competent estimates indicate that in the long run they will be self-liquidating in and of themselves." Further, the memorandum took care to emphasize "that nearly every metropolitan area which is trying to improve its rail transit facilities has had to consider some form of financial aid from tax-supported sources to ensure adequate funds to supplement user resources." Finally, there was explicit understanding that consultants employed in the study would be engaged—and their assignments clearly outlined—on the basis of mutual agreement between the Metropolitan Rapid Transit Commission and the Port Authority.[34]

With the ground rules thus established to ensure the principle of coexistence between transit and auto definitions of transportation needs, the Commission settled down to work. The interstate studies financed by the Port Authority included the making of population and economic forecasts, technical engineering studies of rail transit plans, analyses of immediate rail and bus commuter service problems, and assorted legal, financial, and administrative inquiries. Intrastate studies financed by the two states included a review of commuter travel for all Westchester, Long Island, and Staten Island sectors; an analysis of specific proposals for those sectors; and a study of rapid transit problems within New Jersey.

On January 5, 1958, the Commission's final report was announced.[35] The heart of the document was a recommendation for a permanent bistate rapid transit district to prepare and carry out a general plan for financing, constructing, and operating a coordinated commuter transit system. For the guidance of the proposed district, the MRTC presented four alternative plans, varying in degree of coordination of rail and transit facilities and in cost, but all involving a "loop" system, tying the New Jersey rail system to Manhattan subways at both ends of the Island. The Commission's preferred plan called for the construction of transfer connections with all suburban railroads in New Jersey, a new north-south subway line in Manhattan under Madison Avenue and two new trans-Hudson subway tunnels. Its estimated cost was $500 million, and calculations of its patronage and probable fare schedules left an annual gross operating deficit of about $12 million.[36] Faithful to its memorandum of agreement with the Port Authority, the MRTC recommended that the proposed rapid transit district finance the deficit—theoretically by whatever means it chose, practically through a property tax imposed by the participating counties. Interstate transit improvement was to take place under organizational and revenue arrangements which left the highway agencies unaffected by rail deficits.[37]

The MRTC proposal did not meet with unanimous approval. The Commission had filed a report satisfactory to the Port Authority, and the private railroads were disposed to accept any measure which promised relief for their own deficits. But the municipalities likely to bear the cost, the advocates of a stronger mass transportation system, and groups likely to suffer adverse economic effects immediately set up a hue and cry.

Speaking for the City of New York, Mayor Wagner stated on January 5 that "the City while generally favorable to the over-all idea cannot at this time go on record in favor of the plan as we know it. We're just not in a position to absorb these costs." [38] Three months later, the City's opposition was more specific: the Mayor objected to the basis of representation in the 32-member governing body of the proposed rapid transit district, and to the omission of the New York suburban counties from the plan. He also found the plan's provisions "too general and vague." [39]

New Jersey committees also protested that the MRTC plan dealt with only one part of the problem and one part of the Region, and that it assigned the costs to only one group of beneficiaries. Mayor Charles Witkowski of Jersey City commented that "we want progress but we are not ready to pick up a tab of $800,000 a year or more," and Mayor Leo P. Carlin of Newark warned that his city could not agree to contribute a million dollars a year "unless there is a statewide assessment." Speaking for Middlesex County, Freeholder Karl Metzger observed that the county "could work up very little enthusiasm about putting out $400,000 or $500,000 a year for a plan from which we can't see any gain." [40]

Comments by transit interests were in a similar vein. Herman T. Stichman, trustee of the Hudson & Manhattan Railroad, termed the MRTC plan "impractical and prohibitively costly" and offered his own proposal to coordinate private railway operations with those of his company. This step in his judgment would result in "a system financed and operated by private enterprise with an absolute minimum of deficit operation and tax exemption." Representatives of the New York Transit Authority expressed doubts about the engineering feasibility of tie-ins on the Manhattan part of the system and the financial burdens involved. Sidney H. Bingham, former manager of the Transit Authority, proposed an alternative scheme which would utilize primarily private railroad facilities for the New Jersey commutation.[41]

The opposition of municipalities and transit groups was buttressed by regional planning agencies and by localized political interests likely to be adversely affected by the creation of the district. The Regional Plan Association registered its disapproval and the Metropolitan Regional Council rejected it by formal vote, objecting to the omission of Connecticut from consideration and to the membership provisions.[42] The Jersey City Merchants Council opposed the plan on the ground that it threatened the economy of Jersey City and would place an unfair tax levy on New Jersey residents. The views of other business groups in northern New Jersey were characterized by "the absence of any substantial sentiment for the Plan." [43]

The alternative around which the dissenters came to coalesce was a proposal that the Port Authority assume responsibility for interstate rail as well as automobile commuter service. One articulate critic, Goodhue Livingston, Jr., presented perhaps the most blunt expression of the opposition viewpoint when he proposed "a genuine Port of New York Authority" with jurisdiction "restricted to port operations and air terminals," and a new regional transportation authority. In a letter to W. Averell Harriman, then governor of New York, Livingston wrote: "The Port of New York Authority has all along . . . been stating that they do not want to be concerned even remotely with the operations of rail transit and so probably using the funds they advanced as a lever, influenced the Commission to adopt a very limited but expensive project which dumps the whole cost on the taxpayers' back and thereby keeps their motor toll income inviolate." [44] To most municipalities and transit agencies, the transfer of rail responsibility to the Port Authority represented at once the elimination of their prospective financial burdens and the integration of two heretofore competing systems of transportation.

The issue between the MRTC plan and the alternative of Port Authority operation was never formally joined in New York. In March 1958, the New York legislature passed the Brooks bill to es-

tablish the proposed independent bistate agency and, over the formal
protest of New York City, Governor Harriman approved the legislation on April 24.[45] But in New Jersey, the controversy crystallized
in two separate legal proposals—the so-called Jones and Musto bills,
the first of which incorporated the MRTC plan, while the second
unequivocally placed the responsibility to develop the rapid rail
transportation facilities of the Region in the hands of the Port
Authority.[46]

To the Port Authority, the Musto bill raised the specter of a shot-
gun marriage between rail and auto transportation which would
jeopardize if not destroy its financial capacity. The agency, supported by New York City's Board of Trade and Chamber of Commerce, by commuter organizations such as the Transportation Committee of Bergen County, the Citizens United Transit Committee,
and the North Jersey Commuter Organization, and by auto users
and bus associations, took its stand in favor of the Jones bill which
would carry out the MRTC recommendations.[47] At a legislative hearing the Port Authority contended in a 46-page formal brief that "It
is legally, financially, and contractually impossible for the Port Authority to assume the railroads' increasingly heavy deficit from all
or a part of commuter operations or the cost of development of a new
and comprehensive interstate rail rapid transit system." In the Authority's view, the legislation would not "stand the test of constitutional review and would have a disastrous effect on Port Authority
credit." Rather, the Authority argued that a careful study of the realities of the transportation picture would reveal that "the extent of
real competition between commutation travel by automobile as
against commuting by rail or bus is small." An integrated transportation organization was thus neither necessary nor desirable, for such
integration could come about only if the legislation "included the
grant of power to the super-agency to dictate to each person exactly
how he should travel." [48]

The Authority's contentions were challenged by opponents of the
MRTC plan. Dr. S. J. Flink, economic consultant to the General Assembly, stated in an official report that sufficient legal authority ex-

isted for placing rail facilities under Port Authority management, that "on the basis of a conservative evaluation of its assets, the Port Authority has today an equity of about four hundred million dollars," and that the agency could absorb estimated rail deficits and still show "a sizable annual net surplus." Further, Flink held that the establishment of a single transportation authority was the only effective solution to the Region's problems and that "the Port Authority has the manpower, technical knowhow and managerial experience which are indispensable for the selection of a plan that will fit into the *over-all program* of developing the New York–New Jersey port region." [49] In his arguments, Flink was joined by local public officials and North Jersey business and industrial groups.

The result of the head-on engagement between the two philosophies was a stand-off. Although the MRTC-endorsed Jones bill passed the New Jersey Senate by one vote, the Assembly took no action on either measure. The MRTC plan was being "buried," according to the *New York Times,* "because of widespread local opposition in Northern New Jersey." [50] The legislature shortly after adjourned.

But the stand-off was not long left in terms of such a clear and apparent acknowledgment of failure; camouflaging adjustments and compromises were sought. By early May 1959 the new legislatures in both New York and New Jersey passed bills which authorized continued investigations and some assistance to the rail agencies. One New York bill established a two-man New York–New Jersey Transportation Agency and directed it to devise a plan for the "most efficient long-range use of railroad commuter facilities." The New York legislature also directed the Port Authority to act as a purchasing and leasing agent for the state in furnishing $100 million to three railroads—the New Haven, New York Central, and Long Island—for purchase of passenger cars. The New Jersey legislature established a State Division of Transportation to assist its New York counterpart in offering short-run relief to the railroads. [51] On the surface, at any rate, the tasks of the transportation agencies were becoming intermingled.

Yet, essentially, no major consolidations of responsibility seemed forthcoming. No provisions for the diversion of public revenue to rapid transit were made, nor was the financial position of the Port Authority compromised, for New York State made $20 million available for the purchase-lease arrangement and guaranteed the Authority against any losses. Further, no limitations had been placed on highway facilities, nor the separate identity of the Authorities challenged. The two separate definitions of transportation needs still existed side by side.

Surveying the scene in April 1959 the Regional Plan Association concluded: "There is no group to see if the existing transport system as a whole is working well and to plan needed improvements when it is not. No existing agency is responsible for tracing and evaluating the effects of the changing transport system on the evolving pattern of metropolitan land development. Nor is any agency responsible for anticipating the future requirements of the growing region for all the various forms of transportation." [52] As if to change the Association's criticism into a prophecy, the New Jersey electorate in November 1959 rejected a referendum proposal to transfer surplus from the New Jersey Turnpike to the rapid transit district. Thus the auto agencies had emerged from the fray with their goals, organizations, and finances intact.

Since the demise of the MRTC, some modification of the Port Authority's position has been discernible. Tentatively in 1960, more formally in 1961, the Authority proposed to acquire the Hudson and Manhattan Railroad and to operate the Tubes even if a financial deficit were involved. In its bid of January 27, 1961, the Authority fixed a price of $20.5 million and offered to spend over $60 million in the improvement of equipment and facilities—according to the *New York Times*—"if we are able to satisfy prospective investors by statutory assurances" that the Authority's general reserve fund would not be tapped by "any other or further commuter deficit operations." This action represented a substantial modification of the Authority's 1958 position and indicated a new willingness to consider the commuters' needs. Yet this proposal does not embrace the comprehensive coordination of modes of travel which the Regional Plan Association called for; indeed, it can be interpreted as a plan which precludes or delays such arrangements. It certainly involved no basic sacrifice on the part of the highway system.

Even with this sequel to the MRTC story, then, it would be a most rash observer who predicted an "integrated" transportation system for the Region in the foreseeable future. On the contrary, the play of politics in the transportation field operates to maintain the separate heritage of mass transit and highway development. The transit and rail agencies continue enclosed by a "self-supporting" philosophy which compels them to handle the large volume of unremunerative rush-hour traffic but which deprives them of dependable access to public funds. Fifteen years of postwar experience have made it clear that there is no easy road to rail solvency under the present conditions of stable peak loads, drastic losses in off-hour business, high labor costs, and substantial reduction in patronage with every fare increase. Yet, the illusion persists that commuter railroads and subways can pay their own way, and to date new policies calling for sustained public support have not been translated into action. The companies continue to provide services satisfactory neither to investors, employees, or customers. They are unable to engage in programs of better service which might alter the trends working against them, nor to suspend operations so abruptly as to make the public insist on governmental rescue. The rail portion of the transportation network lives largely on existing capital.

In contrast, the highway agencies work in a situation of financial opulence brought about in part by the preference of the individual consumer and the user-charges he pays and in part by access to public funds which make it unnecessary for the motorist to bear immediately the full cost of the highways he uses. The public funds are derived from sources which are capable of rapid increases in revenue—gasoline taxes and federal grants—and they are supplemented by access to credit, which is more easily available to the Authorities and the states than to the City's transit system or to the railroads. Thus the agencies are in a position continually to expand their operations and to accommodate larger and larger volumes of traffic.

The highway agencies, too, make their decisions and prepare their plans without the direct surveillance of either the Region's constituency or other governmental agencies. While the railroads are operating under the supervision of regulatory agencies, while the transit system is depending on capital funds from the City of New York, the highway agencies work with federal and state agencies which share their objective of program expansion. Neither stockholders nor regulatory commissioners look over the shoulders of the Authorities as they go about their business under broad state and federal grants-of-authority—though Congressional investigations are not unknown.

It is quite possible that the increasing financial plight of rapid transit may result in increased public subsidies to sustain present operations, perhaps to expand them somewhat. Given the record of the last generation, however, it is highly unlikely that this expansion will come at the expense of the highway agencies. The construction of the Narrows Bridge, the completion of the arterial network, the doubledecking of the George Washington Bridge proceed on schedule. Possibly transit service will expand—but so will the highways. The outlook is for piecemeal development of physical facilities with no simultaneous consideration of the consequences of highway construction on other modes of transportation.

So political analysis supports economics in envisioning the Region of the future as one structured by the automobile. The institutions engaged in the movement of vehicular traffic are the best equipped to respond to the economic development and population movements going on about them. Their endeavors are supported by technological innovation, by the policies of state and federal governments, and by the interests of powerful pressure groups. Even a partial reading of the record underwrites Mr. Moses' conviction that the future will arrive on rubber tires.

WATER: NOBODY LOVES A RESERVOIR

The agencies responsible for obtaining water for the Region are basically similar to those which preside over the transportation network. By and large, water facilities pay their own way, receiving revenue from special user-charges and self-liquidating capital outlay funds. Although water *distribution systems* are usually under local municipal management, the key task of developing adequate sources of *supply* is likely to be in the hands of special agencies with special powers and special relationships to the Region's general governments or its electorate. Finally, water systems, both storage and distribution, are once again representatives of a mixed economy, for they are owned and operated in some parts of the Region by private companies, in others by public enterprises.

The provision of water differs in one major respect, however, from the development of a transportation network. Whereas the planning and construction of rail and road facilities takes place primarily within geographical boundaries of the Region, the physical development of the largest sources of water supply must take place outside the Region's twenty-two counties. The Region's own wells and reservoirs can meet only a part of its residential and industrial requirements. Unless technology makes the use of salt water feasible, or offers some other new means for expanding the supply, the search must impinge upon the needs of other metropolitan complexes which depend on the self-same interstate rivers for their supplies. The search also affects other public issues than the provision of water; it becomes intertwined with broader questions concerning the orderly development of river basins in their entirety—the relative emphases on flood control, navigation, electric power, irrigation, and recreation. Thus, it involves the Region's governments in political and organizational problems with which the entire nation has been wrestling at least since the establishment of the Tennessee Valley Authority.

In water politics, therefore, the Region's governments do not deal just with one another. At least twelve federal agencies now have official planning responsibilities concerned with water matters in the Region, and the Corps of Engineers is directly engaged in designing, building, or operating supply structures.[53] Four major departments and seven additional departmental divisions of the State of New York have responsibilities for water supply. For New Jersey, four departments and six divisions have similar duties, and two special agencies—the North Jersey Water Supply Commission and the Passaic Valley Sewage Commission—have important assignments. Whenever water supply problems touch on issues of navigation, flood control, pollution abatement, and watershed protection, two inter-state commissions enter the picture, and so do still other federal and state agencies.[54]

In such a complex, the question of providing an adequate water supply is bound to be far more than a substantive one. Indeed, on the basis of existing engineering studies, there seems little likelihood that a general water shortage will occur in the Region during the next twenty-five years. In the judgment of experts in the Delaware Valley Project of Syracuse University, facilities already on the planning boards of some of the agencies involved will provide supplies suffi-cient for the New York Metropolitan Region's growth through the year 2010.[55] More relevant, in their view, are the questions when, where, and whether the facilities are constructed—whether dams will be actually built or one municipality allowed to tap supplies in another's jurisdictions—and these issues hinge on policy and judicial decisions. In short, though nature favors the New York Metropolitan Region with substantial reserves, and while innovations such as cool-ing towers and desalinization equipment may augment them further, the available water supply within the area or any of its parts is more a function of the existing governmental machinery. Political negotia-tions interpose themselves between the apparently straightforward tasks of locating and building reservoirs, constructing tunnels and aqueducts, and completing distribution facilities.

In these circumstances, two quite different lines of action have ap-peared feasible to the Region's governments. Each municipality within the Region has the legal option to secure out-of-Region sites and construct facilities independently, serving as its own negotiator with the parties-in-interest in the river valleys beyond. Or, it can join in some form of collaborative enterprise on a river-basin or Re-gionwide basis which promises a more unified approach to the allo-cation of available supplies. The latter course commends itself both on the grounds of efficiency and because more comprehensive planning is possible. But it makes the organizational structure more complicated, for under present constitutional arrangements, the state and federal governments become principal participants in the program.

Historically, the Region was committed to the first approach, and for the New York side of the Hudson, the policy has proved sufficient to the present day. In New Jersey, however, for a combination of reasons, the strategy has not sufficed. And, here, the imperfect state of development of river basin or intermunicipal arrangements has served to provoke increasingly serious problems in particular areas. New Jersey residents have been forced to rely on the state government to arrange compromises between water-using jurisdictions and water-supplying jurisdictions, and the process of adjustment has been tortuous.

The relative success in New York appears to have two main reasons: the initial advantage which older and larger cities in the Region have had in pre-empting the largest and most accessible sites, and the later legal authorization for other New York municipalities to share the supplies of their earlier-established neighbors. New York City is the focal point of the system. It supplies not only its own residents but those of many adjacent suburban localities. Hard-pressed for water as early as 1820, the City began the construction of its present facilities in 1842.[56] The present daily delivery of more than a billion gallons of water is the fruit of over a century of planning and acquisition of distant sites and construction. A separate agency within the City government, the Board of Water Supply, has long had the responsibility for locating and developing new sources. The original Croton system is now supplemented by the Bronx-Byram reservoirs, the Catskill waterways, and the Upper Delaware River. All these are linked to the City by some five thousand miles of tunnels and mains. Successful litigation in federal courts has maintained, at least for the time being, the City's access to interstate waters. The City is engaged in more plans for expansion, because the safe yield from its reservoirs is too close to current demands to allow the Water Board to view long periods of drought with equanimity. But when these projected acquisitions are taken into account, the City's billion-dollar investment in waterworks is estimated to provide a supply adequate until the year 2000.[57]

While the City has pioneered in reservoir development, the New York suburbs have found ways to capitalize on the City's long headstart. By state legislation, localities in Westchester and other northern counties have been authorized to tap into the City's tunnels as water flows down from the reservoirs. Nassau and Suffolk Counties, where supplies from local wells have been threatened by salt-water intrusion, have also been negotiating to buy some two thousand acres of watershed along the South Shore of Nassau County, owned by the City and no longer required by its residents.[58] Although the two counties have by no means developed sizable reserves and quarrel sporadically over the allocation of existing supplies, as yet there have been few critical shortages and no persistent ones. For the future, New York City seems likely to support its neighbors by sharing its supply, thus relieving them of the construction expenses which would be prohibitive for suburban settlements to undertake alone.

In New Jersey, the historic pattern of each municipality's "going it alone" in developing water facilities has prevailed—but with less satisfactory results. The state has sizable potential reserves within its own borders; but no single water system, not even that of Newark, has developed those reserves sufficiently to be able easily to share water with its neighbors. A North Jersey Water Supply Commission has made progress in bringing about coordinated arrangements and a State Water Policy and Supply Council has worked since the 1930's to establish general plans. Still, metropolitan New Jersey has depended upon thirty-six separate systems, under both public and private management, to service the counties within the Region. Comparatively small in size and independent in action, these systems have been unable to secure and develop sufficient reserves to meet the growing demands in Northern New Jersey.[59]

Thus, though warnings of impending trouble have been sounded in every one of the more than a hundred studies and reports which have been made on the water problem in Jersey since 1900, no major acquisitions of new sites were completed before 1950. By that time, the dimensions of the problem threatened residential and industrial expansion. For the state as a whole, water consumption rose between 1940 and 1953 from 390 million gallons per day to 593 million and the number of residents "per inch of average rainfall" increased from 93,000 to 104,000. For the nine New Jersey counties within the Region, water consumption in 1953 was 420 million gallons daily, compared to an estimated "safe yield" of 415 million. Engineers projected an even greater disparity for the future, requirements being estimated as 620 million in 1980 and 750 million in the year 2000.[60]

With little prospect for expanding supplies through action of individual municipalities, New Jersey in recent years has been receptive to more comprehensive river-basin arrangements. But a 1950 proposal by the Interstate Commission of the Delaware River Basin for interstate allocations of Delaware water among four states (of which New Jersey was one) was abandoned after New York City took unilateral action to develop its own Upper Delaware supplies. Sporadic bilateral negotiations between New Jersey and Pennsylvania also failed to produce an agreement to construct the so-called Wallpack Bend.[61]

Almost as a last resort, New Jersey's state government itself assumed immediate responsibility for providing more water for its northern counties. This alternative has proved to be an uncertain halfway house, occupied by a welter of conflicting interests and procedures. It is an expedient apparently ill-designed to arrive at a quick decision. Unlike a municipality, the state cannot speak only for water-users anxious for a larger supply from whatever source. Unlike a larger Regional enterprise, it cannot stand aloof from the state electorate—or call on interstate or federal resources or embark on a comprehensive program designed to offer a broad range of benefits. Instead, it had to resolve the conflict of interests between urban water-users and rural water-suppliers within its own legislature— and the water problem was only one of a series of issues on the political agenda. For five years, each proposal for a new site ran the gamut of partisan, ideological, and economic interests, not always relevant to the problem at hand, but always important to the question of who controlled the government. In the end, the state adopted, with modifications, the same plan with which it began—sufficient in the judgment of George Shanklin, state water expert, to meet the area's needs through 1975.[62]

When the plan was first put forward it appeared straightforward enough. In 1953, on the advice of the State Water Supply Council, Governor Robert Meyner recommended the outlay of about $90 million to acquire and develop the site called Round Valley in Hunterdon County, which would supply an estimated 200 million gallons daily.[63] Hunterdon, bordering the Delaware River, is west of the New York Metropolitan Region. After some deliberations, Republican and Democratic members of the legislature reached tentative agreement on this proposal, as well as on plans for water development in southern New Jersey. Early in 1954, legislation was introduced to provide a referendum for a bond issue of $150 million and to establish a new state agency to undertake development.[64]

Partisan agreement was not tantamount to geographical agreement. Though acceptable to the Governor, and initially to both parties in the legislature, the bill did not find favor with the representatives of the areas in which the reservoirs would be built. Senators from five western counties adjacent to Round Valley were concerned lest recreational activities in their lakes and resorts would be eliminated and lest their cranberry industry would suffer. In a 26-man Senate, their opposition swung the balance between party divisions and defeated the bill. A compromise measure, providing for the purchase of the Round Valley site but delaying its development until after further study, passed both houses but in different versions which could not be reconciled in the conference committee of the Assembly and Senate. The Governor's appeals for reconsideration were unsuccessful. The legislature adjourned without taking action. Governor Meyner then called it back for a special session, but it refused to consider any proposal.[65]

In the 1955 legislative session, partisanship joined localism as a prime factor in the struggle over a water program. Governor Meyner called again for action on Round Valley. The caucus of Republicans in the Assembly countered with proposals for a new study and for a Round Valley acquisition bill. The Assembly carried out the caucus plan and passed both measures. But the Senate, again because of opposition from the five western counties, sidetracked the Round Valley bill. It did approve the six-man study commission, of which the Governor was authorized to appoint but a single member. In July the new commission, on recommendation of a professional engineering firm, offered an alternative to Round Valley—the development of the Chimney Rock reservoir in Somerset County. In the judgment of the engineering firm, this site could be developed more cheaply and could utilize water drawn entirely from within the state.[66]

Since the new proposal introduced a new location, it engendered new local opposition; and since it was adjacent to Democratic territory, it changed the partisan battle lines. Opposition arose in the affected cities, the North Jersey Water Supply Commission, and private water companies of the areas. These sources offered a counter-proposal that eight municipalities undertake development of Round Valley, and the Democratic members of the legislature expressed their opposition to Chimney Rock.[67]

At this juncture, the classic legislative problem of conscience versus constituency introduced still another complication. Though all public expression in Somerset County seemed dead set against the Chimney Rock plan, the Republican Senator from Somerset declared himself in favor of the proposal. Given his declaration of intent, the legislature enacted a bill over Democratic opposition, providing for a $60 million bond issue to construct the Chimney Rock reservoir, make additional provisions to maintain water levels in the Raritan Canal, and erect smaller systems. Legislative action alone was not sufficient, however. A referendum was required to add the public at large as a final party in interest. The public proceeded to defeat the Chimney Rock project by 593,000 to 362,000. The rejection was attributed by the *New York Times* to an "anti-borrowing trend, faulty management of the bill, sectionalization, and lack of Democratic enthusiasm." [68]

With the development of internal sites stalemated, the state government in 1956 turned to an attempt to tap out-of-state supplies in the Delaware River. Few Jerseyites objected to the notion of a reservoir in someone else's backyard, and the legislature authorized the purchase of Round Valley for $3 million, subject to the limitation that only out-of-state Delaware River water could be used to fill its reserves. On paper, the plan was attractive to Jerseyites. Unfortunately, as Governor Meyner pointed out, the other states in the Delaware Basin had not agreed to the project, and the Supreme Court had not authorized such interstate water allocations. Political consensus within the state structure had been achieved: the only difficulty was that no water was forthcoming.

In 1957, three major projects having been considered and rejected, and a half-dozen subsidiary schemes proposed and filed away, the state turned back to its own resources. A special advisory group formed by the State Water Resources Advisory Commission and the Department of Conservation and Economic Development presented a new plan designed to provide a basis for compromise. The group recommended the development of still another set of water storage facilities: a reservoir in Hunterdon County and another at Stony Brook, near Princeton in Mercer County, drawing water from the Raritan Canal.[69]

This plan effectively dampened Hunterdon opposition because no local lake water would be used. But it provoked a public explosion from Princeton residents, and by August the legislature had retreated to what now seemed a standard practice of authorizing a special study committee, this time composed of members of the legislature—two Republicans and one Democrat. The committee was instructed to report in 1958, and to make recommendations concerning the development of Round Valley (now without restriction to Delaware River water), and the possibility of compensation to Hunterdon County for losses in its property tax base if Round Valley appeared to be an appropriate site.[70]

At first, this 1957 assignment seemed essentially one of raking old coals and fanning old flames. Before the year had ended, however, nature took a hand. Little rain had fallen throughout the summer, and by September when the committee settled down to work, New Jersey was in the midst of the most severe drought in at least a generation. Trenton's water supply stood at 57 per cent of its reservoir capacity; Jersey City's supply was below 50 per cent; and nine other cities had the lowest reserves ever recorded. The North Jersey Water Supply Commission considered special action to tap the Passaic River; Jersey City's officials talked darkly of rationing water and of bringing it in by tank trucks and milk cartons. Municipalities began to enter into cooperative agreements as their own supplies ran out.[71]

Against this background, the study committee lost little time in proposing a $37 million bond issue, including $21 million for Round Valley, $6 million for a project at Spruce Run, and $3 million to $4 million for Stony Brook.[72] In December the legislature convened in a spirit described as one of urgency and recognition of emergency conditions, and authorized a $40 million bond issue to be voted upon by the people.[73] Two days later rain fell in torrents across the state.

In the following month—January 1958—Governor Meyner proposed an additional $40 million bond issue. The Senate would not grant this request, but it did raise the total issue to about $46 million including $25 million for Round Valley, and the Assembly concurred. With a flurry of support from organizations of such diverse outlooks as the Congress of Industrial Organizations and the New Jersey Taxpayers Association, the campaign for public approval was launched. In November 1958, New Jersey voters approved the proposed issue.[74]

From one perspective this five-year chronicle of a state in search of a reservoir can be viewed as standard operating procedure for an American state government that is wrestling with a controversial and expensive project. Different interests were differently affected; local sportsmen and recreationists had to come to terms with municipal and industrial water-users; competing state and local agencies had to evaluate proposals according to their future prospects for survival; the two parties had to judge the impact of any given plan on their future strength. The Governor, accountable to a statewide electorate, adopted an attitude quite different from a legislature responsible to a bundle of local constituencies. Since there were a number of separate plans to choose from, and since there existed the possibility of reaching outside the state entirely and thereby avoiding the painful prospect of dispossessing Jersey voters, one might consider it natural that the resolution of the issue took time. It is even not surprising that the chronicle ended where it began, at Round Valley—although with important modifications and reservations attached. The participants, the channels of influence, the process of negotiation are familiar components of American state politics.

From the perspective of the New York Metropolitan Region, however, the resolution of the Jersey water problem is best seen as a study of the current pattern of water politics in metropolitan areas. It demonstrates the extent of temporizing which can take place under conditions in which local actions no longer suffice and regional or river-basin institutions are not available. In New Jersey, the halfway house of state government had to deal with an emerging water shortage in essentially non-Regional terms. People outside the New York Metropolitan Region made the key decisions; an electorate much broader than the Region delivered the final approval. Viewed this way, the provision of water to one part of the Region becomes the responsibility of a governmental system which touches only tangentially on Regional problems, and which offers little firm assurance about when and how new facilities will become available.

These cumbersome governmental arrangements need not persist. A long-run solution of the Region's water problems is available in the perfection of interstate river-basin instruments. If the recommendations of current study commissions were accepted, there would emerge a self-supporting, interstate water agency, presiding over the multipurpose development of the Delaware Basin, and closely resembling the transportation authorities in operations though not in territory. It would not be a full-fledged government, but it would be equipped to plan and develop sources with much more responsiveness to economic needs and population requirements than the political system of a single state. Encouraging progress has recently been made in this direction, though actual coordinated development of the Delaware Basin is still years away.

Without the perfection of comprehensive river-basin arrangements, the development of water supplies for large subsectors of the New York Metropolitan Region seems likely to be variously pursued. Given the natural abundance of supply, it is doubtful that any Regionwide shortage will seriously slow economic or population growth. It is even doubtful that serious handicaps will persist for too long in any single part, unless the 1957 drought *was* an indispensable element in the deliberations of New Jersey. What does seem certain is that no businessman or resident can say for sure when certain subareas within the New York Metropolitan Region will develop a safe supply.

NIBBLING AT THE GRAY AREAS

Transportation and water programs, whether under direct government management or carried out by private companies publicly supervised, are traditional responsibilities of the public sector. Their organizational and financial arrangements may vary considerably and their politics may take on quite different forms across the Region, but few people question the appropriateness of public action in these fields. One way or another, the political economy has been involved in them since the process of urbanization began.

In our final exploration of positive public action which influences the Region's growth, however, we deal with a more novel and controversial subject. We deal with governmental programs scarcely a generation old which are concerned with more than providing the private sector with public necessities or with regulating it. They are concerned with altering its physical character, and sometimes on a Regionwide basis. These housing, renewal, and redevelopment programs are a sharp departure from the programs we have just reviewed. They represent new grants of authority, confirmed by judicial decisions only in the last ten or twenty years. They constitute an expansion of public activity that is still questionable in the view of many and still provokes political debate about the propriety of it all.

Besides being new and controversial, the physical development activities involve us in another set of arrangements and relations, another process of decision-making, another type of electorate. Regional transportation and water programs involve all three levels of government in the federal system, to be sure, and they bring the operations of many agencies to bear in their resolution. In each field, however, municipal and state governments play a decisive role in making policy and pay a large share of the bills. In the field of physical development, the responsibilities of the national government loom large. The participation of Regional units hinges on whether they capitalize on the opportunities Washington offers.

Three sets of federal programs now help determine how the physical transformation of the Region takes place.[75] The oldest set is the federal activities concerned with housing. This includes the federal mortgage insurance and secondary mortgage programs underwriting private construction; it also includes public low-cost housing and related activities. The second is the urban redevelopment and renewal program, an outgrowth of public housing but since World War II a program with quite different objectives. It focuses on the renewal of property in the older parts of the Region, principally by making private investment easier and more rewarding. Last, tentative steps have been taken by Washington to encourage general land-use planning on a Regional scale. This newest program undertakes to establish a broad framework for guiding the physical development of the Region as a whole, and to coordinate the largely defensive municipal programs outlined in the preceding chapter. These three sets of federal programs, evolving slowly and not always consistently, now alter the pattern of construction which the private economic system carries out.

We will not tarry long with federal housing insurance programs, those of the Federal Housing Administration, Veterans Administration, and the like. Though their effect is as persuasive in the New York Region as throughout the nation, their operation is neither susceptible to much interregional variation nor indeed to substantial participation by local governments or agencies.[76] The programs, having stemmed largely from such national events as the foreclosures of the early 1930's, the resulting President's Conference on Home Building and Home Ownership in 1931, the later New Deal legislation, and the still later increase in the number of veterans, are directed toward national objectives.

Moreover, home insurance and guarantees do not substitute public construction for private construction. On the contrary, by increasing the credit capacity of individual home-buyers, they work through private banking and lending institutions to support the marketplace. True, federal policies with respect to the amount of insurance available, the extent of public liability, the approval of individual applications, and the inspection of construction help determine practices in the construction industry. Federal policies also alter credit activities, encourage or discourage particular forms of residential development, and ease or complicate local public-service problems. By and large, however, their impact is indirect, putting money in the hands of individual home-buyers, builders, and bankers, affecting private decisions to borrow or to lend. Government, in this instance, is discreetly in the background.

Federal public low-cost housing, on the other hand, involves the government in direct design, construction, and operation of housing projects; and its effective operation hinges on cooperation within the Region. The federal government works directly with municipalities, usually through the instrument of semi-independent municipal housing authorities. Under the present law—the Housing Act of 1937 as amended—Washington assumes 90 per cent of capital costs of authorized housing projects and makes annual subsidy payments to cover operating expenditures at rent levels federally established.[77] But, though the program is direct in its impact, its significance seems to be rapidly dwindling. Today, the much more ambitious ventures popularly known as redevelopment and renewal have combined to overshadow public housing in magnitude and popular attention.

It is in these newer activities that the prospects for widespread, systematic influence on physical development now center, and it is here that the greatest differences occur among metropolitan areas and among parts of the New York Metropolitan Region. The federal urban redevelopment and renewal program had its origin in the 1949 Housing Act. In that statute the goal of achieving a "decent home" for every American was broadened to the concept of a "decent environment." [78] Accordingly, Title I of the Act went beyond slum-clearance activities to establish the now familiar tools of land assembly and clearance, write-downs, and redevelopment procedures. Later amendments to the basic legislation sought to do more than "redevelop" individual sites; it aimed at urban "renewal" through widespread rebuilding and rehabilitation of blighted and obsolescent areas in older cities, and the conservation of urban neighborhoods on the verge of decline. The long-run objective of all this legislation was to establish a systematic process of putting urban land—whether residential, commercial, or industrial—to uses appropriate to its location.

Over the last ten years the 1949 Act, successively amended and refined, has evolved into a highly complex set of intergovernmental financial, administrative, and political relationships. Participating municipalities are to prepare what are popularly known as "workable programs"—comprehensive renewal plans on a citywide basis—instead of individual projects. They can apply for demonstration grants to perfect new administration and planning techniques to initiate pilot and model projects. They can mesh their renewal activities with the federal mortgage insurance programs so that special loans are available for private property improvements in blighted areas.

The 1954 amendments to the Act introduced what we called the third set of federal programs—the one relating to comprehensive land-use planning on a metropolitan area basis. Section 701 of the 1954 statute provided financial aid for local, metropolitan, and regional planning agencies to assist in "the preparation of metropolitan housing market analyses and the integration of the renewal and development plans, programs, codes and controls of the numerous local governments in their areas." [79] This aid marks the first time that public support was given to systematic economic studies, population forecasts, land-use plans, area-wide analyses for the location of community facilities and for the development of more uniform proposals for subdivision and zoning. It also represents the first effort to view housing and redevelopment programs in individual areas and private construction activities from a common Regional perspective. These metropolitan planning activities, however, remain in embryonic form, and it is the second set of programs—redevelopment and renewal—that most concerns us here.

In redevelopment and renewal the role of Washington is preeminent. Federal legislation is the sparkplug for most local and state action; federal money accounts for most of the public spending, and federal policies and regulations guide the administrative processes. To a very large extent Presidential budgetary proposals and Congressional authorizations fix the gross amount of capital funds available for renewal projects, just as they determine the number of low-rent dwelling units built annually and the magnitude of mortgage money available for residential housing. Federal administrative requirements are sufficiently detailed to bring forth local complaints that there is no "presumption in favor of the competence of municipal officials." [80] In the New York Metropolitan Region, as in any other part of the country, the tempo of renewal depends in the first instance on the national political climate. A Korean War, a new Administration, a Congressional election, a Presidential veto can quickly and decisively alter the operations.

Yet local action remains crucial in the renewal program. Though national legislation, money, and direction make the program possible, municipalities, assisted in various ways by state and special agencies, carry it out. The capacity of these agencies to use federal assistance has a decisive bearing on the shape of the final program. The alacrity with which municipalities establish their redevelopment authorities, the support they receive from their states, the imagination they show in utilizing the many separate parts of the federal scheme, the relations they establish with the federal bureaucracy serve to distinguish the performance record of the New York Metropolitan Region from that of other metropolitan areas, and parts of the Region from one another. As time goes on, the variations in political administrative skill and sophistication at the local level transforms the federal program into a series of distinct local enterprises. So an estimate of the success or failure of the entire program hinges as much on an accurate reading of local capabilities within the Region as it does on a judgment of the size of future federal appropriations.

We can begin to gauge the probable impact of the program on different parts of the Region by taking the by now familiar step of contrasting the New York side of the Hudson with that of New Jersey. At both the state and local levels, New York brings to renewal and planning activities a unique heritage of initiative and willingness to capitalize on opportunities. As far back as the turn of the century, the governments of New York State and New York City encouraged low-cost housing programs, and by World War I they had become the first governments in the United States to be involved officially in these activities. In 1923 the state established a Commission of Housing and Regional Planning, and in 1926 it became the first state to authorize the establishment of limited-dividend and cooperative housing ventures, designed to facilitate private group investment. In the 1930's New York not only accommodated itself to New Deal programs, but also adopted a public housing amendment to the state constitution in 1938 which again made it a pioneer in the field.[81] This amendment authorized state loans and subsidies to localities for housing projects—paralleling federal programs—and also conferred municipal powers of eminent domain and condemnation to be used in housing programs.

In 1939, the State Public Housing Law codified and extended these developments and established state housing aid programs to municipalities, which were independent of the federal programs. The law continued limited-dividend and cooperative housing companies; introduced loan programs for improving existing multiple dwellings; authorized municipalities to start their own programs. By 1960, state low-cost housing programs in the Region provided in New York City alone close to 38,000 dwelling units, and smaller projects were completed or underway in Hempstead, North Hempstead, Mount Vernon, Newburgh, New Rochelle, Port Chester, White Plains, and Yonkers.[82]

To the particular legacy of the state, New York City has added its own program, with distinctive objectives and methods of operation. For publicly supported housing, the City has introduced the so-called middle-income "no cash subsidy" project, designed to expand the range of the usual federal and state programs, and it has carried on an independent program in the traditional low-rent housing field. By January 1, 1960, the City program consisted of twenty-nine projects of 27,493 dwelling units.[83]

More important, the City has used available federal funds to a much greater degree per capita than any other city within the Region. Since the earliest New Deal days, when the close personal ties between Mayor La Guardia and President Roosevelt helped assure a steady flow of relief and housing funds, New York City has always led the nation in its proportional share of federal funds for direct housing and development activities.[84] In January 1958 the City had twenty-one Title I projects completed, under contract, or in the planning stage, covering 606 acres of land and scheduled to provide over 38,000 new dwelling units. The long-range total program, including projects identified for planning, called for the clearance of 831 acres of land and the construction of 54,000 dwelling units.[85] So far as combined housing and renewal activities were concerned, the City, with 5 per cent of the United States population, had completed 8.5 per cent of all federally aided public housing apartments, had 15.1 per cent of all those under construction, and 16.9 per cent of all those under contract.[86]

The City is special not just in terms of money—but in the treatment it receives. The 1949 federal law set the maximum share of any single state at 10 per cent of the total national authorization of $500 million for Title I activities. The City, however, proposed and the Congress enacted a 1953 amendment which made available an additional $25 million for New York City alone. In 1955, when

Congress voted another authorization of $500 million, the City's normal share was increased by $39 million—this time from the President's discretionary fund. It later arrived at a "general understanding" with the Housing and Home Finance Agency to increase its share of the write-down funds to $110 million and to receive at least 10 per cent of the funds authorized by Congress in 1957.[87]

Given these differences in quantity and quality of activity, the New York City renewal enterprise appears as a thing unto itself, within the Region and the nation—the ultimate of what can be expected in the way of a local response. The interpretation of most observers has been that a peculiar combination of history, effective formal organizational arrangements, and energetic informal arrangements have produced a unique and an extraordinarily effective program. So far as the formal organization is concerned, the position of the Mayor has frequently been singled out as an important factor. In New York City a Mayor equipped with substantial powers and facing a weak Council vies chiefly with the Board of Estimate for political leadership—and a determined Mayor can usually triumph over even this powerful body. Legally the decisive voice in municipal affairs, the Mayor is also the central political figure, for assembly district and county leaders look to him and not to other officials in the City as the prime source of patronage and support. And, while law and politics combine to give him power to act, the public's longstanding support for housing and development activities gives him an incentive to expand these programs. Local opposition exists, of course—usually in the person of the City Comptroller in his role of guardian of the taxpayer—and from time to time it has been intensified by allegations of scandal in the program's management. But to date the opposition has been ineffective; and the Mayor, endowed with both the incentive and the capacity to act, and supported by a highly professional staff, can make decisions rapidly and with final effect.[88]

Indeed, some complain that renewal decisions in the City come so rapidly and quietly that even proponents of renewal and housing are often not aware of new developments. "Ordinarily, in New York," two astute observers have written, "it is possible to protest the location of a public housing project only *after* the decision has been virtually made. Such preliminary planning as is done is usually completed before a project proposed is submitted to the City Planning Commission and the Board of Estimate and the groundwork for the project's acceptance by the Board is laid in advance. Thus the Citizens' Housing and Planning Council of New York is occupied not so much with appealing for new projects, as with getting an opportunity to be heard before the Board of Estimate on projects already planned. Sometimes, the Council is unable to get any information about a project until the planning is almost done." [89]

To the comparative strength and order of the City's formal structure, many add the particular administrative arrangements which have long existed in the City. We have met these arrangements before in the person of Robert Moses. Until 1960 when he became head of the 1964 World Fair, Moses was as much a key figure in housing and renewal as he was in transportation. He long served as chairman of the Committee on Slum Clearance—the agency first in charge of clearance and rebuilding under Title I. Since 1942 he served on the City Planning Commission, which reviews housing and redevelopment projects for conformity to the City's more general land-use plans, carries out renewal analyses, and approves sites for related public facilities. He was associated since New Deal days with the City Housing Authority, which constructs and operates all public housing projects, whether federal, state, or city. Given these strategic posts, it is not surprising that in the mid-1950's he was described as the key factor accounting for the City's activities:

Since 1934, a gifted man named Robert Moses has come to be the undisputed head of what is virtually a parallel government of matters concerning public works and related activities. Moses' only salaried job is Park Commissioner, but he has managed to get formal or informal control of several key agencies, and, by placing his engineers, architects and other followers in strategic positions and by rewarding his friends and punishing his enemies among the host of contractors, consultants and politicians who depend, in one way or another, on the operation he controls, he has managed to build what Chicago politicians would call an

"organization," albeit, one which is generally supposed to be "clean."
City administrations come and go, but Moses keeps his tight grip on
countless committees, boards, authorities, and commissions, and Moses is
an exceedingly high-handed man.[90]

From this combination of formal City structure and informal
Moses "organization" has evolved a local renewal enterprise which
at times has appeared at least equal and sometimes superior to its
federal counterpart in political skill. In what has been known in renewal circles as the "unique" New York strategy, the City is the
only municipality in the United States empowered to offer full pay
to the directors of the local housing authority. It is also exceptional
in the way it has screened, selected, and received commitments from
the private developers. In New York these arrangements are usually
completed prior to the clearing of sites or public action. The private
sponsors—rather than the municipality—are required to demolish
existing buildings and relocate tenants. And the City has been accustomed to negotiating its own sale prices with private sponsors,
sometimes in apparent contradiction to rules and regulations.

In the Lincoln Square project, for example, the City first recommended that Fordham University be charged $8.00 per square foot
for the site it was acquiring in the area. Later the City announced
a new negotiated price of $6.75. Shortly afterwards the Federal
Housing and Home Finance Agency declared the price unaccepta-
ble. It insisted that at least two independent re-use appraisals be
made before the revised resale price could be approved, and it at-
tacked the City's practice of private clearance and tenant relocation.
Mr. Moses' response was that the federal demands were "unprece-
dented, unnecessary, and may cause a six months delay," and, in the
end, he appeared to have his way. Although the federal agency rejected two land appraisals submitted by the City and directed that
three federally chosen appraisals be made in their place, it held
$27,331,325 in reserve for the Lincoln project—the exact sum to the
dollar required by the negotiated rate of $6.75 per square foot. After
further negotiation, in place of its original demands for other appraisals, the federal agency accepted a new joint estimate based upon

the City's two proposals. Ultimately, it accepted a $7.00 estimate, $1.00 less per square foot than the proposal originally recommended by the City itself.[91]

In the words of the *New York Times:*

> Mr. Cole [the then Administrator of the Housing and Home Finance Agency] had better face the fact as F.D.R. had to, that New York City is not going to drop Bob Moses as a public servant as long as he is willing to keep working for the city. . . . Maybe some other system would have worked better here on urban renewal, than the "unique" New York system. That can only be a matter of speculation. What we do know is that, in general, New York's slum clearance progress has been unequaled and that in the memory of living man on the New York scene, there has never been the equal of Bob Moses for getting things done. The Federal Government is not going to change Mr. Moses. It had better try to get along with him for that is the way we will travel farthest fastest for the public good.[92]

Lincoln Square has not been the last example of the City's exceptional performance. On May 4, 1959, when the Slum Clearance Committee announced two new projects, Bellevue South and Park Row Extension, with an estimated federal contribution of $30 million, the regional office of the Housing and Home Finance Agency revealed that it had no knowledge of the projects. "If they want to use our money," said Walter S. Fried, the regional administrator, "it's only polite to tell us." [93]

The City's programs are not, of course, free from charges of manipulation and skullduggery—familiar by-products of any large-scale development activities—and they have their coordination problems. The year 1959 saw the development of full-blown revelations in periodicals—charges of financial manipulation and irresponsible alliances, as well as bitter criticism of the tenant relocation practices.[94] But the City's special methods avoid the financial risk of acquiring a site which might not be attractive to private capital and minimize the political liabilities which often occur in the process of tenant relocation. On balance, the City seems to possess experienced talent, established procedures, and tested organization, which does more than acquire—and use—available federal revenue. It often shapes the

federal program to its own purposes. It strives "to take full advantage of assistance," and it attributes program delays to "man failure,
largely chargeable to Washington." [95]

The New York City pattern of renewal stands in sharp contrast to
renewal enterprises elsewhere in the Region. The net result of so
much activity and effort in the five boroughs is that no other city
has approached the City's per capita record. Newark, after a series of
postwar governmental reorganizations, is now an active but far more
"regular" member of the federal team.[96] And Edison, Elizabeth, Hoboken, Morristown, Long Branch, New Brunswick, Passaic, Paterson, Perth Amboy, and Union City had entered the program by 1957.
Most of their projects, however, were still in the planning stage, and
the total public cost for all authorized projects in the State of New
Jersey amounted to only $56 million.[97]

In the three years beginning in 1957, the rate of progress stepped
up rapidly, indicating that New York's "unique practices" might
no longer be quite so distinctive. The cost of authorized projects for
New Jersey as a whole had risen to $69 million, and an additional
$244 million was involved in plans already completed.[98] As a har-
binger of even greater expectations, recent estimates for the New
Jersey portion of the Region alone call for $300 million to be spent
in the next five years and perhaps a billion dollars in the ten years
to follow. Newark now boasts of having "more urban renewal under way or planned than any city of a comparable size in the United
States." [99]

Yet though increasing administrative experience and skill hint at
a growing parity between New Jersey and New York cities, New Jersey has still other handicaps. The culprit which is blamed most frequently is the state's tax system. The director of the Newark redevelopment program wrote a popular version of the effect of Jersey's
narrow tax base in 1957:

> The cost of local government, most of it for education, is loaded on real
> property. . . . The result is that real-estate taxes are much higher in New
> Jersey cities than in New York or Philadelphia. Property taxes in New
> Jersey cities cause blight and prevent new construction or rebuilding. Re-

development programs of the size and scope that is needed, will not be possible until the State shifts some of the cost of education from real property to other forms of taxation.[100]

To the depressant influence of the tax system can be added another familiar characteristic of the Jersey scene: the fact that its renewal effort is divided among a number of municipalities, and that professional staff and administrative and organizational talents of the sort available in New York City or Newark are hard to come by in the smaller cities. Renewal agencies in many of these cities seem to chafe—not to override federal regulations. They complain of "cumbersome procedures," "tight centralization," "inadequate staffing," and "detailed controls that go far beyond the conditions intended by Congress." [101] As they do so, they testify to how hard it is for small organizations, in a field where trained personnel is short, to master politically and administratively intricate activity.

Even if these liabilities in finance and size were overcome, one would still be entitled to question the impact of the effort as presently conceived. When all the programs within the Region are lumped together, the net effect, measured against requirements, seems small. As for New Jersey, in the words of one local renewal expert, "The dike being built in this State to stop the flood of obsolescence consists of a dozen cities out of hundreds with needs, 10,000 families out of a million involved, 1,000 acres out of the tens of thousands required and gross project costs of some $80 million out of the billions necessary." [102] Even New York City's performance approaches the picayune when set against the public goals established for redevelopment. The 831 acres involved in all present or identified projects in New York City have to be contrasted to the 5000 acres which the Committee on Slum Clearance called the worst slums within the five boroughs. And, according to the Committee on Slum Clearance, "it is unrealistic to imagine that these can be absolutely cleared and entirely new structures substituted in any foreseeable time. The cost would be simply staggering, running into many billions of dollars. . . . The real job will have to be done by raising standards in the Multiple Dwelling and other controlling laws and regulations and by offering substantial inducements to private owners and developers to go ahead on their own." [103]

In effect, the present public programs to shape directly the physical development of the Region have to be discounted in three important ways. First, on a national level, financial support to attack seriously the renewal problems of the Region has not been forthcoming. Though population densities in slum areas of New York City are decreasing, the amount of obsolete real estate is not. And, for other old cities in the Region, as other volumes in the New York Metropolitan Region Study have indicated, the number of low-income residents is increasing as they follow the industrial jobs outward from New York City toward suburban areas.

This movement emphasizes the second obstacle in the program. Not only are the federal grants clearly insufficient in terms of total Regional requirements, but the political and administrative structures of most municipalities are not geared to obtain whatever funds the national government does make available. And the process involved in turning a renewal proposal into reality appears tortuous indeed. At least so far, it has taken a rare combination of personal talent, organizational experience, and political sagacity to see a specific plan through the long obstacle course to completion—the legal complications involved in land assembly, the discovery of a willing and appropriate sponsor, the politically explosive task of relocating tenants, the consequent disruption of long established neighborhood social and political organizations, and the technical difficulties in rezoning and dovetailing public and private facilities within a given area. It is not surprising that usually within the Region these programs have proceeded in fits and starts, in a manner commensurate with the talent and ability the governments can muster, and often depending upon the man and the hour fortuitously meeting in a suitable locale.

Third and finally, one must recall that the program still relies for its success on private action. Once cleared, the site chosen for renewal activities must still seem a good investment to a private business man. Quite obviously, government help in securing a downtown location in Manhattan or Newark will be welcomed. Clearly, a banker can see sense in investing in rehabilitation activities next-door to Wall Street. But one wonders how attractive the program will seem when it leaves the central business district and moves to concentrate on the gray areas of largely residential neighborhoods. Perhaps suburbanites in Middlesex County stand poised to reenter Union City once new accommodations are available, but a prudent investor may be entitled to wonder. Therefore, to the scarcity of federal funds, and the shortage of local talent on which the organizational success depends, is added an economic question: whether the very scheme of renewal as presently authorized is feasible. Taken together, these limitations and questions seem to make it certain that not all parts of the Region where renewal is appropriate will undertake these programs. And, even in the parts that do, drastic changes in methods and magnitudes would have to occur in order to thwart the trends toward obsolescence and blight.

UNDERWRITING DIFFUSION

Programs for transportation, water, and physical development are not the only public activities that affect the distribution of jobs and people within the Region. Other factors, such as public recreational and cultural facilities, special educational institutions, and interstate regulatory efforts in air and pollution control, help determine the relative attractiveness of the New York Region vis-à-vis other metropolitan areas in the country, and the relative attractiveness of different parts of the Region for residential or industrial location. But the three fields we chose for discussion are the ones in which institutional arrangements have been most clearly developed, and the ones in which the characteristics of the particular political systems involved are most susceptible to summary. On the basis of those three, what conclusions can we draw about the consequences for the private sector and the shape of Regional development?

The principal conclusion is that the present array of programs works for the continued diffusion of households and firms.

In transportation it is true that two separate philosophies and two sets of values still exist, and that the advocates of mass transportation are also advocates of maintaining population and business in the Region's central parts. They continue to argue for improved transit facilities which would allow New York City to be "remade into a pleasant and efficient place for working and living in many refashioned and integrated neighborhoods." And they continue to predict that such policies "should keep more middle income families from leaving for the suburbs." [104]

But, however appealing or repellent such an image may be, the philosophy seems to run against present trends. At the present time, the capacity of the mass transit agencies to formulate, finance, and carry out their plans is a poor second to that of the highway transportation agencies. It is true that signs of partial blending of responsibilities appear more frequently: highway agencies find it appropriate to consider taking over some transit programs; governors and mayors look more favorably on proposals to waive the property taxes of commuting railroads. Yet these developments have been only marginal. Certainly they do not occur at the expense of the automobile users. And, as more bridges, expressways, and circumferential routes are constructed, as new industrial locations are opened up, the result is that new patterns of movement become possible and new areas for residential development become available. The growing transportation network accelerates the diffusion process begun by the automobile and strengthened by shortages of space in the old cities and changes in the Region's economic structure. Nothing short of a massive flow of public funds to support mass transit could conceivably check this trend.

More slowly, but still moving in the same direction, the political process concerned with the development of water supply increases suburban access to reservoirs. The elapsed time required to complete arrangements in this field is much longer, of course, and the initial advantage of the older cities much greater. But, though the machinery seems clumsy and the conflicts among localities wanting water and localities possessing water are likely to continue, even in New Jersey water in adequate amounts appears forthcoming. A particular subarea in the Region may suffer a temporary disadvantage and this may be important for a particular firm at a particular time. But the record does not indicate that suburban communities will have to depend entirely on their own resources to meet the expenses involved in providing new distribution lines. Although no river basin adjacent to the Region has yet been developed according to a comprehensive plan, Delaware River water will be tapped before downstream mains run dry.

As for renewal activities, the efforts seem too little and too difficult. The federal housing insurance programs, working through the marketplace instead of public institutions, swell the volume of suburban construction. At the same time, federal appropriations to redevelop city sites are puny in comparison. And the necessity to mesh local political and administrative processes with federal requirements further impedes the operations of these programs in many localities where their applicability seems urgent.

Of course this promotion of what has been called "regional homogenization" is not a conscious, deliberate act of public policy. If one thing is apparent from our survey of the Region's public program, it is that few decisions are made on the basis of their effect upon the Region as a whole. Rather, the result is the net outcome of a series of public decisions made by largely separate political processes, each understandable in its own way, but each representing only a piece of the puzzle. Rarely do the decisions in one field take into account the activities in other fields. Rarely are the immediate objectives of the participants the same, and rarely are the consequences of their activities upon the course of Regional development accurately anticipated. The results of public action at the Regional level are unpremeditated, the products of accident, not of design, or at least not of a design that takes the broad shape of the Region into account.

Finally, and not unnaturally, the public programs expanding most rapidly in the Region are those that exhibit an operating philosophy most closely akin to a market economy. The public agencies that define needs according to the criteria of the individual consumer, that

have revenues dependent on direct-user charges, or that aim toward
the satisfaction of the purchaser are the agencies that make the most
influential decisions. The highway transportation agencies, the mortgage programs of the Federal Housing Administration and Veterans Administration proceed on the same philosophy of supply and
demand that governs the behavior of private firms. In their political
philosophy they are Manchesterian liberals, defining their public in
terms of the individual buyer and striving to give the buyer what he
wants. In contrast, renewal agencies and programs for comprehensive development of water resources carry a more corporate concept
of community, and represent a notion of public interest which is
not the same as an aggregation of individual wants. Because these
institutions and procedures are organized on a different basis from
the marketplace, they seem to experience a greater difficulty in
finding revenue or winning public sanction.

All this is not surprising, for the ideological environment of the
Region's governments remains that of the market economy and limited government activity. The final result is that a public sector committed to this ideology by financing and structure offers no countervailing influence against the trends generated in the private sector.
On the contrary, committed to the principle that changes in the private sector are generally for the best, the Regional agencies move to
support the present lines of development. They underwrite and accelerate the process of scatteration.

5

The Political Economy
of the Future

THE SYSTEMS WITHIN THE SECTOR

For all the emphasis on matters of quantity—levels of expenditures and revenues, numbers of public employees, miles of highways, units of substandard housing—the chapters which have gone before yield not surprisingly a qualitative conclusion. The most significant fact about the governments of the New York Region circa 1960 is not the size of the public budgets, the number of dollars allocated or about to be allocated to one program or another, or the trends in these budgets and allocations. The most significant fact is that two different types of political systems rule the public sector today—the local governments and the Regional enterprises.

The inference to be drawn from this finding is that these systems, by the attitudes of the participants, the nature of the political processes, and the rules of the political game, strengthen the economic trends in being. They leave most of the important decisions for Regional development to the private marketplace. They work in ways which by and large encourage firms and households to continue "doing what comes naturally."

To be sure, the two systems arrive at their positions of negative influence by quite separate routes. That system which we have subsumed under the title of "local governments"—the units of general jurisdiction and their satellites, the small special-purpose districts—is ineffective in the aggregate principally because its parts tend to cancel one another out. The system of quasi-governmental agencies, the Authorities and public corporations with programs which leap over municipal boundary lines, buttresses the marketplace more as a matter of conscious design. In this instance considerations of institutional survival often tend toward programs which accelerate trends already underway. But the net effect remains the same: public policy rarely seems to be the initiating force in the pattern of population settlement or economic growth.

There is nothing mysterious, of course, about why this vacuum in public policy occurs. For all their frantic bustlings with economic development programs, land-use controls, and building regulations, each local government, even that of New York City, commands only a small portion of the Region's territory. As each strives to preserve its own local identity, doctrines of municipal mercantilism become natural lines of action. Indeed they are close to being the only politically palatable policies so long as both a desire for high quality urban services *and* continued independence make up a common municipal credo. Yet, from the point of view of the Region, no common policy emerges from the welter of elaborately and individually concocted strategies of manipulation and maneuver. Instead, there is only a number of options from which businessmen and households can choose.

In a different way, but just as understandably, the present development of agencies with more or less Regional responsibilities makes public direction of economic growth difficult. In the oligopolistic sphere of the transportation giants, the half-way house of water politics, and in the complex realm of intergovernmental housing activities, the program most likely to succeed is the one that supports—not contradicts—the marketplace. Success seems to smile on the transport agencies that favor the auto, the housing project that reclaims a potentially profitable downtown site, the water resources program which responds to a present need rather than anticipating—and helping shape—the future pattern of development. Though these agencies are concerned with questions of over-all Regional policy with a vengeance, typically they ride with, rather than oppose, the main currents in the private sector.

It is these characteristics of the political systems that allow us to discount the programs and policies of local governments so heavily. So long as the individual strategies of individual muncipalities are condemned to frustration because of the sheer number of their neighbors, so long as prudence dictates that Regional institutions abet the economic forces already at work, public programs and public policies are of little consequence. Costs of urban government may continue to rise, but they will not substantially influence the preference patterns of families and locational choices of entrepreneurs. The most stringent policies of land-use control or the most ardent wooing of industries will not in the end determine the broad pattern of settlement. While these systems continue, the economist is safe in basing his projections on a consideration of the economic factors involved in Regional growth.

CHECKLIST FOR A REVOLUTION

But will the political systems continue to function in 1970 or 1980 or 1985 as they have today? Is it plausible to expect that the changes in living and working patterns projected elsewhere in this Study will take place while political styles remain unaffected? Already, in Dade County, Florida, one metropolitan area in the United States has effected a comprehensive structural reorganization and there are more modest but nonetheless significant reforms in other metropolitan centers. Already, one distinguished scholar of urban affairs speaks of "a vast and growing dissatisfaction with life in and around the great cities" and suggests that popular action is impending.[1] Within the New York Region itself in recent years, new governmental agencies have been established, new procedures for intergovernmental collaboration have developed, and new proposals for more fundamental rearrangements have been put forward. With such apparent signals of impending change flying, is it conceivable that twenty-five years will pass without the emergence of a new ideology and structure of public bodies, equipped with new capacities and motivations to intervene in the affairs of the private sector? In short, is not the gravest danger in sketching the Region of the future that of underestimating—or even ignoring—the prospects of revolution?

This sort of proposition is a difficult one to tackle—but it is not an impossible one. It is difficult because the question is not how much government but what kind of government, and in this instance the projection of trends "as they are" may confuse rather than clarify the issue. But the proposition remains manageable, for there is nothing inherently unpredictable about the process of radical change. We are not called upon to contemplate a disorderly or violent future for the New York Region; we are not involved in the business of forecasting municipal socialism or conjuring up visions of irate citizens marching on City Hall. We are asked instead to consider whether certain major stresses and strains in the public sector will require transformations in political habits and major new governmental arrangements—not marginal changes but changes of the character not seen since the boroughs of New York City formed a more perfect union or the Port of New York Authority was established.

Conceived in these terms, the inquiry becomes both a familiar and a limited one. It is familiar because we are covering ground for the New York Region which has been carefully examined elsewhere before in the 100-odd studies of the conditions requiring governmental reorganization in metropolitan areas which have been authorized since World War II. So the situation in New York has strong parallels to Miami and Toronto where reorganizations were put into effect and to St. Louis and Cleveland where they were rejected.

The inquiry is limited, because three specific stresses are involved in the New York situation. We are concerned first with the capacity of the present systems to remain financially solvent given the pattern of population movement and economic change projected elsewhere in the New York Metropolitan Region Study. Second, we need to make a judgment about the ability of the systems to improve service levels, at least at a rate approximating that since World War II, against the background of new public demands and

new expectations of government. Finally, we have to evaluate the
sporadic displays of public dissatisfaction over the ways the Region
is developing and judge how serious is the inclination for widespread public intervention.

If we can establish a plausible case that the present systems can
handle these problems, then our prognosis will be against a local
revolution. For our presumption is that the governments in the New
York Region will continue doing business as usual unless there is
compelling evidence that a breakdown is at hand. Ideological satisfaction, historical lethargy, and the calculus of politics are on the
side of the status quo. Prudent politicians, committed to the present
systems as "going concerns" and uneasy at the uncertainties of
change, will, we expect, make minimal—not maximum—adjustments.

THE BURNING ISSUES: (1) THE CASE FOR
MUNICIPAL BANKRUPTCY

By all odds, the most widely publicized basis for expecting dramatic changes in the structure of the Region's governments and the
reallocation of duties and responsibility is the one built upon the
so-called "gaslight government" thesis. The bare bones of this position are that the revenue base of local government is hopelessly an-
tiquated, narrow, inefficient, and inadequate. Local revenues—so the
argument runs—are far less sensitive to changes in income or pro-
duction than are federal or state taxes. Particularly the property tax
fails to expand its yield proportionately with other revenues, and yet
the structure of local government is such that other tax sources are
even less politically or administratively feasible. As a consequence,
the Region's governments are rapidly approaching the point where
they cannot provide even the additional services required by population growth or the extension of urban settlement. With such a rigid
tax base they face fiscal disaster—unless there occurs a major over-
haul, at least in the revenue system and more likely in the formal
structure of government.

In one sense, this argument is only a Regional variation of a national analysis: a conviction that the Region's plight is symptomatic of nationwide conditions. Otto Eckstein, for example, projecting net cash expenditures of all state and local governments in the United States to 1968 on the bases of "past policy decisions and the interplay of political and economic forces," arrives at a "medium projection" in current dollars of $53.7 billion, in comparison with the 1958 total of $36.2 billion. On the assumption that present revenue rates and sources will remain unchanged, he forecasts a state and local deficit of $3.4 billion by 1968—a ten-year increase of $1.7 billion. Eckstein believes that, if conditions of inflation intensify, the situation will become even worse, for "property tax assessments notoriously lag behind value changes; gasoline and other specific taxes also lag; only income and general sales taxes may have a better than proportionate response." Even without inflation, an average increase in tax rates of 8 per cent would be required between 1958 and 1963 to erase the deficit.[2]

But, if local governments everywhere are headed for deficit spending, their prospects for borrowing the money they need also seem dim. Paralleling Eckstein's estimates of total expenditures and revenue for the future, Harry L. Severson has projected new construction costs, program by program, for the next decade. He arrives at a capital outlay total for state and local governments in 1968 of $25.2 billion, and estimates the new state and local bond offerings of that year at $16.3.[3] Both of those figures are more than double the 1958 levels. But even as the rate or volume of borrowing increases, the position of these governments in the security market grows worse. Fiscal experts attribute this partly to the depressant effect that expanded offerings would have on the market. Another reason is that the tax-exemption proviso of local bonds is no longer the drawing card it once was. "The natural size of the market has been narrowing while the demand for funds has been broadening. State and local governments have had to bargain away most of the advantages of tax exemptions to investors. Prospects for an increased interest rate, greater difficulty in securing investors in the marketing of general obligation bonds seem to compound the financial troubles of the local unit. The lone investor with the large income who was forced to state and local purchases in order to reserve some of his earnings from the National Treasury no longer is sufficient to handle the volume of offerings now current. The relative bargaining position of borrower and lender has consequently shifted and major reforms seem necessary if this source of finance is to prove adequate to the demands ahead." [4]

At the level of the New York Metropolitan Region, this national analysis is, by the testimony of many observers, doubled in spades. Not since the twenties, for example, has New York City been able to receive a clean bill of financial health from any of the numerous state or municipal investigating commissions. Typically, the City is usually characterized as operating in a financial strait jacket, with a tax base that cannot meet even the requirements of normal growth. So, the Temporary Commission on the Fiscal Affairs of the State Government concluded in 1955 that, by 1961, the City would require $511 million more than in the 1954–55 budget and that only about one-half of the increase could be received from the existing tax levies.[5] (As it turned out, the predictions came true three years before the 1961 target date.) Continuing the tradition, the Commission on Governmental Operations of the City of New York, established in 1959, observed that between 1949 and 1958 the City's total operating costs increased by almost 82 per cent while the property tax base estimated at market value expanded by only 56 per cent and the residents' personal income after income tax withholdings rose by only 23 per cent.[6]

The City's capital outlay program is similarly in tight circumstances. In 1958 the Planning Commission set the capital requirements for the City at $300 million annually for a "barely minimum capital program." An adequate program over the next ten years, in the Commission's judgment, would call for a yearly expenditure of $380 million and even this would only "permit reasonable progress in meeting our real needs without frills. It makes no allowance for increased costs and it would not permit any major additional transit expenses." In contrast the actual capital expenditure had not exceeded $200 million in any postwar year to 1958 and is not budgeted to go much higher in the years immediately ahead.[7]

The largest city in the Region is not the only one that appears, on the surface, to have reached the limits of its revenue yields. Surveying in 1959 the postwar experience of the Region's suburban governments, Merrill Folsom reports a growing concern over the present level of taxation among officials and residents; cries of "strangulation" as "the real estate tax burden is being shifted from the urban industrial areas to the new homes of commuters"; and statements that "taxes are becoming overwhelming." Within affluent Westchester County, where real estate levies increased from $61.5 to $136.7 million between 1948 and 1958, Folsom calculated that at current levels, an average property owner's lifetime taxes on real estate will be $7,710.[8]

Less impressionistically, Samuel F. Thomas supplements Folsom's finding, focusing on the extraordinary growth in school expenditures in Nassau County. Between 1945 and 1954, Thomas reports, school operating expenditures rose over 300 per cent and total school expenditures went up 657 per cent. In the one year between 1953–54 and 1954–55 the school operating expenditures rose by one third, leaving Thomas to suggest "that the tax burden on the real estate owner in Nassau County is greater and is increasing at a faster pace than the tax burden on the property owner in New York City."[9]

Perhaps the bluntest warning of tax insufficiency in New York has come from New York State's Commissioner of Education, James E. Allen, Jr. Anticipating necessary educational outlays in New York in 1965 at double their 1958 level, Allen estimates that— even having made "liberal allowances for the growth of real property valuation" in the meantime—local property tax rates would have to increase by about 40 per cent to finance new school budgets. In his judgment "the real estate tax will not suffice for meeting the educational burdens of the years immediately ahead."[10]

The same cries of tax crises echo with special intensity in New Jersey. With a much heavier dependence on the property tax, the

Garden State has doubled the amount so levied between 1948 and 1958. The New Jersey Commission on State Tax Policy in its 1958 report concludes, "The policy of no new taxes has succeeded only in part. Its success has been limited largely to the legislative halls. Its effect may well have been to commit New Jersey to the support of its governmental services primarily from the property tax to the point of no return." [11]

PAPER TIGERS IN PUBLIC FINANCE

But what precisely is "the point of no return" in estimating the capacity of a tax system? One is not disposed to ignore steadily rising tax rates nor prophecies of disasters when issued by responsible observers. Nonetheless, the minor and often underemphasized premise of the municipal bankruptcy argument is that there is somewhere an economic or political peril point beyond which taxes cannot go without the system collapsing. Specifically there is the notion that Eckstein's 8 per cent increase in effective taxes (that is, tax levels expressed as a percentage of tax base, either income or market property value) is very hard to come by in the world of practical affairs.

Yet, actually, the facts do not bear out this contention. Once expenditure and revenue trends are laid along trends in economic growth, more than a little sunshine breaks through the gloom. On a national basis in 1958, after a decade of dramatic growth in absolute terms, total expenditures of local governments amounted to 5.8 per cent of the gross national product—about the same as in 1927. State and local capital expenditures in the same period closely paralleled earlier experience; they totaled 2.4 per cent of the gross national product in 1955 as contrasted to 2.1 per cent in 1927.[12]

Nor do the years ahead appear to place substantially more drastic burdens on the economy. Eckstein's projections of expenditures assume that state and local expenditures will move in the 1958–1968 period from 8.3 per cent of the gross national product to 8.6 per cent—certainly not an extraordinary rise.[13] Making similar forecasts, Dick Netzer arrives at a 1970 "moderate" projection in the range of between 8.4 and 8.9 per cent of the gross national product.[14] His "substantial" projection—the highest range of expenditures which he believes possible—is between 10 and 10.6 per cent. Other analyses project a 1970 state-local ratio of expenditures to gross national product at approximately 10 per cent.[15]

When we move to the most accurate indicators of "available" revenues—real property valuations and tax rates expressed as a percentage of market value—the desperate straits of local fiscal capacity seem even less desperate. Despite the persuasive logical arguments to the contrary, nationwide the property tax has proven far from sluggish in recent years. Netzer estimates that between 1946 and 1957 the percentage change in the property tax base for all state and local governments was about 151 per cent, an increase just about equal to that of the gross national product. During the same period, the increase in the average effective tax rate—as a proportion of value—has been about 5 per cent, and between 1946 and 1952 the effective tax rates across the country appear actually to have declined.[16]

Once again, the evidence which can be assembled on a Regional basis supports a conclusion that the experience of the New York Metropolitan Region parallels that of the nation. As a proportion of personal income, total local government *expenditures* rose between 1945 and 1955 from 5.9 per cent to 9 per cent for the total Region, from 5.7 per cent to 10.3 per cent for New York City, from 7.0 to 9.3 per cent for other New York governments and from 5.9 per cent to 6.4 per cent for New Jersey units. No dramatic signs of upheaval in local *revenue* burdens appeared. As Table 4 indicates, total property tax levies show no sharply rising trend relative to personal income outside New York City. Further, our investigations in New York State indicate that total local property taxes as a percentage of market value declined between 1950 and 1955 an average of 30 per cent for the governments in the counties outside New York City. A further indication of the "water" remaining in the existing tax structure is the fact that in 1951 the average ratio of the assessed valuation to market value for the New Jersey counties of the Region was 33.1

Table 4 Total Property Tax Revenue of Local Governments
Compared with Personal Income [a] of Population,
New York Metropolitan Region [b]

	Personal income (millions)	Local property taxes (millions)	Property taxes as percentage of income
Region			
1945	$20,287	$ 619	3.05
1950	27,876	998	3.58
1955	35,766	1,495	4.17
New York City			
1945	13,124	300	2.28
1950	16,247	541	3.32
1955	18,663	763	4.08
Other New York counties			
1945	2,412	112	4.64
1950	4,328	161	3.71
1955	6,814	305	4.47
New Jersey counties			
1945	4,751	207	4.35
1950	7,301	296	4.05
1955	10,289	427	4.15

[a] Personal income figures for 1945 and 1950 were interpolated from New York Metropolitan Region Study estimates for 1939, 1947, and 1955.

[b] Excluding Fairfield County, Connecticut, for which figures are not available.

per cent and in 1957 was 28.7 per cent.[17] Throughout a decade of substantial population changes and pent-up demands for public services spilling over from the war years, New Jersey has maintained its policy of "no new taxes" because it extracted over one-half billion dollars in additional revenue from the taxes it already had.

It is true that local school taxes on real property rose considerably, in absolute terms, an average of 121 percent between 1950 and 1955.[18] But when these school taxes are shown as a percentage of personal income and of market value of property (where these figures were available), the increase is not so sharp. Here the New York experience again approximated that of the nation: local school taxes doubled, but in the relatively low range of from 1.5 to 3.0 per cent of personal income.

In summary, these figures suggest that however intense the spending pressures in the Region's public sector generated by urbanization and growth since World War II may appear for the Region as a whole, they have certainly not brought about a massive diversion of income or capital to public purposes. More important, in an economic sense (except possibly for a long-term shift in consumer expenditures away from housing expenditures and a consequent slowing down in the accumulation of taxable property values) the resilience of public revenue does not seem as low as is often supposed. For the "gaps" between projected expenditures and projected revenues, more often than not in the postwar period, have been filled by an increase in revenue rather than a reduction in expenditures, demonstrating an elasticity in taxes not suspected when the trends of expenditures and revenues are extrapolated independently of one another. In the end, the case for municipal bankruptcy rests on the incapacity of the political process to divert funds to public policy—not on "an objective economic constraint to taxes . . . or a measureable limit on the fraction of economic activity that a community may wish to channel through the public sector." [19]

But this supposed political incapacity has not shown itself in the New York Metropolitan Region. In New York City, beginning with the complete reorganization of grants-in-aid under the Moore Plan in 1946, continuing in the state's uniform reassessment of local property values, and extending to Governor Rockefeller's proposal to equip the local school districts with general powers of taxation, again and again the size of the revenue structure has been expanded.[20] Less dramatically, New Jersey has moved in the same direction: first, by a grant-in-aid breakthrough so far as education is concerned; second, by the business earnings tax in 1958; third, by the court rulings on assessments which in effect have doubled the taxing

capacity of all local jurisdictions. When these state actions are cou-
pled with the adoption of local sales and nuisance taxes at the
county and municipal level, and with much heavier rates of borrowing, it is clear that over-all the political process has displayed few
signs of incapacity to adjust. Simultaneously, it has indicated little
disposition to undergo comprehensive or fundamental structural or
financial reform.

It is quite true that this picture of the Regional public sector as a
whole does not fit equally well all parts of the Region. On a relative
basis, not only New York City but the older municipalities in the
inlying New Jersey counties have experienced conditions of increasing stringency. In the six years between 1951 and 1957, Jersey City,
Newark, Elizabeth, Paterson, Bayonne, and Hoboken have all faced
increased tax rates against a background of tax bases which were either rising much more slowly or actually declining. These six registered changes of between 2.2 per cent and 45.9 per cent in the local
property tax rate per thousand dollars of full market value. In the
case of Hoboken and Bayonne, where the increases were 45.9 per
cent and 12.2 per cent respectively, these changes were accompanied
by absolute losses in both assessed and market value. Clearly, these
cities have not found the last few years easy going.

Yet these municipalities still seem more the exception than the
rule—there is little evidence that the division between the haves and
the have-nots in other parts of the Region grows worse. On the contrary, what little evidence can be assembled hints at an opposite process underway. When New York towns were compared in the estimated per capita full market value of taxable property for the years
1945, 1950, and 1955, no trend toward greater disparities among the
governments' revenue base was detectable. Although there is an increasing spread in the values of these series (as indicated in the increase in the standard deviation from $1180 in 1945 to $2350 in 1955),
the degree of dispersion relative to their average level remains
roughly the same.[21]

Very probably even the absolute increase in the ranges of these
values reflects more the Regionwide growth in property holdings

and the impact of inflation than any tendency toward an increasing "clustering" of values. One can reason from this pattern that, though differences in residential values among localities continue to grow, the process of commercial and industrial diffusion works in the opposite direction. New shopping centers and new industrial plants leaven the sprawl of comparatively low-value residential settlement in Bergen, Rockland, and Suffolk Counties to offer tax relief to beleaguered officials.

Clearly we are on tenuous ground either in forecasting that the older cities will muddle through or that the respective positions of the "haves" and "have-nots" will stay about the same. For one thing, a ten-year time is too short to determine reliably what is happening to the spread in municipal tax bases. For another, as Chapter 3 indicates, municipalities *try* very hard to acquire that kind of residential and industrial development which returns more in taxes than it costs in public services, and intent becomes entangled with effect. Undoubtedly once a government scores an initial success in this strategy a snowballing tendency may get underway—for it is easier for "them that has" not only to "get" but to get more. Still there are few signs, as we have seen, that these intentions are generally matched by deeds. To the contrary, a gradual bunching of effective tax rates is underway, and a leveling out in the per capita differences in respective tax bases. As another volume in this Study has pointed out: "The scope for variation in the tax levels of different areas contained within a single state is narrowing. More and more of the total tax bill is coming to be represented by state and federal taxes, correspondingly less of it by local taxes . . . on top of this, the leveling of population densities in the Region of the future may well add to the general equalization of local tax rates." [22]

THE BURNING ISSUES: (2) THE DEMAND
FOR SERVICES

If one can feel sanguine about the future supply of public monies in the Region, what other pressures might drive the governments to radical reform? Paradoxically enough, the very fact that public budgets *can* be balanced is often taken as a distress signal. The second major indictment of the present systems is that expenditures are set now and in the future at far too low a level. Malnutrition, not galloping consumption, according to this argument, is the fatal ailment of the public sector.

This is by no means a new argument in the United States, but it is an especially fashionable one right now. Its main thrust is that the American economy suffers from underspending so far as social investment and services are concerned; that national prosperity depends on channeling more resources to the support of government. Or, in one of the more pungent phrases of its advocates, the present mechanisms for allocating resources between the public and private sectors pay too much attention to "private wants" and not enough to "public needs." [23]

One can catch a sense of what the New Spenders regard as appropriate expenditure levels by reviewing the "needs" established by professional specialists in the main public programs. Writing in 1955, and concerned with projecting government expenditures to 1960, Wilie Kilpatrick and Robert Drury attributed past changes in expenditures to such relatively impersonal and typical forces as prices, population growth, age distribution, income, and urbanization. Looking to the future, however, they distinguished between demands and needs and provided two 1960 estimates: the "probable" and the "needed," according to the lights of experts in the public programs involved. Wherever a "direct measure of need" was available, the authors employed it, usually maintaining the same ratio between probable and needed expenditures for 1960 as existed in 1950. In their calculations, total state and local expenditures in 1960, using 1950 prices, would "probably" total $37 billion, whereas $42 billion would be actually "needed." Thus, a series of "deficiencies"—the gaps between the probable and the needed—appeared: $1 billion for schools, $165 million for highways, $455 million for welfare and corrections, and so on, adding up to a grand total of over $5 billion.[24]

The same sort of balance, this time for public investment rather than annual spending, was struck in 1957 by the Special Assistant to the President for Public Works Planning. His office estimated a backlog of $204 billion worth of public facilities required by 1965, including $92 billion for highways, $42 billion for education, $22 billion for hospitals, and $25 billion for water and sewage. In effect, the Special Assistant called for construction spending at the rate of $20 billion at a time when the annual rate was 42 per cent of that amount.[25]

Yet, just as with the bankruptcy argument, the starvation thesis fails to come to grips with the reality of the problems of the public sector. Estimates of needs can put dollar signs on the expectations of experts concerned about the quality of public service today—but they cannot turn the preferences of the experts into the preferences of the public. Even if they could, the popular preferences would not be immediately registered on the governments involved. At best, what the estimates give us are standards by which to evaluate services. They never free us from the problems of determining whether any given set of standards actually expresses preferences—or whether any set of standards is likely to be realized. Thus, one can readily admit that the impersonal forces of population growth, industrialization, density, and so forth push up the demand for public services, without arriving at the conclusion that failure to meet certain defined standards courts political disaster. One can concede that while schools are crowded there will be articulated demands for additional classrooms—and that while streams are polluted, there will be judicial decisions requiring the installation of more disposal systems—and still not accept the proposition that these voices and decisions will inexorably prevail. No greater mistake can be made than to suppose that the apparently objective and impersonal chronicling of "requirements" is anything more than presumptive evidence that some individuals are unhappy about the present state of affairs.

What is most relevant in estimating the relation of service levels to political stability is not their deviation from utopia but an understanding of the drift of present affairs in terms of the temper of the Region's residents. What we need to know are not the opinions of agitators as much as the general record of recent accomplishments.

By and large, are public services showing some signs of improving quality that can be determined in any reasonably objective way? Are the most "pressing needs" being fulfilled first? Are the politically active and influential elements in the Region's constituencies mollified by the recent trend of events?

On all these counts, on the basis of the evidence which is available, the record of the Region suggests that the systems are more likely to survive than go under. So far as the over-all trends are concerned, it seems clear that improvements in the quality of public services are being registered. Between 1945 and 1955, the average per capita operating expenditure for the Region in constant 1954 dollars rose from \$160.71 to \$221.90, an increase of 35.1 per cent.[26]

Undoubtedly some of this increase may have been due to the growing complications of providing a roughly constant level of services under more difficult circumstances—extra police assignments in the slums of older cities, for instance, or more fire engines for a new suburban development. Some could also be set down to increased factor costs—changes in real wages and fringe benefits without any improvement in the services involved. But even if we take these aspects into account for the Region as a whole, there has been, in fact, an increase in services—in more policemen per 1000 population in New York City, more hospital beds in Newark, more teachers per thousand pupils in the New York suburbs, more teachers with an A.B. degree in the New Jersey suburbs. Fire rating improved in Long Island towns; the average age of the subway cars declined; school property value per pupil across the Region almost doubled. Even in those older cities with stable or declining populations, significant changes in major services seem to have occurred. Between 1947 and 1957, the number of firemen in Yonkers, Elizabeth, Newark, and New York City increased 19, 20, 18, and 65 per cent respectively. The number of policemen rose 32, 27, 17, and 46 per cent. In short, if, as experts in municipal finance have long contended, the citizen gets what he pays for—if service standards are principally a function of money—quality has improved for almost every service in every part of the Region. On a per person, constant dollar basis, more money has been put to public purposes at a faster rate than in any other ten-year period in the Region's history.[27]

If the Region's over-all performance shows up favorably, what about the record for the services which loom most important in the public eye? As far as the largest public program—education—is concerned, absolutely and proportionately more money has gone into this activity than any other. Between 1955–56 and 1959–60 the average school operating expenditure per pupil in New York State has risen from $378 to $491; and during the 1959–60 school year the foundation "minimum" program amount of $356 was exceeded in 95 per cent of major school districts. Indeed, if one were disposed to accept the referenda on school bond issues as a true expression of the public will, the decision would be inescapable in New York that school progress has been too rapid. For the 1958–59 school year, 38 per cent of all bond issues put to a vote failed to carry.[28]

If the quality of municipal services seems at least to be holding steady, and schools improving rapidly, prospects are just as good for improvements in another sensitive area, transportation. At any rate, facilities for the movement of automobile and air traffic are being constructed at a rate and on standards of service which have never been undertaken before. No one could accuse the Port of New York Authority, for example, of lack of imagination and enterprise in its planning and building of the new Idlewild Airport. The designs of the new bridges and expressways similarly display continuing pursuit of engineering excellence. The gross annual operating expenditures of the Port Authority between 1945 and 1955 increased 170 per cent—compared to an increase by the City of New York of about 80 per cent, and an average increase of 120 per cent in nonschool operating expenditures outside New York City. Only the suburban school districts have registered a greater percentage rise on the average, topping the 200 per cent mark in their expenditure increases during the same period.[29]

Of course, as we have pointed out in earlier chapters, both the school districts and the transportation authorities operate in very special circumstances. The districts have developed sophisticated and financially remunerative relations with state authorities, resulting in large and growing grants-in-aid programs. The transportation agencies are supported by user charges which feed on larger and larger volumes of traffic or substantial federal grants. In both instances, public officials responsible for the programs are able to a considerable degree to define "needs" according to their own standards and then proceed to satisfy them. Given these capabilities, it is not surprising that these programs function on a self-starter basis and their records of improving standards of service are the best in the Region.

As in the case of the revenue question, then, the problem of public expenditures in the Region turns out at rock bottom to be one of political attitudes and behavior. Just as any allocation of resources between the public and the private sectors from 1 to 100 per cent is theoretically possible, so, given public desires which are intense enough, almost any "need" can be fulfilled. In Lyle Fitch's words, "Fiscal stress in the modern American community is often more psychological than economic." [30] All that our expenditure calculations can yield is the knowledge that, in ways more or less related to the type of government involved, public spending has been increasing, and that one is justified again, with some qualifications, in inferring that quality has been upgraded in public programs. Whether the quality is good "enough" and the responsiveness rapid "enough" are issues which no expenditure series or professional criteria of excellence can answer.

POLITICAL PAYOFFS IN THE GOING SYSTEMS

We have been seeking evidence that a substantial change in the nature of public ideology and organization impends in the New York Region—one which will alter the trends which economic analysis has identified. The burden of the foregoing two sections has been that the indices customarily employed to gauge the effectiveness of the present system are not really relevant to the issue. The Region's governments theoretically can never go bankrupt, and they can never achieve the utopian standards that program specialists advocate.

But even if we took the indices seriously, the recent history of the Region would give us little cause for alarm. No "cruel burden" present or impending seems to rest upon the taxpayer, even if the most pessimistic estimates of new levies are accepted. No abnormally low service standards prevail, at least when considered in historical perspective. What has occurred—when one considers criticism of school conditions in New York City or renewal programs in New Jersey—is a sizable redefinition of what we consider "adequate" today, at least in experts' eyes. What obviously exists is a body of opinion which wants more funds allocated to the public sector and more positive public policies toward the use of natural resources in the Region, the planning of the transportation network, and the rebuilding of the Region's centrally located cities. The question is whether or not that body of opinion will be politically effective enough in the next twenty-five years to accomplish its objectives.

We should be as specific as possible here about what the revolution would constitute now that it seems clear it will not come with Hegelian naturalness. It would involve, first off, a much more rapid diversion of resources to the public sector: at a rate which, say, diverted at least one-half of all productivity gains to government rather than private spending. More important, however, it would involve the establishment of a governmental structure which possessed the jurisdiction and the authority to make decisions about alternative forms of Regional development, more or less consciously and more or less comprehensively. More specifically, there would be some type of Regional organization empowered to set aside land for recreational purposes on the basis of a Regional plan and not on the sporadic acquisitions of states, localities, and independent authorities or bequests by private citizens. There would be some type of Regional organization empowered to subsidize commuter transportation, if this were in accord with a general plan. And, to be fully satisfactory to the body of opinion which Jesse Burkhead has termed the "view with alarm" school of metropolitan affairs, the organization should probably be responsible to a Regional electorate and draw revenue from a common revenue pool.

To sketch the skeleton of a government sufficient to redirect the pattern of economic development in the Region—even in the minimum terms above—is to indicate at once the rocky road to reform. For, if the dissidents are to be effective, they must attract a sizable number of politically influential supporters; they must gain the acquiescence of the majority of the Region's residents; and, finally, they must overcome formidable legal, constitutional, and political obstacles, to make the groundswell of opinion legally applicable. These are difficult tasks. Slow evolution over the next twenty-five years, not decisive action to alter the main lines of development, seems the course of least resistance.

Perhaps the most formidable obstacle to changing either the structure or the philosophy of the Region's governments would be the assembling of a coalition of effective political figures. On the basis of the strategies and policies treated earlier in the book, it is hard even to conceive how such a coalition might come about. At the outset, three governors, the mayor of New York City, and the chief office-holders of the 17 counties surrounding the City would have to be persuaded that their present performance in their offices was unsatisfactory; that their failure was due to severe structural deficiencies in the present organization; and that only the creation of new arrangements would solve the problems they face.

That these officials know they have problems is already clear. Since 1956, the Metropolitan Regional Council has included in its 30-man body the top elected officials of all the counties and major cities of the Region as well as a number of smaller municipalities.[31] As an informed, consultative association, the Council has been able both to develop common policies with respect to some matters of law enforcement and traffic control and to initiate major investigations into Regional problems. It has been hailed therefore as having a "great potential for becoming an official regional leadership institution." [32]

The potential exists—but so far the evolution of the Council into an agency with the capacity to set goals, analyze resources, and recommend development policies has been slow. It remains a confederation, requiring unanimous consent from all its members before taking any important step. For two years, one of its committees held hearings to determine if it should acquire legal status. But the upshot of this self-analysis remains inconclusive, for while the Council has ultimately decided that its role should be legitimized, a strong minority is reported as reluctant to see the organization gain official recognition. Some outside groups have suggested that the Council take on operating responsibilities. Among these groups were the Citizens' Union, the Metropolitan Committee on Planning, and the Association of Real Estate Syndicators. But the more noteworthy of the Council's supporters—the Regional Plan Association of New York, the Citizens Budget Committee, and the State Citizen Council—have carefully refrained from suggesting that it acquire independent financial resources or assume major operating responsibilities.

Meantime, there are few signs that the usual pattern of political behavior is undergoing a metamorphosis. Officials continue to cling to their favorite slogan "cooperation" as the panacea for the very real conflicts of interests which exist. The conflicts themselves, however, show few signs of diminishing. A new state study committee has been created to criticize the City's administration and to cast doubt about the capacity of the largest governmental organization in the Region to conduct its own affairs. Recent mayors of the City and the recent comptrollers of the state have continued in the tradition of their predecessors to dispute openly the program needs of the City government. The City and the Port Authority continue to announce and activate separate programs for port development. The New Jersey municipalities and the Port Authority continue to disagree on their respective responsibilities with respect to a metropolitan district plan for pooling transit revenues. As between the states themselves, problems over the taxation of New Jersey residents by New York, of air pollution control, and the strain of persistent crises in mass transportation have led to predictions of "an era of hostile rivalry such as has not existed since Colonial days." Said Walter Jones, New Jersey state senator and Republican party leader in

Bergen County, "The very purposes of the bistate compact establishing the Port of New York Authority are in grave danger. A desire
for vengeance is in the air." [33] Given these performances, one is dis-
inclined to believe that major surrenders of existing prerogatives are
close at hand.

In the less formal circles of political activity, much the same characteristics of divisiveness are on display. The business community, in
various garbs, has been represented as concerned with economic
development across the Region. So far, however, this concern has
evidenced itself principally with respect to maintaining or increasing land values in Manhattan and Newark and to urging the limited development of the Metropolitan Regional Council. The renewal projects which the private interests have sparked directly are
located in areas where the forces of regeneration already exist (as
with the Downtown-Lower Manhattan Association) or where matters of special institutional concern are apparent (Morningside adjacent to Columbia University or the Bloomingdale Neighborhood
Conservation Project). So far as other Regional problems are concerned, the failure of private concerns to provide financial support
for the Metropolitan Rapid Transit Commission emphasized the
difficulties which even vitally concerned interests have in mobilizing
themselves to attack this issue. As for general developmental plans,
even private associations dedicated to progress in government and
planning find it difficult to agree. Thus, the Regional Plan Association and the City Club of New York criticize each other's analyses
and reports, almost before they are published.

Other elements of diversity and insularity also underscore the difficulty of coordinate action among the political activists. Within the
City, the predominant majority party has more than its usual number
of factions—its leadership undergoing serious attack from members
claiming that racial favoritism intrudes on party councils and from
those concerned with issues of party integrity and policy. The governors of the three states meet cautiously but inconclusively on transportation and other matters; to date they prefer to work separately
on the resolution of the problems. And suburban party figures show

little enthusiasm for closer collaboration with their neighbors if new election districts are involved. Indeed, in many matters, suburban governments go their separate ways, impervious to entreaties of party or state loyalties.

So, in November 1959, Democratic Hudson County, fearing local revenue losses, opposed Democratic Governor Meyner in his proposal to divert turnpike funds to mass transit purposes.[34] So, in January 1960, the Republican New York legislators were reported "cool" to a Republican governor's proposal to give school districts local taxing power, the first reason being their feeling that "school board members in many areas do not exhibit enough independence as taxpayers representatives, tending rather to be 'yes men' for school superintendents." [35] Except for study committees, a thesis that the existing leadership in the Region stands poised for reform and reorganization, restrained only by lack of public understanding, hardly seems plausible. It is easy to see how incumbents might suffer in a major reshuffle; it is hard to see who would get ahead.

If the Region's leadership shows little inclination to take giant strides, it is not likely to be pushed by the Region's electorate. No massive mumblings demanding reform seem at hand. As far as one can detect, there are no insurgent elements in either party demanding "metropolitan government"; no civic associations in Long Island, Rockland, or Monmouth seeking union now with New York City. To be sure, a formal proposal for a change in governmental structure was made in 1959, coming on the heels of Governor Rockefeller's tax proposals, but it was scarcely a move toward unity. On the contrary, at that time the cry went out—and rapidly waned—for New York City to secede from the state and establish itself as a separate commonwealth.[36] Elsewhere attitudes toward metropolitan reform appear to have paralleled those expressed in Bergen County in 1958 when a survey asking what should be done about metropolitan problems of transportation, planning, and resource development disclosed that most voters felt they were "somebody else's headache." [37] Apathy, not anxiety, seems to be the prevalent popular mood. Political change when public problems become pressing seems quite possible. But the anticipation of problems by the localities and the development of policies and structures to meet them is another matter.

It is possible, of course, that the stimulus for reform may come from political institutions at higher echelons in the American federal system. Over a period of years, the state governments may take to heart the injunction of one study commission after another that their programs and policies are inextricably intertwined with those of the local governments in the Region. They may also accept the commissions' recommendations that the activities of the Regional enterprises authorized by state law need to be more effectively coordinated and rationalized. Alternatively the federal government might be persuaded to apply its not inconsiderable influence in the shaping of the pattern of development within the Region. If Washington adopted standards in its home loan and guaranty programs which considered the impact of new housing developments on the suburban community concerned, as well as the effect upon the homeowner and the lender, the character of residential settlement might be quite different. If the Congress were to provide federal aid for mass transportation as well as for highways, the location of both homes and factories would be further affected. If renewal and development programs, and assistance in the fields of water resources and open space, were conducted according to metropolitan rather than municipal plans, the federal influence could be felt in still a more comprehensive way. In each instance, these developments might take place without so direct and obvious a challenge to the going political systems that exist within the Region itself.

The prospects seem even more substantial that informal nongovernmental concern with the course of Regional economic development will sharply increase. There are strong traditions in the Region for private concern with metropolitan planning; for educational and philanthropic activities designed to offer alternative courses of action which are professionally prepared; and for the sounding of alarms at what appear to be untoward governmental proposals. These traditions may now trigger off a rapid evolution of quasi-public, quasi-private programs which reflect many interests but which require no formal grants of authority. These programs could move to strengthen the prospects of coordinated guidance of urban growth.

As for the probability of actions within the formal systems themselves, however, the odds seem smaller. Certainly the evidence we have just cited concerning the disinclination of the professional political leaders to move rapidly and the unconcern of the electorate should come as no surprise. For the expectations of the reformers do violence to what we know about the objectives and mode of operation of the Region's political systems. In actuality, what the reformers suggest should take place is the establishment of institutions which will "ensure the Region's optimum development" and "maximize the usefulness of the Region's human and material resources." The goal they see as both desirable and possible for the Region's government is a major and continuing concern with the shape of the Region's development.

Yet the plain fact is, of course, that few inhabitants of the Region, or of the nation for that matter, have ever looked to their local governments to "optimize" or "maximize" anything. On the contrary, people have regarded these units as necessary but not especially admirable service units to provide programs which did not seem supportable through private enterprise. It has never been in the Region's tradition to charge local government with the responsiblity for physical and economic development. The price mechanism and the marketplace are our chosen instruments for those purposes.

We seem, now, somehow concerned at the end-products issuing from the instruments on which we have relied. And, somewhat wistfully and somewhat vaguely, we think that possibly a system of human relationships neither designed nor oriented toward that purpose can be restructured to do better. We wish this restructured system, possibly, to reconsider the transportation or land-use or water-use or recreational activities that the marketplace has encouraged. We wish it to come to grips with problems in blight, obsolescence, and poverty which the marketplace has not solved. And we would prefer it to do so quickly.

Yet, to these new purposes, we endow the system with no special urgency. On the contrary, we devise ways and means—through grants-in-aid, minimal boundary changes, new sources of revenue, and new contractual relationships—for the old set of institutions and working arrangements to survive, to improve their services, and to adjust bit by bit to changing circumstances. We make sure that in extreme crises some palliative action is taken. Wherever we can, we pattern the agency organization after the very mechanism we have found defective—and then express concern when these agencies act like their ancestors. If, in any given part of the Region, public service levels fall too low, or conditions of blight and obsolescence become too severe for our taste, many of us simply move out farther into the suburbs. This is in the great American pioneering tradition of abandoning settlements we have despoiled.

It is possible, of course, that even under these circumstances of ambivalence, drastic changes will occur. Leadership may forswear present power and prerogative; the public may adopt a new consciousness toward their neighbors and embrace an ideology of metropolitan citizenship. Both may seek not the tolerable environment, but the best conditions of Regional growth—a New Yorker's interpretation of the *arete* of the Greek city-state.

In a discipline as uncertain and rudimentary in its techniques of prediction as political science, we do not dismiss these possibilities out of hand. We simply record that we know of no other time when a revolution took place when the existing system was solidly established and its citizens, as they understood the goals of their domestic society, content.

APPENDICES

NOTES

INDEX

Appendix A
Governmental Financial Statistics:
Definitions and Compilations

The assembly and analysis of financial statistics covering local government activity in the New York Metropolitan Region posed special problems of comparability among the units of government in the three states involved and over time; also problems of completeness of coverage and of reliability of reporting. Some of the issues were resolved by making special arrangements of the data; some could never be adequately handled. Two days of interviewing state officials and reviewing the records in Connecticut, for example, led to the conclusion that detailed comparison of Connecticut's government expenditures and revenues with those of New York and New Jersey was not possible. A study of the published and unpublished data of the Governments Division, United States Bureau of the Census, made it plain that it was not feasible to reconstruct these series on a Regional basis for years earlier than 1952. A final complication was that the different ways in which public functions and programs were assigned to local government units in New York and New Jersey often made direct comparisons of unit activities inappropriate.

In these circumstances a number of separate sources of data were used and different series were constructed to utilize the existing reports for specific purposes. First, where the objective was simply to indicate current magnitudes in local government spending and taxing for the Region as a whole, or for all local governments within a county, figures from the U.S. *1957 Census of Governments* were used. It was from the Census that the expenditure map in Chapter 2 (Chart 6) was drawn. These statistics have the virtue of a common classification system for all parts of the Region, and uniformity in coverage and reporting. However, they were not useful over time so far as the Region is concerned. In Chart 1, for example, we spliced the 1957 Census figures into comparable series drawn from state reports. Further, the Census figures could not be used to compare local finance at levels below the county.

When it was necessary to construct Regional time series, state financial reports were used—for New York, the Special Report on Municipal Affairs of the State Comptroller; for New Jersey, the report of the Division of Local Government, Department of the Treasury. This was the case in the first fifteen years reported in Chart 1. These sources were also used in Chapter 3 in the text where county-to-county comparisons were made. Occasionally these series were supplemented by the annual reports of the departments of education in the two states and of the New York City Comptroller. None of the reports, state or national, provided comparable series for the years before 1945. Accordingly, most of our series do not go back before that year.

In addition to the series which reported gross financial magnitudes and financial activity over time, a third major need was to study local government operations below the county level. So long as county aggregates alone were used, relations between population characteristics and financial patterns "washed out" in the combining of the records of the many local units. Yet once we dropped below the county, the legal responsibilities of the local governments in New York and New Jersey differed so sharply that direct comparisons were impossible.

To solve this problem, an artificial reporting unit for New York was constructed, based on the town. The town is an actual local unit of government in New York, although presently it is assigned relatively few functions. We used it to assemble all financial data on a less-than-county basis. For any given town, total local expenditures or revenues were defined as the sum of those of the town itself and of the villages, fire districts, school and special improvement districts in the town—plus the town's share of county expenditures or revenues, allocated on the basis of the ratio which the town's assessed valuation bore to that of the county's. (Ratios were also calculated on a population basis and found to be similar in their allocation effects.) The revenues and expenditures of cities which in New York are responsible for town, village, special district, and often some county functions—were reported in a separate series.

In New Jersey, the five authorized types of municipalities are all comparable in the range of public services they offer. Therefore, the municipality was made the basic reporting unit, whether or not its legal title was town, borough, village, township, or city. To municipal revenues and expenditures, we added school revenues and expenditures; special-district taxes (which also served as an estimate of special-district expenditures); and total expenditures and required payments of municipally operated utilities (minus the sum classified as the surplus to municipal operations). County figures were allocated in the same way as in New York: in the proportion that the municipalities' assessed valuation bore to total county assessed valuation.

So constructed, the New York town and the New Jersey municipality represented a similar range of public services and similar types of expenditures and revenues. Their experiences could be compared, with the expectation that the same "packages" of public activities were involved.

Since the New York classification system was the "simplest" (reporting expenditures according to current operations, capital outlay, debt service and transfers, and revenue according to real estate taxes, state and federal aid, and other revenue), perforce it became our basis of classification. New Jersey reported in much greater detail, but we combined the items to compare with New York experience. Definitions and explanations of the classifications are provided in each state's reports and are comparable.

On the basis of this joint classification system, eight series of data were assembled, four of expenditures and four of revenues.

1. *Total Expenditures:* a series consisting of all monies spent within the town or municipality regardless of the local spending unit. In instances where the chart or table in the text specifically

states, these monies include capital outlay (for purposes of indicating gross magnitudes). Otherwise—principally in the text of Chapter 3—capital outlay is *always* excluded, so that these large expenditures which occur sporadically over time would not have a distorting effect.

2. *Total Municipal* * *Expenditures:* a series covering all expenditures of the "general-purpose" local governments (that is, excluding school and other special districts and county expenditures). Again, capital outlay items are included only when the chart or table specifically says so. Otherwise they are excluded.

3. *Municipal Operating Expenditures:* a series restricted to general-purpose governments again, and designed to cover the day-to-day costs of government—salaries, wages, exhaustible supplies and equipment. Capital outlay and debt service charges are *always* excluded.

4. *Total Municipal Debt Service:* a series reflecting interest and principal payments on long-term debt for municipalities, including debts of public utilities but excluding short-term borrowings. This series is the best available indicator for the general level of capital construction costs which local units are carrying over a considerable period of time. It serves to correct the impression of exaggerated magnitudes which the irregular capital outlay charges convey.

5. *Total Property Taxes:* a series covering all property taxes for all units, including counties, expressed on a town and municipality basis.

6. *Total Local Property Taxes:* a series covering all property taxes for the general-purpose governments, excluding county and school and other special taxes.

7. *Other Municipal Revenue:* a series again limited to general-purpose units and consisting of fees, licenses, and other miscellaneous revenues.

---

* In this book we occasionally use the term "nonschool" as a substitute for "municipal" (whether in connection with *Total Municipal Expenditures* or *Municipal Operating Expenditures*) in order to emphasize the distinction between municipal and school spending. For example, Chart 4 and Table B-4.

8. *State and Federal Aid to Municipalities:* a series consisting of grants-in-aid and other assistance payments made to general-purpose units only.

Special tabulations of the revenues and expenditures for the school districts were compiled separately for use in the factor analysis (see Appendix B) and to compare their rate of growth to those of general-purpose municipalities. Sources here were the annual reports of the states' departments of education. New York City figures were almost always taken from the Reports of the City Comptroller or Dun and Bradstreet, though the lack of comparable data prevented us from including New York City in our eight major series.

These series made it possible to compare levels of expenditures and revenues between the two states with the assurance that essentially the same programs and activities were involved. Expressed in "per capita" and "per cent change" terms, they enabled us to explore the widely different experience within single counties and to establish much more sensitive associations with population and economic data. Within New York State, they made possible the subregional comparisons analyzed in Chapter 3.

Figures of assessed property valuations and estimated market values for New York and New Jersey are taken from the state reports of the New York Comptroller and New Jersey Department of the Treasury of recent years. The New Jersey Tax Policy Commission reports were an additional and valuable source, as were the records of the New York State Equalization Board.

Where estimates of market value are used for New York prior to 1953 (when the first reliable samplings became available) the procedure was to maintain the same ratio between market and assessed value as existed in later years (thereby probably understating the market valuation). These estimates were also checked against a weighted index of economic characteristics (income, value added by manufacture, and so on) which has been used to simulate market property value in the calculations of state aid in school "minimum foundation" programs. The specific formula used is that employed by the State of Florida, which we judge to be the most accurate for our purposes. The details of calculation in this formula were made available by the Florida State Superintendent of Public Instruction.

We report in Tables A-1 through A-8 the absolute totals of our eight series, arranged by counties, for the New Jersey and New York portions of the New York Metropolitan Region, to indicate the base for the more elaborate calculations included in the charts and tables of the text. Figures for the individual towns and municipalities, also totals for the Inner and Outer zones of the Region, as well as statistics expressed on per capita and per cent change bases, may be consulted in unpublished form. They are deposited at the Regional Plan Association, Inc., New York City.

Tables A-1 through A-8 give figures for sixteen of the Region's twenty-two counties, since Fairfield County, Connecticut, and the five counties making up New York City are not included.

Table A-1 Total Expenditures, by Counties

	1945	1950	1955
NEW JERSEY			
Bergen	$ 31,112,924	$ 54,168,126	$ 84,977,049
Essex	78,944,015	123,705,270	161,392,638
Hudson	72,794,047	100,985,858	118,342,435
Middlesex	17,822,713	28,130,755	47,544,923
Monmouth	15,313,362	23,923,141	35,934,662
Morris	9,473,277	17,372,231	29,131,472
Passaic	23,103,309	36,069,704	45,603,302
Somerset	4,655,772	8,345,598	13,428,282
Union	26,777,833	48,347,568	65,467,690
Total, nine New Jersey counties ...	279,997,252	441,048,251	601,822,453
NEW YORK			
Dutchess	8,224,766	14,066,622	21,821,815
Nassau	50,427,656	117,304,216	253,511,753
Orange	9,438,197	16,323,326	24,088,504
Putnam	1,944,688	3,703,428	6,105,445
Rockland	4,439,122	9,616,970	12,938,726
Suffolk	17,898,447	35,641,398	70,853,617
Westchester	75,640,499	113,530,789	159,106,089
Total, seven New York counties ...	168,013,375	310,186,749	548,425,949
TOTAL, sixteen counties	448,010,627	751,235,000	1,150,248,402

Table A-2 Total Municipal Expenditures, by Counties

	1945	1950	1955
NEW JERSEY			
Bergen	$ 13,286,035	$ 19,411,052	$ 29,571,430
Essex	41,023,365	54,088,464	65,136,557
Hudson	35,865,090	46,620,142	53,738,306
Middlesex	7,178,303	10,384,313	16,656,086
Monmouth	6,523,406	8,635,312	11,882,164
Morris	3,034,824	4,695,530	7,082,161
Passaic	10,288,639	13,588,931	17,196,281
Somerset	1,583,738	2,426,904	3,640,382
Union	12,229,532	17,342,605	24,788,680
Total, nine New			
Jersey counties	131,012,932	177,193,253	229,692,047
NEW YORK			
Dutchess	3,615,529	5,550,566	6,847,423
Nassau	12,477,573	21,728,204	40,380,987
Orange	3,912,043	6,128,293	8,217,292
Putnam	490,944	882,199	1,376,261
Rockland	1,555,427	2,544,529	4,100,498
Suffolk	5,423,229	9,240,023	18,007,901
Westchester	34,083,522	41,528,435	54,465,464
Total, seven New			
York counties	61,558,267	87,602,249	133,395,826
TOTAL, sixteen			
counties	192,571,199	264,795,502	363,087,873

Table A-3 Municipal Operating Expenditures, by Counties

	1945	1950	1955
NEW JERSEY			
Bergen	$ 9,501,848	$ 15,664,748	$ 25,371,397
Essex	29,653,741	44,805,522	56,391,963
Hudson	25,845,987	37,766,375	45,200,947
Middlesex	5,009,393	8,243,491	13,541,012
Monmouth	4,759,572	6,997,485	10,265,999
Morris	2,555,155	4,184,616	6,546,626
Passaic	7,095,310	10,643,705	14,488,486
Somerset	1,356,599	2,213,643	3,463,050
Union	8,736,013	14,005,980	21,075,391
Total, nine New Jersey counties	94,513,618	144,525,565	196,344,871
NEW YORK			
Dutchess	2,979,294	4,977,790	6,256,824
Nassau	9,334,156	16,331,745	30,256,246
Orange	3,305,456	5,431,628	7,083,503
Putnam	455,358	748,773	1,259,393
Rockland	1,359,198	2,202,909	3,478,839
Suffolk	4,742,926	8,284,906	16,146,159
Westchester	20,390,660	28,864,997	41,980,124
Total, seven New York counties	42,567,048	66,842,748	106,461,088
TOTAL, sixteen counties	137,080,666	211,368,313	302,805,959

Table A-4 Total Municipal Debt Service, by Counties

	1945	1950	1955
NEW JERSEY			
Bergen	$ 3,951,163	$ 3,941,618	$ 4,515,809
Essex	13,010,830	11,485,203	10,412,126
Hudson	11,515,554	10,325,820	10,398,147
Middlesex	2,413,268	2,366,480	3,461,543
Monmouth	1,930,370	1,836,049	1,823,729
Morris	710,657	732,235	829,098
Passaic	3,242,631	3,026,096	2,857,950
Somerset	246,684	234,536	231,951
Union	3,847,499	3,671,551	4,021,570
Total, nine New Jersey counties	40,868,656	37,619,588	38,551,923
NEW YORK			
Dutchess	636,235	572,776	590,599
Nassau	3,143,417	5,396,459	10,124,741
Orange	606,587	696,665	1,133,789
Putnam	35,586	133,426	116,868
Rockland	196,229	341,620	621,659
Suffolk	680,303	955,117	1,861,742
Westchester	13,692,862	12,663,438	12,485,340
Total, seven New York counties	18,991,219	20,759,501	26,934,738
TOTAL, sixteen counties	59,859,875	58,379,089	65,486,661

Table A-5 Total Property Taxes, by Counties

	1945	1950	1955
NEW JERSEY			
Bergen	$ 24,381,641	$ 35,305,583	$ 60,207,572
Essex	64,861,553	88,012,257	119,098,783
Hudson	49,216,115	71,726,112	86,226,049
Middlesex	11,577,574	17,189,577	29,797,794
Monmouth	9,804,676	13,991,787	22,548,979
Morris	5,740,427	9,731,647	18,661,499
Passaic	16,971,398	23,314,258	32,376,756
Somerset	2,927,237	5,089,832	8,954,622
Union	21,365,322	31,288,838	49,258,695
Total, nine New			
Jersey counties	206,845,943	295,649,891	427,130,749
NEW YORK			
Dutchess	4,896,157	6,435,105	10,387,308
Nassau	35,229,774	52,949,776	132,821,464
Orange	5,089,864	7,367,468	11,537,465
Putnam	1,227,332	2,323,949	3,603,553
Rockland	3,352,226	5,349,027	9,142,477
Suffolk	11,349,686	20,624,695	45,312,820
Westchester	50,729,357	66,293,340	92,652,248
Total, seven New			
York counties	111,874,396	161,343,360	305,457,335
TOTAL, sixteen			
counties	318,720,339	456,993,251	732,588,084

Table A-6 Total Local Property Taxes, by Counties

	1945	1950	1955
NEW JERSEY			
Bergen .... $	9,287,568	$ 14,387,158	$ 20,917,951
Essex	30,217,717	46,090,253	54,678,142
Hudson	16,262,603	36,982,029	41,790,812
Middlesex	3,509,191	5,730,772	8,262,556
Monmouth	3,706,993	5,365,325	7,851,798
Morris	1,555,277	3,124,435	4,812,378
Passaic	6,199,627	10,605,993	12,154,822
Somerset	885,048	1,573,248	2,247,156
Union	7,932,540	13,865,178	18,478,314
Total, nine New Jersey counties	79,556,564	137,724,391	171,188,929
NEW YORK			
Dutchess	2,021,485	2,595,999	3,426,682
Nassau	6,790,170	11,737,023	18,609,332
Orange	2,269,798	3,106,428	4,064,984
Putnam	358,182	698,632	1,006,455
Rockland	1,020,644	1,488,747	2,440,726
Suffolk	3,768,646	6,508,908	12,080,654
Westchester	22,975,320	26,265,776	33,570,673
Total, seven New York counties	39,204,245	52,401,513	75,199,506
TOTAL, sixteen counties	118,760,809	190,125,904	246,388,435

Table A-7 Other Municipal Revenue, by Counties

	1945	1950	1955
NEW JERSEY			
Bergen	$ 3,748,797	$ 6,351,528	$ 10,424,130
Essex	8,866,769	15,916,432	18,509,528
Hudson	15,621,994	10,547,298	15,673,209
Middlesex	2,809,559	4,874,647	8,229,732
Monmouth	2,421,052	3,577,486	5,505,164
Morris	1,293,541	1,870,261	3,222,382
Passaic	2,765,348	3,839,118	5,648,478
Somerset	600,950	917,453	1,566,717
Union	2,955,896	4,667,988	6,719,485
Total, nine New Jersey counties	41,083,906	52,562,211	75,498,825
NEW YORK			
Dutchess	721,491	1,686,835	2,060,044
Nassau	5,166,938	6,003,400	11,759,564
Orange	628,980	1,381,845	1,643,204
Putnam	165,301	80,914	112,228
Rockland	516,150	375,070	779,711
Suffolk	1,581,595	1,083,117	2,371,528
Westchester	5,659,278	7,932,254	11,202,877
Total, seven New York counties	14,439,733	18,543,435	29,929,156
TOTAL, sixteen counties	55,523,639	71,105,646	105,427,981

Table A-8   State and Federal Aid to Municipalities, by Counties

	1945	1950	1955
NEW JERSEY			
Bergen	n.a.	$ 385,259	$ 457,945
Essex	n.a.	625,561	510,916
Hudson	n.a.	475,621	432,256
Middlesex	n.a.	315,423	380,456
Monmouth	n.a.	269,690	320,190
Morris	n.a.	252,209	274,506
Passaic	n.a.	322,165	320,969
Somerset	n.a.	187,730	248,011
Union	n.a.	344,309	364,529
Total, nine New Jersey			
counties	n.a.	3,177,967	3,309,778
NEW YORK			
Dutchess	$ 334,632	1,260,250	1,510,798
Nassau	69,438	4,731,728	6,047,760
Orange	333,151	1,376,826	1,799,150
Putnam	43,385	110,434	156,149
Rockland	52,985	486,756	659,331
Suffolk	213,818	1,586,689	2,687,546
Westchester	784,968	4,719,711	5,506,241
Total, seven New York			
counties	1,832,377	14,272,394	18,366,975
TOTAL, sixteen counties ...	n.a.	17,450,361	21,676,753

n.a. = not available.

Appendix B

The Application of Factor Analysis to Municipal Finance

I. THE CHOICE OF MODELS

In Chapter 2 we reported the results of an ambitious attempt to relate variations in the level and pattern of local government expenditures to the differences in community environments. Beginning on page 32, we described our sample of 64 middle-sized New Jersey municipalities, and in Chart 2 we listed all 64 and showed their locations on a map. Beginning on page 34, we explained in nontechnical language that our method was factor analysis, and that it involved boiling down twenty community characteristics into seven meaningful factors which we labeled COMMUNITY SIZE, INDUSTRIALIZATION, HOUSING DENSITY, AGE, LOW-INCOME PREVALENCE, RESIDENTIAL AFFLUENCE, and LAND RESERVE. In Chart 3 we showed the relation of these indices to total operating expenditures; in Chart 4 to twelve particular *types* of expenditures; and in Chart 12 to "tax effort." The purpose of this appendix is to give the technical reader a further discussion of our procedure.

Our intention did not go so far as the building of a formal model of the interaction of local finance with its environment, and lack of data prevented our giving attention to causal links over time. The analysis throughout is static, cross-sectional, and essentially exploratory.

The purpose was to explore two questions. First, in what strategic and relevant respects do communities of a portion of a metropolitan area differ from one another? And second, to what extent, and how, are expenditures for the several municipal functions related to community differences so conceptualized? By "strategic and relevant" community differences we mean specifically those differences in the socio-economic environment that are thought to imply different patterns of demand for public services and different capacities to afford them.

A statistical model commonly used to state in a formal fashion the two questions just posed has been that of multiple regression. This method warrants some use in situations where only a handful of explanatory variables can be marshaled for analysis. We ourselves resorted to it in a brief test of smaller New Jersey communities (see page 41). One is on safe ground with multiple regression if he can hypothesize that the expenditure differences among communities result directly from the variation in the *observable* characteristics of the environment, in the sense that the total mileage of streets in a city may be expected to have a direct bearing upon the level of municipal outlays for their upkeep. But, in many studies employing the multiple regression model, explanatory hypotheses involve factors which are not necessarily directly observable. For example, the level of maintenance costs is likely to reflect also the residents' expectations of a certain quality of service, and this, we suspect, may be a function of something we conceptualize as their "affluence." Also, "density" is another useful abstraction difficult to cope with in a simple model. In the regression equation these latent but conceptually highly relevant dimensions of variance are represented by what the investigator arbitrarily assumes are their best indirect measures. The regression he is now really concerned with is not upon the total variance of a predictor variable but merely upon that part which correlates perfectly with a hypothetical dimension. The problem of weighting thus becomes crucial. A systematic examination of the hazards of arbitrary schemes of weighting leads to the conclusion that we cannot move from the manifest variables which we observe to the hypothetical "strategic and relevant" factors which we need, unless we follow some procedure that takes into account the structure of relations among the manifest variables (observable community characteristics).

Our requirements would seem to be best met by the technique of factor analysis, a type of multivariate analysis which has had a long history of development and application in psychology and related disciplines of social science.*

II. THE SAMPLE OF VARIABLES

1 SOCIO-ECONOMIC VARIABLES

Two considerations were controlling in the selection of variables for the factor analysis of socio-economic characteristics of communities.

First, in order to get results that are not overly sensitive to the inclusion or exclusion of one or more variables—that is, to obtain weights for any given variable which tend to stay invariant whether or not other variables are added or deleted—factor analysis requires that each dimension considered of significance to the analysis be adequately determined in terms of the observed variation. This means that each such dimension should account for at least as much variance as any directly observed variable and preferably for more, and that, in turn, the communalities of all variables be generally as high as possible. In contrast to the simple analysis of regression, factor analysis calls for the most extensive possible sampling of the measures indicative of the underlying dimensions of covariation.

The second consideration is that, while factor analysis frowns upon an a priori definition and weighting of the hypothetical dimensions of variance, it is nonetheless true that no more comes out of a factor analysis than has been put into it. It is essential that the choice of variables be guided by theoretical criteria of relevance, and that the domain of variation of interest be carefully rationalized.

Twenty measures were chosen for factor analysis in an attempt to provide a somewhat more extensive description of fiscal capacities

---

* There exists a vast literature on the methodology and technique of factor analysis. The reader interested in a relatively nontechnical presentation of the subject is encouraged to consult R. B. Cattell, *Factor Analysis* (New York, 1952), especially chapters 1 and 20. For a thorough, up-to-date treatment of factor analysis, see Harry H. Harman, *Modern Factor Analysis* (Chicago, 1960).

and service needs of municipal jurisdictions than has been so far attempted. The selection is clearly limited to variables that were available with sufficiently complete coverage for the sample of 64 municipalities, and generally focuses on the year 1955. Our twenty observable variables, designated as x_1 through x_{20}, are as follows:

x_1 *Population* (*estimated*), *1955,* linearly extrapolated from 1954 estimates in Regional Plan Association (RPA), *Bulletin 85.*

x_2 *Per cent population change, 1945–1955,* base-year estimate linearly interpolated from 1940 and 1950 U. S. Census data.

x_3 *Area in square miles, 1955.*

x_4 *Net density, 1954,* defined as the ratio of the number of dwelling units to built-up residential land in acres, based on data from RPA Land-Use Survey, 1954.

x_5 *Per cent saturation, 1954,* that is, the percentage of saturation of residential capacity, defined as the ratio of built-up residential land to the sum of built-up residential land and vacant land zoned residential, based on data from RPA Land-Use Survey, 1954.

x_6 *Per cent residential land in multifamily buildings, 1954,* based on data from RPA Land-Use Survey, 1954.

x_7 *Per cent land in industrial use, 1954,* based on data from RPA Land-Use Survey, 1954.

x_8 *Full valuation of residential property, 1955.* This is the estimated market value of residential property, based on property type distributions given in Ninth Report of the New Jersey Commission on State Tax Policy (1958); assessed valuation figures from 18th Annual Report of New Jersey Division of Local Government (for 1955); and 1955 equalization rates supplied by New Jersey Taxpayers Association. For each community, estimates of the tax yield in 1957 (the nearest year available) from each type of property when assessed at 100 per cent of market value were divided by the total gross taxes (that is, tax return prior to adjustment for the several exemptions), and the resulting ratios were applied to the total 1955 assessed valuation adjusted to market value. The 1957 full tax return by types of property was estimated by the staff of the New Jersey Commission on State Tax Policy.

x_9 *Full valuation of business property, 1955;* estimated market value of business property; same sources as for x_8.

x_{10} *Full valuation of vacant land, 1955;* estimated market value of vacant land; same sources as for x_8.

x_{11} *State aid to municipalities, 1955,* principally state aid for road repairs, street lighting, and capital roads construction ("formula funds"). Source: 18th Annual Report of New Jersey Division of Local Government (for 1955).

x_{12} *State aid to schools, 1954–55,* from Fourth Annual Report of New Jersey Department of Education.

x_{13} *Per cent "other" in total revenue, 1955.* This represents the proportion of total revenue due to cash receipts other than property taxes and state aid; same source as for x_{11}.

x_{14} *Average daily enrollment in day schools, 1954–55;* data reported by New Jersey Taxpayers Association.

x_{15} *Per cent population 65 years old and over, 1950,* from U. S. Census of Population.

x_{16} *Median school years completed, persons 25 years old and over, 1950,* from U. S. Census of Population.

x_{17} *Per cent population 14 years old and less, 1950,* from U. S. Census of Population.

x_{18} *Per cent residents employed in manufacturing, 1950,* from U. S. Census of Population.

x_{19} *Median income, families and unrelated individuals, 1949,* from U. S. Census of Population.

x_{20} *Per cent families and unrelated individuals having incomes less than $2000, 1949,* from U. S. Census of Population.

No observations were available on the last six variables—those taken from the U. S. Census—for fifteen jurisdictions in the sample of 64. (These places, historically designated as "townships" and therefore excluded from the detailed reporting for "urban places," are Cedar Grove, Cranford, Hillside, Livingston, Lyndhurst, Maplewood, Millburn, North Bergen, Saddle Brook, Scotch Plains, Springfield, Teaneck, Union, Wayne, and Weehawken.) It seemed impractical to drop these variables from analysis, especially since preliminary tests had indicated that in that case at least three key dimensions could not have been adequately determined in the full-dress analysis. Reducing the sample of municipalities to 49, on the other hand, would have wasted information available for the fifteen municipalities on the remaining variables. Varying the sample size in computing correlation coefficients was objectionable on technical grounds. In the procedure we actually employed, multiple regression techniques were used to obtain a preliminary set of Census variable estimates for each of the fifteen municipalities from its observed values on the remaining nineteen variables (excluding summary indices y_{13} and y_{14}; see Table B-2). In order to avoid upward bias from the use of error-free estimates in the computation of correlation coefficients for the full sample, these preliminary estimates, expressed in standard deviation units, were augmented by a random error component, consisting of a normal deviate times the normalized standard error of estimate for a given variable, and converted back into original units.*

The means and standard deviations for the twenty socio-economic variables are shown in Table B-1.

❼ FISCAL VARIABLES

Relatively complete documentation of the municipal expenditures by function was available for our 64 communities through the Annual Report of the New Jersey Division of Local Government. Excluded from consideration were (1) capital outlay, which is generally subject to significant year-to-year fluctuations, and (2) functions representing outlays for which only a small fraction of the municipalities were responsible (for example, hospitals). As a meaningful reflection of the past investment in the municipal and school

---

* A second transformation excluded the error component and was intended for use in estimating dimension scores for each individual community; preliminary estimates were merely brought to unit standard deviation by dividing each score by the corresponding multiple correlation coefficient of the estimate. These coefficients—indicating roughly the success of estimation were x_{15}, 0.78; x_{16}, 0.91; x_{17}, 0.85; x_{18}, 0.87; x_{19}, 0.88; and x_{20}, 0.89.

Table B-1 Means and Standard Deviations for Twenty
Socio-Economic Variables

		Mean	Standard deviation
x_1	Population	27,516	17,439
x_2	Per cent population change	38.87	45.23
x_3	Area in square miles	4.69	3.91
x_4	Net density (ratio)	8.68	8.01
x_5	Per cent saturation	72.29	19.04
x_6	Per cent multifamily buildings	16.61	28.04
x_7	Per cent land industrial	6.01	7.88
x_8	Residential valuation (thousands)	$66,497	$37,218
x_9	Business valuation (thousands)	$54,302	$52,815
x_{10}	Vacant land valuation (thousands)	$2,674	$2,234
x_{11}	State aid to municipalities	$16,955	$10,325
x_{12}	State aid to schools	$247,717	$148,753
x_{13}	Per cent "other" in revenue	30.58	11.31
x_{14}	Average daily enrollment	3,778	2,061
x_{15}	Per cent population 65 and over	7.85	2.06
x_{16}	Median school years completed	10.59	1.42
x_{17}	Per cent population 14 and under	23.55	3.08
x_{18}	Per cent residents in manufacturing	37.72	10.69
x_{19}	Median income	$3,983	$621
x_{20}	Per cent earning under $2,000	18.18	5.69

Note: The figures above are based on the sample of 64 middle-sized New
Jersey municipalities listed in Chart 2 (Chapter 2), except that the figures for
the last six, x_{15} through x_{20}, are based on the 49 municipalities for which
U. S. Census data have been published.

plant we have employed debt service, combining payments of interest and payments on the principal in one measure.

Levels of taxation were also calculated for the 64-community cross-
section. The "tax effort," as explained in Chart 12 (Chapter 2), was
defined as the ratio of local property taxes (county, school, and municipal) to the estimated market value of taxable property.

The functional expenditures selected for analysis are for 1955.
They are listed in Table B-2 with their mean values and standard
deviations for the 64-community cross-section as a whole.

Table B-2 Means and Standard Deviations for Fiscal Variables

(in dollars, except for y_{13})

		Means	Standard deviation
y_1	General government	189,214	141,398
y_2	Fire protection	218,466	222,415
y_3	Police	305,913	218,706
y_4	Streets	154,700	92,690
y_5	Sanitation	155,452	124,906
y_6	Health	34,188	31,379
y_7	Welfare	27,550	42,302
y_8	Recreation	57,038	56,356
y_9	Libraries and civic services	43,747	42,901
y_{10}	Nonschool debt service	190,561	187,471
y_{11}	Schools, except debt service	1,397,660	829,830
y_{12}	School debt service	154,395	105,523
y_{13}	"Tax effort" (per cent)	2.292	.945
y_{14}	Total local expenditures	3,047,090	2,026,840

Note: In Chapter 2, our seven hypothetical indices of community characteristics (based upon the twenty variables listed in Table B–1) are related to y_1 through y_{12} in Chart 4; to y_{13} in Chart 12; and to y_{14} in Chart 3.

In selecting measures of the dependent variables for one particular year (1955), we have assumed that a strong trend component tends to dominate most municipal functions, and that, therefore, substituting some weighted or unweighted average calculated over the years, say 1954–1956, would not appreciably improve the reliability of our single-year estimates. The merit of this assumption was subsequently probed in respect of welfare expenditures, which are especially sensitive to business-cycle fluctuation. We separately correlated welfare expenditures in the 49 Census-recognized communities for 1952, 1953, 1954, 1955, and 1956 with the "per cent families and unrelated individuals having incomes less than $2000 in 1949" ($x_{20}$). We found the correlations to range from 0.45 in 1953 to 0.60 in 1955, with the systematic element of the five-year trend (first principal component) correlating 0.53. Though the estimates in the case of welfare expenditures could have clearly been improved if the year-to-year disturbances had been suppressed, welfare expenditures were the sole municipal function behaving in a somewhat erratic manner.

Contrary to the practice in most public-finance research, we have not deflated the expenditure variables by a measure of population size. The model itself, we expected, would control the differences in size among jurisdictions. Deflation by population implicitly involves assumptions about the homogeneity and linearity of the relation between expenditure variates and population, assumptions which are hardly tenable. There are applications for per capita expenditure variables, particularly in regression analysis, where possible heteroscedasticities may thus be mitigated, but there is little merit in extending the practice to correlation models.

III. THE MODEL APPLIED

For our specific exercise a matrix of zero-order product moment correlation coefficients was initially computed for the full set of variables.* Partitioned into three parts, relating the independent (socioeconomic) and dependent (fiscal) variables separately and then jointly, this matrix is presented in Tables B-3, B-4, and B-5.

Our model posited a straightforward regression relation according to which variations in municipal expenditure levels were said to "depend" upon the dimensions of community differences. We have therefore factored only the submatrix containing the correlations of independent variables. We had, however, defined as the common part of each independent variable that part which perfectly covaried with variables from both the independent and dependent domains. Thus unities in the leading diagonal were reduced to the squared

* All requisite computations were performed on an IBM Type 650 EDPM at the Littauer Statistical Laboratory, Harvard University. We availed ourselves principally of the following programs: A. E. Beaton, C. R. Baker, K. L. Kelley, "Correlation Analysis" (unpublished; Harvard University, 1959); A. E. Beaton, K. L. Kelley, "Matrix Package II" (unpublished; Harvard University, 1959); W. W. Piper, *A Program for the Solution of Secular Equations* (General Electric Laboratory Report No. 56–RL–1503, March 1956); and S. Vandenberg and D. Lamphiear, *Varimax and Quartimax Factor Analysis Rotation Program* (University of Michigan, 1958).

multiple correlations between a given variable and the remaining 31 variables of both types (excluding the summary indices y_{13} and y_{14}) as the preferred estimates of significant common variance. The squared multiple correlations so defined would seem to yield better over-all systematic estimates of communalities than might have been the case with, say, the highest off-diagonal correlations.*

The reduced correlation matrix was resolved into fifteen principal-axes factors. As a reflection of inconsistencies introduced into the correlation matrix by the estimates of communalities, five latent roots emerged negative. However, the error variance thus introduced was estimated to be of the order of less than 0.6 per cent of the original trace and held unlikely to affect subsequent results within the bounds of reporting accuracy. The ten largest factors, jointly contributing over 98 per cent of the original trace, were retained for rotation. The loadings of the independent variables on the ten principal axes of their common factor space are given in Table B-6. Inspection of the residuals below the main diagonal in Table B-3 reveals that these ten factors reproduce the original correlations within a negligible margin of error.

Principal-axes factors, however, were not intended as a final solution. To maximize the parsimony and interpretability of the factorial structure, a coordinate solution of the simple structure type was indicated. But on this we have imposed the restriction of orthogonality. In what remains essentially an exploratory enterprise, noncorrelated factors would seem to provide the simplest and most readily interpretable frame of reference.

Rotation to simple structure was performed analytically under the

* It has been shown by P. S. Dwyer, in "The Contribution of an Orthogonal Multiple Factor Solution to Multiple Correlation," *Psychometrika*, 4:163–171 (1939), and more recently by Louis Guttman, " 'Best Possible' Systematic Estimates of Communalities," *Psychometrika*, 21:273–285 (1956), that squared multiple correlations represent an objective lower bound to communalities. The use of squared multiple correlations in the leading diagonal *instead* of communalities was recently recommended by Charles Wrigley, "The Distinction between Common and Specific Variance in Factor Theory," *British Journal of Statistical Psychology*, 10:81–98 (1957).

normal varimax criterion recently proposed by H. F. Kaiser. This criterion calls for maximization of the variance of squared loadings of the normalized common parts of variables on a factor. The procedure optimally renders a simple and distinctive account of each factor in terms of a small number of variables with which it is highly correlated. Similar clarity is reciprocally attained in the factorial description of each variable. Experience with normal varimax is reported to have shown that it yields a factor solution which "does not seem to deviate systematically from what may be considered the best orthogonal simple structure." * Table B-7 gives the transformation matrix which effects the rotation to normal varimax. The new solution follows in Table B-8.

The functional expenditure variables were next "regressed" on the explanatory varimax factors. The results are given in Table B-9. Correlations between these variables and the varimax factors were obtained according to the standard procedure due to Dwyer and Mosier for the determination of factor loadings of variables which originally have not been included in a factored matrix.** The percentages of variance used in Charts 3, 4, and 12 (our Chapter 2) were derived from Table B-9 as explained in that table.

* Henry F. Kaiser, "The Varimax Criterion for Analytic Rotation in Factor Analysis," *Psychometrika*, 23:187–200 (1958).

** C. I. Mosier, "A Note on Dwyer: The Determination of the Factor Loadings of a Given Test," *Psychometrika*, 3:297–299 (1938).

Table B-3 Correlations of Socio-Economic Variables

Socio-economic variables	x_1	x_2	x_3	x_4	x_5	x_6	x_7	x_8	x_9	x_{10}	x_{11}	x_{12}	x_{13}	x_{14}	x_{15}	x_{16}	x_{17}	x_{18}	x_{19}	x_{20}
x_1 Population	98	−38	11	41	38	49	32	45	81	08	83	85	−29	91	04	−34	−34	25	−45	30
x_2 Pct. population change	00	77	24	−43	−63	−33	−31	−05	−34	25	−50	−35	41	−36	−26	29	47	−23	33	−29
x_3 Area in square miles	00	00	87	32	−66	−26	−10	41	17	81	08	13	43	23	08	07	09	−08	05	09
x_4 Net density	00	00	00	96	48	81	51	−39	32	−31	53	37	−26	23	−02	−61	−36	29	−57	40
x_5 Pct. saturation	00	00	01	00	91	45	31	−08	25	−66	36	31	−50	27	11	−35	−36	24	−40	16
x_6 Pct. multifamily buildings	00	00	02	00	01	91	16	−23	31	−23	58	42	−40	32	15	−48	−50	15	−50	45
x_7 Pct. land industrial	00	00	00	00	00	00	86	−20	57	−20	27	27	00	25	−23	−56	−00	55	−41	11
x_8 Residential valuation	−02	01	00	00	02	00	00	95	26	47	29	41	−03	63	24	39	−06	−24	24	01
x_9 Business valuation	00	00	00	00	00	00	00	00	95	07	73	66	−18	76	−09	−43	−19	39	−42	22
x_{10} Vacant land valuation	00	00	−01	01	00	−01	00	00	00	93	08	10	33	18	25	07	−09	−20	−01	18
x_{11} State aid to municipalities	−01	00	−02	01	−01	−01	00	01	00	00	91	72	−32	75	17	−41	−41	28	−44	32
x_{12} State aid to schools	00	00	−01	−01	−01	00	00	−01	00	00	00	93	−27	88	−12	−40	−19	36	−40	18
x_{13} Pct. "other" in revenue	00	00	00	00	00	00	00	00	00	−01	00	00	71	−24	−11	08	32	−16	10	−14
x_{14} Average daily enrollment	00	00	00	−01	00	00	00	00	00	00	00	00	00	97	02	−21	−24	18	−29	28
x_{15} Pct. pop. 65 and over	00	02	00	00	00	01	01	00	−01	00	01	02	00	−01	84	16	−54	−49	−06	58
x_{16} Median school yrs. compl.	02	01	00	00	01	00	00	00	00	00	00	−01	−01	00	−02	89	26	−63	76	−22
x_{17} Pct. pop. 14 and under	01	02	−01	00	01	00	00	01	00	00	02	00	−02	−01	04	−01	75	10	43	−57
x_{18} Pct. residents in mfg.	00	01	01	−02	00	01	01	00	−01	−01	01	00	00	00	01	00	01	79	−34	−25
x_{19} Median income	01	00	00	−01	−01	01	00	00	00	00	−01	01	00	01	02	−01	−01	00	86	−53
x_{20} Pct. earning under $2,000	00	01	00	00	00	00	00	00	00	−01	00	00	00	01	01	00	00	01	00	89

Decimal points are omitted. Zero-order correlations are in the upper right half of the matrix. Below the principal diagonal are given residuals after factor analysis. Squared multiple correlations between a given variable and all other variables, dependent and independent, serving as predictors, are entered in the principal diagonal for each variable as a measure of its significant "common variance."

Table B-4 Correlations of Fiscal Variables

Fiscal variables	y_1	y_2	y_3	y_4	y_5	y_6	y_7	y_8	y_9	y_{10}	y_{11}	y_{12}	y_{13}	y_{14}
y_1 General government	95	91	94	79	79	84	63	85	71	76	87	37	66	94
y_2 Fire protection	02	98	97	80	83	84	66	83	76	73	88	88	66	95
y_3 Police	05	02	99	80	85	88	68	85	76	76	87	32	67	94
y_4 Streets	01	−00	00	89	69	77	47	77	78	70	89	50	39	88
y_5 Sanitation	01	−00	02	−04	86	78	56	73	73	63	79	24	47	85
y_6 Health	05	−01	02	03	02	93	67	79	79	57	83	30	55	87
y_7 Welfare	00	−01	−02	03	03	04	79	56	44	54	53	02	76	61
y_8 Recreation	02	−04	−01	−01	−01	04	01	94	66	68	83	45	61	86
y_9 Libraries and civic services	04	00	01	−03	02	09	02	−05	92	49	80	43	33	81
y_{10} Nonschool debt service	04	03	06	07	01	−05	07	04	−02	83	69	20	54	75
y_{11} Schools, except debt service	03	00	01	01	−01	03	01	01	02	01	99	62	48	97
y_{12} School debt service	02	00	−01	−03	−07	00	00	02	00	−06	02	88	45	53
y_{13} "Tax effort"	*	*	*	*	*	*	*	*	*	*	*	*	*	57
y_{14} Total local expenditures	*	*	*	*	*	*	*	*	*	*	*	*	*	*

Decimal points are omitted. Asterisk means correlations not computed.

Zero-order correlations are in the upper right half of the matrix. Below the principal diagonal are given residuals after factor analysis. Squared multiple correlations between a given variable and all other variables, dependent and independent, serving as predictors (variables y_{13} and y_{14} have been omitted, however) are entered in the principal diagonal for each variable as a measure of its significant "common variance."

[229]

Table B-5 Correlations of Fiscal Variables with Socio-Economic Variables

	Socio-economic variables	y_1	y_2	y_3	y_4	y_5	y_6	y_7	y_8	y_9	y_{10}	y_{11}	y_{12}	y_{13}	y_{14}
x_1	Population	89	88	90	81	86	85	58	78	79	72	95	42	52	95
x_2	Pct. population change	−41	−47	−46	−37	−41	−39	−40	−39	−38	−40	−39	−02	−44	−43
x_3	Area in square miles	03	07	03	25	−01	06	−14	07	09	03	23	55	−21	15
x_4	Net density	57	58	59	26	44	46	69	51	15	47	31	−17	87	44
x_5	Pct. saturation	39	40	40	22	40	38	43	30	35	34	29	−23	45	35
x_6	Pct. multifamily buildings	54	58	57	27	44	45	64	42	27	40	37	−07	83	47
x_7	Pct. land industrial	50	49	51	38	42	39	34	40	22	44	29	−08	31	39
x_8	Residential valuation	27	27	22	50	28	22	−12	35	50	25	59	77	−19	46
x_9	Business valuation	77	85	85	79	81	77	46	73	68	84	81	34	31	85
x_{10}	Vacant land valuation	−01	00	00	18	−01	−04	−21	06	03	06	15	48	−25	09
x_{11}	State aid to municipalities	74	81	78	71	74	71	57	77	62	60	81	37	59	82
x_{12}	State aid to schools	75	71	72	74	64	71	51	66	53	58	86	45	49	82
x_{13}	Pct. "other" in revenue	−31	−32	−31	−26	−28	−30	−28	−35	−27	−31	−27	08	−44	29
x_{14}	Average daily enrollment	81	81	80	85	73	75	45	76	72	66	96	60	40	92
x_{15}	Pct. pop. 65 and over	02	12	08	02	01	03	05	10	29	−02	08	12	18	08
x_{16}	Median school yrs. compl.	−42	−39	−43	−23	−33	−33	−47	−23	02	−42	−22	25	−43	31
x_{17}	Pct. pop. 14 and under	−34	−36	−36	−24	−27	−37	−34	−33	−37	−30	−27	04	−39	32
x_{18}	Pct. residents in mfg.	26	20	23	21	24	23	16	11	−07	24	18	−13	16	20
x_{19}	Median income	−48	−50	−56	−31	−45	−50	−61	−33	−27	−50	−32	19	−50	42
x_{20}	Pct. earning under $2,000	40	48	49	30	31	45	55	44	40	27	31	11	53	39

Decimal points are omitted.

Table B-6 Principal-Axes Factor Loadings for Socio-Economic Variables

PRINCIPAL-AXES FACTORS

Socio-economic variables	F_1	F_2	F_3	F_4	F_5	F_6	F_7	F_8	F_9	F_{10}
x_1 Population	84	-41	11	19	-11	-10	-08	04	-10	04
x_2 Pct. population change	-61	-14	24	-20	-37	-14	-20	17	-10	18
x_3 Area in square miles	-14	-76	19	-42	02	07	12	-04	04	-11
x_4 Net density	73	41	-07	-25	-25	-20	20	-19	11	06
x_5 Pct. saturation	62	46	-20	40	21	02	-19	-13	-08	04
x_6 Pct. multifamily buildings	71	23	-28	-14	-47	-02	11	-01	-04	06
x_7 Pct. land industrial	52	24	44	-20	40	-30	14	00	11	17
x_8 Residential valuation	07	-82	-07	43	12	01	-07	-13	04	17
x_9 Business valuation	74	-31	33	03	16	-19	10	29	-16	-04
x_{10} Vacant land valuation	-14	-79	-02	-46	00	21	08	-02	06	13
x_{11} State aid to municipalities	83	-29	-01	07	-11	04	22	-03	-19	-10
x_{12} State aid to schools	76	-37	25	18	-19	08	-15	-12	15	-06
x_{13} Pct. "other" in revenue	-42	-21	25	-43	09	-27	-10	-32	-20	-06
x_{14} Average daily enrollment	73	-57	14	27	-05	-09	-11	-02	08	-03
x_{15} Pct. pop. 65 and over	09	-24	-80	-11	24	00	10	-02	-10	02
x_{16} Median school yrs. compl.	-65	-29	-29	47	-05	-23	11	04	07	-05
x_{17} Pct. pop. 14 and under	-50	04	59	15	-08	-20	-03	-03	08	-12
x_{18} Pct. residents in mfg.	42	27	63	-05	11	32	09	04	05	00
x_{19} Median income	-69	-14	02	47	-08	-09	34	-02	04	03
x_{20} Pct. earning under $2,000	45	-15	-59	-41	08	-22	-14	15	21	-10
Absolute contribution of factor	689	351	250	188	83	59	45	33	27	18
Pct. contribution of factor	39	20	14	11	05	03	03	02	01	01
Cumul. pct. of common variance	39	59	73	83	88	91	94	95	97	98

Decimal points are omitted.

[231]

Table B-7 Transformation Matrix from Principal-Axes to the Normal Varimax Solution

	V_1	V_2	V_3	V_4	V_5	V_6	V_7	V_8	V_9	V_{10}
F_1	68	24	−24	−43	−37	−22	15	14	−04	−03
F_2	−57	68	18	−28	−28	−12	05	08	−05	−02
F_3	19	−16	85	−29	14	−30	−03	−10	−05	07
F_4	35	56	24	53	29	16	13	26	07	16
F_5	−10	10	−31	−14	66	−54	35	−11	−00	05
F_6	−10	−16	02	−46	21	49	31	49	13	34
F_7	−13	−27	04	36	−39	−35	45	27	−30	37
F_8	−02	−04	−05	−03	21	−15	−47	61	−54	−21
F_9	−07	−15	11	10	−07	−19	21	42	55	−62
F_{10}	−04	−00	−11	02	−06	−34	−52	19	54	52

Decimal points are omitted.

Socio-economic variables	Community size V1	Land reserve V2	Age V3	Residential affluence V4	Housing density V5	Industrialization V6	V7	V8	V9	Low-income prevalence V10	Communality[b]
x1 Population	93	06	13	-16	18	10	04	-05	04	-03	96
x2 Pct. population change	-29	-35	-34	16	-08	-18	59	16	00	01	76
x3 Area in square miles	20	-87	02	00	-16	-01	-05	17	04	03	85
x4 Net density	18	27	13	-32	80	28	-13	-00	-06	08	96
x5 Pct. saturation	27	82	22	-23	08	09	-19	-08	-10	-06	92
x6 Pct. multifamily buildings	29	23	26	-24	77	-08	04	-17	06	00	90
x7 Pct. land industrial	18	14	-12	-37	12	79	-10	07	00	03	87
x8 Residential valuation	65	-26	16	41	-38	-08	-02	00	-28	-16	94
x9 Business valuation	76	-03	02	-24	03	43	02	-06	34	-01	95
x10 Vacant land valuation	15	-89	23	-02	-14	-08	07	04	-13	-08	93
x11 State aid to municipalities	76	00	21	-18	34	05	-22	-09	-21	-15	89
x12 State aid to schools	87	-01	-09	-24	18	-04	-12	-09	-15	11	91
x13 Pct. "other" in revenue	-22	-40	-14	00	-12	07	10	67	-01	00	71
x14 Average daily enrollment	97	-05	07	-03	03	08	-06	-06	-07	10	97
x15 Pct. pop. 65 and over	-02	-06	85	19	-01	-08	-12	00	01	-05	79
x16 Median school yrs. compl.	-15	-05	00	85	-30	-21	07	00	-02	04	89
x17 Pct. pop. 14 and under	-17	-08	-71	21	-21	06	09	19	02	11	70
x18 Pct. residents in mfg.	17	08	-45	-59	04	27	-22	-22	04	-13	78
x19 Median income	-25	09	-31	76	-22	-10	-05	-08	00	-19	85
x20 Pct. earning under $2,000	15	-08	74	-14	25	10	05	-01	01	46	89
Absolute contribution of factor	471	275	253	249	191	112	58	66	31	37	1743
Pct. contribution of factor	27	16	15	14	11	06	03	04	02	02	100

Note: Decimal points are omitted.

[a] Varimax factor V_3 and factors V_5 to V_{10} have been reflected.

[b] The proportion of the variance of a socio-economic variable that is associated with all ten varimax factors.

Table B-9 Correlations of Fiscal Variables with Explanatory Varimax Factors

VARIMAX FACTORS[a]

Fiscal variables	Community size V_1	Land reserve V_2	Age V_3	Residential affluence V_4	Housing density V_5	Industrialization V_6	V_7	V_8	V_9	Low-income prevalence V_{10}	Communality[b]
y_1 General government	77	08	15	−16	31	33	04	−11	−03	11	88
y_2 Fire protection	78	07	24	−11	32	35	02	−08	18	13	96
y_3 Police	77	09	22	−19	30	35	02	−08	15	18	95
y_4 Streets	82	−11	09	−05	03	28	−08	−16	05	12	83
y_5 Sanitation	76	13	14	−15	16	28	04	−05	20	00	78
y_6 Health	74	10	18	−20	17	21	02	−09	19	24	81
y_7 Welfare	42	22	20	−29	46	09	−06	02	10	39	74
y_8 Recreation	73	01	21	05	29	36	−03	−18	06	14	84
y_9 Libraries & civic svcs.	75	14	38	13	−07	19	06	−03	21	08	84
y_{10} Nonschool debt svc.	61	05	14	−25	18	30	02	−15	−11	00	62
y_{11} Schools, exc. debt svc.	96	−04	12	−01	10	14	−07	−06	02	07	98
y_{12} School debt svc.	61	−44	02	37	−08	02	−07	05	−14	01	74
y_{13} "Tax effort"	33	20	20	−15	77	09	−16	−19	−05	31	97
y_{14} Total local expends.	91	01	17	−08	19	23	−03	−06	07	09	97
Absolute contrib'n of factor[c]	654	32	45	44	70	84	03	12	22	31	997
Pct. contrib'n of factor[c]	67	03	05	04	07	08	00	01	02	03	100

Note: Decimal points are omitted.

[a] The seven labeled factors, that is, V_1, V_2, V_3, V_4, V_5, V_6, and V_{10}, are the indices discussed in Chapter 2 and used in Charts 3, 4 and 12. The percentages of variance used in those charts are the squares of the corresponding coefficients in the above table. The "unexplained" percentages in those charts include not only the difference between 100 and the communality (last column, above) but also the variance accounted for by the three factors disregarded in the interpretation, namely V_7, V_8, and V_9.

[b] The proportion of the variance of a fiscal variable that is associated with all ten varimax factors.

Notes

CHAPTER I: THE POLITICAL ECONOMY OF A METROPOLITAN AREA

1. This and the following paragraphs draw from R. Werner, *Tammany Hall* (New York, 1928); L. Riordon, *Plunkitt of Tammany Hall* (New York, 1948); Lincoln Steffens, *Autobiography* (New York, 1931), and other standard works on American city politics. In particular, the draft report of Mark D. Hirsch entitled *Reflections on Urban History and Politics with Special Reference to New York City, 1865–1900* (mimeographed; New York, 1958) is acknowledged.

2. Werner, p. 303.

3. *Ibid.*, p. 483.

4. Steffens; see especially Chapter VIII.

5. Werner, p. 502.

6. *Ibid*, p. xx.

7. Solomon Fabricant, *The Trend of Government Activity in the United States since 1900* (New York, 1952), p. 191. See also U. S. Bureau of the Census, *Historical Review of State and Local Government Finances* (Washington, 1948).

8. Fabricant, p. 7.

9. Regional Plan Association, *Bulletin 86* (1956).

10. Grover Cleveland, *Second Inaugural Address*, quoted in Fabricant, p. 7.

11. Arnold M. Soloway, "Growth of Government in the Last 50 Years: an Analytical Review," published in *Federal Expenditure Policy for Economic Growth and Stability*, Joint Economic Committee, 85th Cong., 1st sess., 1957.

12. Quotations are from Arthur M. Schlesinger, Jr., *Crisis of the Old Order* (Boston, 1957), pp. 458–459.

13. Soloway. General sources for government expenditure include the previously cited U. S. Bureau of the Census, *Historical Review of State and Local Government Finances;* and J. Frederic Dewhurst and associates, *America's Needs and Resources,* Twentieth Century Fund (New York, 1955).

14. Lyle C. Fitch, *Technical Memorandum #7* of the Mayor's Commission on Organization and Management of New York City (mimeographed, 1953); F. Dodd McHugh, *Financing New York City's Future Permanent Improvements,* prepared for the Mayor's Committee on City Planning (WPA Project 465-97-3-96; New York, 1938); and unpublished monograph by Elaine Pearlstine, Domestic Research Division of the Federal Reserve Bank of New York, entitled "Postwar State Finances, All States, New York, and New Jersey," December 1949.

15. City of New York, *Foundations for Better Government, First Annual Report of Mayor Robert F. Wagner to the City Council and to the People of

New York City (1954) and his subsequent reports. Descriptions of New York public programs and facilities here and in the paragraphs which follow are taken from these reports plus special departmental publications and the *1958 Statistical Guide for New York City,* published by the Department of Commerce and Public Events.

16. Nassau County, Office of the Executive, "Your County Nassau" (1957); Town of Hempstead, "Hempstead: America's Largest Township" (1957).

17. See, for example, Westchester County Department of Planning, "The Status of Municipal Planning in Westchester, 1957" (White Plains, 1957).

18. Harold Lasswell, "Strategies of Inquiry: The Rational Use of Observation," in Daniel Lerner, ed., *The Human Meaning of The Social Sciences* (New York, 1959), p. 98. In general this section is based on an analytical framework common in contemporary political analysis. See, for example, David B. Truman, *The Governmental Process* (New York, 1951), or Robert A. Dahl, *A Preface to Democratic Theory* (Chicago, 1956).

19. For an analysis paralleling in many ways the one presented here, see Jesse Burkhead, "Informing Government with Economics," *Public Administration Review,* 18:4 (Autumn 1958). This discussion of the differences between the public and private sectors is in contrast to such theoretical expositions of how the political economy might behave as Paul A. Samuelson, "The Pure Theory of Public Expenditure," *Review of Economics and Statistics,* 36:387 (November 1954); Charles Tiebout, "A Pure Theory of Local Expenditures," *The Journal of Political Economy,* 64:5 (October 1956); Anthony Downs, *An Economic Theory of Democracy* (New York, 1957); Francis Bator, *The Question of Government Spending* (New York, 1960).

20. Wallace S. Sayre and Herbert Kaufman, *Governing New York City: Politics in the Metropolis* (New York, 1960).

21. Norton E. Long, "The Local Community as an Ecology of Games," *The American Journal of Sociology,* 64:3 (November 1958).

22. For definitions and numbers of local governments, we rely principally on *U. S. Census of Governments: 1957,* Vol. 1: No. 1, *Governments in the United States;* No. 2, *Local Government in Standard Metropolitan Areas;* No. 3, *Local Government Structure.* See also Audrey M. Davies, *Political Units in the New York Metropolitan Region* (mimeographed; New York: Institute of Public Administration, March 1959).

23. State of New Jersey, "The General Property Tax in 1958: Toward a Balanced Tax Structure," *Ninth Report of the Commission on State Tax Policy* (Trenton, 1958), p. 8.

24. State of New York, Temporary Commission on the Fiscal Affairs of State Government, *A Program for Continued Progress in Fiscal Management* (Albany, 1955), p. 669.

25. The New York State–New York City Fiscal Relations Committee, *A Report to the Governor of the State of New York and the Mayor of the City of New York* (New York, 1956), p. 10.

26. Sayre and Kaufman, "Introduction."

27. Merrill Folsom, interview, June 16, 1959.

28. Wendell Pigman, "The Democratic Party in Hudson County" (unpublished M. A. thesis; Princeton University, 1958).

29. William E. Oriol, "Where Is Bergen Headed?" reprint from *Bergen Evening Record*, Aug. 12–17, 1957.

CHAPTER 2: PRESSURES ON THE PUBLIC SECTOR

1. An extensive literature of state and local public finance is now in existence. The major recent publications on which we have relied heavily in this chapter are Solomon Fabricant, *The Trend of Government Activity in the United States since 1900* (New York, 1952); J. Frederic Dewhurst and associates, *America's Needs and Resources,* Twentieth Century Fund (New York, 1955), particularly chapter 18 by Wilie Kilpatrick and Robert Drury; Arnold M. Soloway, "Growth of Government in the Last 50 Years: an Analytical Review," in *Federal Expenditure Policy for Economic Growth and Stability,* Joint Economic Committee, 85th Cong., 1st sess., 1957; Lyle C. Fitch, *Technical Memorandum #7* of the Mayor's Commission on Organization and Management of New York City (mimeographed, 1953); Harvey Brazer, *City Expenditure in the United States,* National Bureau of Economic Research, Occasional Paper 48 (New York, 1959); Werner Z. Hirsch, *Three Studies in the Measurement of the Impact of Metropolitan Growth,* Resources for the Future, Inc. (Washington, 1959); Cleveland Metropolitan Services Commission, *Government Costs: Questions for Community Decision* (Cleveland, 1959); Seymour Sacks, "The Pattern of Local Finances in the Cleveland Metropolitan Area" (mimeographed staff paper of Cleveland Metropolitan Services Commission, Dec. 23, 1958); Stanley Scott and Edward L. Feder, *Factors Associated with Variations in Municipal Expenditure Levels: a Statistical Study of California Cities* (Berkeley, Cal., 1957).

2. Fabricant, p. 151.

3. Fabricant, p. 9.

4. Edgar M. Hoover and Raymond Vernon, *Anatomy of a Metropolis* (Cambridge: Harvard University Press, 1959), chap. 8.

5. "Surging Growth Has Sober Side," *New Brunswick Sunday Home News* (Jan. 25, 1959); Town of Greenwich, Connecticut, *Horseneck Extended,* Summary of the Annual Report, 1957.

6. William E. Oriol, "Where Is Bergen Headed?" reprint from *Bergen Evening Record,* Aug. 12–17, 1957. The figures on Teaneck and Teterboro are in the fourth article of the series.

CHAPTER 3: RESPONSES OF THE LOCAL GOVERNMENTS

1. State of New Jersey, Commission on State Tax Policy, *Ninth Report* (Trenton, 1958).

2. This comparison is based on the 1945, 1950, and 1955 issues of *Special Report on Municipal Affairs of the State Comptroller of New York.* For a

description of how market values were estimated for the earlier years, see our Appendix A.

3. State of New Jersey, Commission on State Tax Policy, *Fifth Report* (Trenton, 1950), and *Ninth Report* (Trenton, 1958). See also report of Harry V. Osborne, Jr., Deputy Administrator of Taxation, "Investigations of Assessments, City of Passaic," as printed in the *Herald-News,* Passaic-Clifton, New Jersey, July 11, 1951.

4. State of New Jersey, Commission on State Tax Policy, *Sixth Report* (Trenton, 1953), chap. V, pp. 103–120.

5. State of New Jersey, Commission on State Tax Policy, *Ninth Report* (Trenton, 1958), p. 139.

6. State of New York, *Report of the Temporary Commission on the Fiscal Affairs of State Government* (Albany, 1955), Vol. II, p. 666.

7. *Ibid.,* p. 616.

8. U. S. *1957 Census of Governments,* Vol. I, No. 1, and Vol. VI, Nos. 28 and 30. See also *Special Report on Municipal Affairs of the State Comptroller of New York* for 1945, 1950, and 1955; State of New Jersey, annual reports of the Commissioner of Education for 1954–55, 1955–56, and 1956–57; and Dun and Bradstreet, Municipal Credit Surveys, with special reference to school districts. For a detailed study on New Jersey school districts see Commission on State Tax Policy, *Public School Financing in New Jersey* (Trenton, 1954).

9. These figures are from a series constructed by the New York Metropolitan Region Study from reports by the Comptroller of the State of New York and by the New Jersey Department of the Treasury, as explained in our Appendix A.

10. For a comparison of the relevant definitions, see U. S. *1957 Census of Governments,* Vol. I, No. 1, and the Temporary State Commission on the Coordination of State Activities, *Staff Report on Public Authorities Under New York State* (Albany, 1956), chap. I.

11. State of New Jersey, Commission on State Tax Policy, *Sixth Report* (Trenton, 1953), chap. V.

12. Regional Plan Association, *Bulletin 86* (1956). This paragraph and those following rely heavily on that bulletin as well as upon conversations with the professional staff of the RPA for the summary of current doctrines about zoning.

13. The New Jersey Commission's report was issued at Trenton in 1957. See also Hofstra College Bureau of Business and Community Research, *Long Island Industrial Survey* (Hempstead, 1956).

14. "City Says Suburbs Bar Its Workers," *New York Times* (July 6, 1959).

15. For example, Hofstra College, just cited, part I.

16. U. S. *1957 Census of Governments,* Vol. VI, Nos. 28 and 30. As usual in this chapter, noncomparability of financial reporting units prevented our including Fairfield County in the Region totals.

17. See note 9. See also New Jersey Taxpayers Association, *Notes on Gov-*

ernment, an occasional publication which details (as in Nos. 27, 28, 32) state grants-in-aid for major purposes.

18. For a general description of the New York grant program see the mimeographed report of the State Department of Audit and Control, August 1956, entitled "State Aid to Local Government." The U. S. *1957 Census of Governments* provides comparative analysis, and an authoritative summary of the grant programs is found in Lynton K. Caldwell, *The Government and Administration of New York* (New York, 1954).

19. New Jersey Taxpayers Association, *Notes on Government,* No. 32.

20. For a general analysis of the effects of New York grants-in-aid upon governmental operations within the Region see Arch Dotson, "Metropolitan Aspects of New York State–New York City Fiscal Relations," a consultant memorandum in the 1956 report of the New York State–New York City Fiscal Relations Committee.

21. See note 9.

22. Carl S. Shoup, "New York City's Need for Fiscal Powers," consultant memorandum in the 1956 report of the New York State–New York City Fiscal Relations Committee. Much of the material for this section is drawn from this report, and from three other major recent studies, made by: the Mayor's Committee on Management Survey of the City of New York (1950–1953); the Temporary State Commission to Study the Organizational Structure of the Government of the City of New York (1953–1954); and the Commission on Governmental Operations of the City of New York, whose report is entitled "New York City in Transition," Feb. 1, 1960.

23. An able summary of these tax and debt limit requirements is found in Vol. II, chap. IV, of the *Report of the Temporary Commission on the Fiscal Affairs of State Government* (Albany, 1955).

24. Regional Plan Association, *Bulletin 86* (1956).

25. City of New York, First Annual Report of Mayor Wagner, 1954.

26. Joseph F. Maloney, "Preliminary Report on Reasons for Large Public Housing Program in New York City" (mimeographed, March 1958).

27. New York City Committee on Slum Clearance, *Slum Clearance Program Under Title I of the Federal Housing Act of 1949* (July 15, 1957), p. 20.

28. For a general discussion of these differentials, see Dotson (our note 20).

29. New York State Comptroller, special analysis of finances in metropolitan areas, mimeographed, 1957.

30. Calculations from U. S. *1957 Census of Governments.*

31. See note 20.

32. New York City, *Annual Report of the Comptroller, Fiscal Year 1956–57.*

33. 1956 report of Temporary Commission on the Fiscal Affairs of State Government, chap. IV. See also the annual reports of the Mayor and the special reports cited in note 22.

34. Herbert Kaufman, "Gotham in the Air Age," in Harold Stein, ed., *A Case Book on Public Administration and Policy* (New York, 1952).

35. For a detailed analysis of the establishment of the Transit Authority,

see William L. Miller, "The New York Subway Crisis" (unpublished senior thesis; Harvard University, 1956).

36. A summary treatment of the Triborough Authority's program is found in William Reid and Joseph M. Leiper, "Integrated Transportation" (1956), a consultant memorandum of the New York State–New York City Fiscal Relations Committee.

37. The Mayor's Committee on Management Survey of the City of New York and the Commission on Governmental Operations of the City of New York have given special emphasis to this situation.

38. Among the main sources for the description and analysis of Westchester are interviews with Merrill Folsom, the county's *New York Times* correspondent; William Cassella of the National Municipal League; and Robert T. Daland of the University of North Carolina. I have also had the opportunity to review Professor Daland's draft manuscript, "A Political System in Suburbia: The Politics of Autonomy," an authoritative treatment of the county. The quotations are taken from a letter from Daland to the author.

39. Regional Plan Association files, and Westchester County, *The Status of Municipal Planning* (1957).

40. See note 9.

41. Regional Plan Association, *Bulletin 86* (1956). See also the *New York Herald Tribune's* two special feature series on Suburbia in April 1955 and April 1959.

42. Robert Moses, "The Future of Nassau and Western Suffolk: Introductory Remarks," in *The Problems of Growth in Nassau and Western Suffolk: A Planning Forum, Hofstra College* (Hempstead, 1955), p. 3.

43. Samuel F. Thomas, "Nassau County: Its Governments and Their Expenditure and Revenue Patterns," draft report of a project of the New York Area Research Council of the City College of New York (mimeographed, 1957), p. 24.

44. *Ibid.*, Part II, Section B.

45. See note 20.

46. See note 9.

47. *Newsday,* series entitled "Suffolk Needs a Charter," article of Aug. 13, 1957. See also Suffolk County Planning Board, "Progress Report" (Patchogue, 1957).

48. *Newsday,* Aug. 8, 1957.

49. *Ibid.,* Sept. 9.

50. *Ibid.,* Sept. 9.

51. See note 9.

52. See note 9.

53. See note 9.

54. *New York Herald Tribune* (April 26, 1959).

55. See note 9.

56. State of New Jersey, Commission to Study Laws Affecting Industrial Development, *Report* (Trenton, 1957), p. 58. See also First Annual Report of the Advisory Planning Commission to the Legislature and Governor of the

State of New Jersey, Feb. 1, 1957; New Jersey Municipal Planning Enabling Act of 1953 (Laws 1953: Chapter 433); New Jersey County and Regional Planning Enabling Act of 1935 (Laws 1935: Chapter 251); New Jersey State Planning Act (Laws 1934: Chapter 178); New Jersey Municipal Zoning Enabling Act (Laws 1928: Chapter 274); New Jersey State Planning Bureau, *Zoning in New Jersey* (Trenton, 1956).

57. Statistics provided by B. Chavooshian, director, State Planning Bureau, Trenton, N. J.

58. Harry Heher, "Zoning Administration in New Jersey," *New Jersey Municipalities,* Vol. XXXIV, No. 2 (February 1957), and Passaic-Bergen Community Planning Association, *Existing Uses of Land* (mimeographed; Wallington, N. J., 1954).

59. Based on county planning reports and consultant memoranda for Bergen, Somerset, Middlesex, Monmouth, Morris, and Passaic counties, 1950–1957.

60. State of New Jersey, Commission on State Tax Policy, *Sixth Report* (Trenton, 1953), pp. 55, xix. See also James A. Arnold, Jr., "New Jersey Property Tax in 1957," *New Jersey Municipalities,* Vol. XXXIV, No. 8 (November 1957).

61. See note 9.

62. Orlando F. Furno, *Twenty Years of Teachers Salaries in the Schools of the Metropolitan School Study Council* (New York, 1958).

63. U. S. *1957 Census of Governments,* Vol. I.

64. See note 9.

65. State of New Jersey, Commission on State Tax Policy, *Ninth Report* (Trenton, 1958), chap. I.

66. State of New Jersey, *Annual Report of the Commission of Education* (Trenton, 1957–58).

67. *Newsday,* Aug. 21, 1957.

68. *Ibid.*

CHAPTER 4: THE WORLD OF THE METROPOLITAN GIANTS

1. For a representative chronicle of the character and extent of inter-municipality cooperation see State of New York Joint Legislative Committee on Metropolitan Area Study, *Municipal Cooperation: A Digest of the Law of New York Permitting Intergovernmental Service Arrangements Among Municipalities of the State* (mimeographed, 1958).

2. Harrison E. Salisbury, "The Commuter Crisis," first of a series of three articles, *New York Times* (March 2, 1959).

3. Prime source material about the Region's highway facilities is found in the Port of New York Authority and the Triborough Bridge and Tunnel Authority, *Joint Study of Arterial Facilities* (January 1955); special analysis by the Office of the Secretariat, Metropolitan Regional Council, "Present and Proposed Highway Construction in the Metropolitan Area," reported in the

Council's *Bulletin* (January 1960); Joint Report of the New York Metropolitan Rapid Transit Commission and the New Jersey Metropolitan Rapid Transit Commission, *The Problem of Providing Improved Mass Transportation between the City of New York and New Jersey–Westchester–Long Island* (March 3, 1954). For transit and rail facilities, see the Joint Report just cited and subsequent staff and interim reports of the successor agency to these two commissions, the Metropolitan Rapid Transit Commission, established in 1954 (to be referred to as MRTC). In particular see the staff report of December 1957 and the interim reports of Feb. 18, 1955, March 1, 1956, and Jan. 31, 1957. See also City of New York, *Statistical Guide,* issued annually, and the report of the New York State–New York City Fiscal Relations Committee, November 1956, especially the memorandum of William Reid and Joseph M. Leiper and those of Philip Golden, Bertram H. Lindman, and Wilfred Owen.

4. MRTC (Metropolitan Rapid Transit Commission), *Report* (January 1958), pp. 14, 15–17. See also Salisbury series cited above, and series by Tom Barrett, "Plight of Jersey Commuters," *New York Herald Tribune* (Feb. 4–9, 1959). Staff analyses of the Comprehensive Planning Office, Port Development Department, Port of New York Authority, also are valuable sources.

5. MRTC, *Staff Report* (December 1957), p. 6. See also Salisbury, cited above.

6. MRTC, *Staff Report* (December 1957), p. 7.

7. Barrett, cited in note 4.

8. MRTC, *Staff Report* (December 1957), p. 9.

9. Barrett, Feb. 4, 1959.

10. MRTC, *Staff Report* (December 1957), p. 9.

11. See the joint MRTC report of March 3, 1954 (cited in note 3), p. 99.

12. Annual reports of Mayor Wagner.

13. *Ibid.* Additional information respecting the City's transit capital improvement needs and programs was gained in interviews with staff of the City Planning Commission and the City Administrator during the summers of 1957 and 1958.

14. Fourth Annual Report of Mayor Wagner (1957), p. 115.

15. The annual reports of the Port of New York Authority are the basic sources used in detailing this agency's operations. Summary data are also found in the MRTC reports and the consultant memoranda in the November 1956 report of the New York State–New York City Fiscal Relations Committee.

16. Annual reports of the Triborough Bridge and Tunnel Authority, with same supplementary data as described in note 15.

17. *Joint Study* of January 1955 (cited in note 3), pp. 6, 7.

18. Although Mr. Moses' public activities are widely reported, the official sources respecting the offices mentioned here are the Mayor's annual reports, and the Temporary State Commission on the Coordination of State Activities, *Staff Report on Public Authorities* (Albany, 1956).

19. See report of New York State–New York City Fiscal Relations Committee, November 1956, in particular the consultant memorandum of Wil-

liam Reid and Joseph M. Leiper, "Integrated Transportation." For an especially able presentation of the management philosophy and outlook in the Port of New York Authority, see Austin J. Tobin, "Engineering and Management Decisions in the Port of New York Authority" (speech before the American Society for Engineering Education; Ithaca, N. Y., June 19, 1957).

20. *Joint Report* of the New York MRTC and the New Jersey MRTC, March 3, 1954, p. 78.

21. Port of New York Authority, *Statement by Commissioners* with respect to Assembly Bill No. 16, before the Committee on Federal and Interstate Relations and the Committee on Highways, Transportation and Public Utilities of the House of Assembly of the State of New Jersey, Nov. 24, 1958, Trenton, N. J., pp. 40, 41.

22. Herman T. Stichman, *An Efficient Method for Providing Direct Rapid Transit Commutation between Suburban Residential and City Employment Areas in Metropolitan New Jersey, Connecticut and New York without Physical Transfer and at Minimum Cost, with Aid to Commerce, Railroads and Municipal Living* (printed statement in connection with MRTC hearings in 1958).

23. Fourth Annual Report of Mayor Wagner (1957), p. 114.

24. See, for example, Port of New York Authority, cited in note 21, pp. 38–43, and *Joint Report* of New York MRTC and New Jersey MRTC, March 3, 1954, pp. 77–79.

25. Report of New York State–New York City Fiscal Relations Committee, November 1956, pp. 29–33.

26. Port of New York Authority, 1959 annual report.

27. Joint Study of January 1955 (cited in note 3), p. 7.

28. Fourth Annual Report of Mayor Wagner (1957), p. 111.

29. See note 25.

30. For a general explanation of the City's role in these conflicts, see Wallace S. Sayre and Herbert Kaufman, *Governing New York City: Politics in the Metropolis* (New York, 1960).

31. The MRTC came into being June 14, 1954, as a bistate agency created by Chapter 801, Laws of 1954, of the State of New York and Chapter 44, Laws of 1954, of the State of New Jersey.

32. MRTC, *Interim Report* (Feb. 18, 1955), pp. 9, 11.

33. *Ibid.*, pp. 15, 18.

34. *Ibid.*, pp. 45, 46.

35. MRTC, *Rapid Transit for the New York–New Jersey Metropolitan Area* (January 1958). See also the Project Director, *Report to the Commission* (May 20, 1957).

36. MRTC'S 1958 report, just cited, p. 36. Considerable disagreement exists among transportation experts concerning the magnitude of the probable deficit. The $12 million here quoted was a popular estimate.

37. *Ibid.*, p. 6.

38. As quoted in *New York Times* (Jan. 8, 1958), p. 1.

39. *New York Times* (April 24, 1958), p. 35.

40. *Ibid.* (Jan. 8, 1958), p. 1.

41. *Ibid.* (Jan. 7, 1958), p. 1, for Stichman and Bingham statements.

42. *Ibid.* (Feb. 10, 1958), pp. 25 and 29.

43. *Ibid.* (Jan. 13, 1958), p. 16.

44 *Ibid.* (Dec. 25, 1957), p. 25.

45. *Ibid.* (April 25, 1958), p. 1.

46. For detailed analysis of these bills, formally Senate Bill No. 50, and Assembly Bills No. 16 and 115, as well as the views of proponents and opponents, see the transcript of the first and second public hearings before the Assembly Committee on Federal and Interstate Relations and Assembly Committee on Highways, Transportation and Public Utilities, held on Nov. 24, 1958, and Dec. 3, 1958, Trenton, N. J., as well as the appendix thereto.

47. *Ibid.* See index for list of witnesses.

48. Statement cited in note 21, letter of transmittal.

49. S. J. Flink, "Report on the Port of New York Authority and Rapid Transit in the Metropolitan Region," mimeographed, Nov. 5, 1958, Section V, as reproduced in the appendix to the public hearings cited in note 46.

50. *New York Times* (Dec. 9, 1958), p. 25.

51. *Ibid.* (May 4, 1959), p. 1.

52. Regional Plan Association news release for Monday, April 20, 1959.

53. The basic sources for the analysis of public water programs in the Region are (1) Syracuse University, Delaware Valley Project, *The Problem of Water Resources Administration with Special Reference to the Delaware River Basin* (Syracuse, 1960), and the interim draft analyses which preceded it; and (2) Interstate Commission on the Delaware River Basin, *Report on the Utilization of the Waters of the Delaware River Basin* (Philadelphia, 1950); (3) *Tippetts-Abbett-McCarthy-Stratton Survey of New Jersey Water Resources Development for the Legislative Commission on Water Supply* (Trenton, 1955); and (4) *Report of the North Jersey District Water Supply Commission* (Trenton, 1954). A well-presented summary of developments is found in the New Jersey Taxpayers Association, "Series of Informational Memoranda on the Water Supply Problem," submitted to the Legislative Commission on Water Supply, mimeographed, 1956. This packet includes a document entitled "Water Supply Studies in New Jersey," which contains a comprehensive bibliography of water supply materials issued under official or private auspices since 1900.

54. Syracuse University, just cited. See especially the draft entitled "An Administrative Structure for Water Resources Management" (February 1959), p. 6.

55. Syracuse University, "Financing a Delaware Resources Program" (April 1959), pp. 16–24.

56. See the annual reports of New York City Board of Water Supply, and for a popular account of the development of the City's system, Henry LaCossitt, "The World's Biggest Thirst," *Saturday Evening Post* (September 10, 1955). Connecticut physical water supply conditions appear to parallel New York's. See State of Connecticut, "Water Resources of Connecticut," Report

to the General Assembly by the Water Resources Commission (Hartford, 1957).

57. LaCossitt, as cited above.

58. County of Nassau, *Your County, Nassau* (Hempstead, 1959); also Long Island State Park Commission, "Report on City Water Supply System in Nassau County to the Board of Estimate of the City of New York" (March 23, 1959).

59. New Jersey Taxpayers Association (cited in note 53), Informational Memorandum #3.

60. Taxpayers Association, Memorandum #5.

61. Taxpayers Association, Memorandum #3.

62. "Crises of Growth in North Jersey," *New York Times* (Jan. 31, 1960).

63. Taxpayers Association, Memorandum #4.

64. *New York Times* (March 28, 1954). In general the account of legislative action is based on *Times* reports, as specified in that newspaper's index.

65. *Ibid.* (Sept. 18, 1954), p. 16.

66. *Ibid.* (July 25, 1955), p. 15.

67. *Ibid.* (Aug. 23, 1955), p. 25.

68. *Ibid.* (Sept. 10, 1955), p. 26.

69. *Ibid.* (June 2, 1956), p. 21.

70. *Ibid.* (May 5, 1957), p. 78.

71. *Ibid.* (Sept. 11, 1957), p. 19.

72. *Ibid.* (Nov. 16, 1957), p. 11.

73. *Ibid.* (Dec. 17, 1957), p. 37.

74. *Ibid.* (Nov. 5, 1958), p. 27.

75. For a general introduction to federal housing and redevelopment programs, see such standard works as Miles Colean, *Renewing Our Cities* (New York, 1953); Martin Meyerson and Edward C. Banfield, *Politics, Planning and the Public Interest* (Glencoe, Ill., 1955); and Coleman Woodbury, *The Future of Cities and Urban Redevelopment* (Chicago, 1956).

76. For an analysis of the present impact of these programs, see Robert H. Connery and Richard H. Leach, *The Federal Government and Metropolitan Areas* (Cambridge, Mass., 1960).

77. For a brief review of applicable federal legislation, see the New York City Committee on Slum Clearance, *Slum Clearance Program Under Title I of the Federal Housing Act of 1949* (July 15, 1957), p. 1.

78. Colean, cited above, Chapter I. See also Committee for Economic Development, *Guiding Metropolitan Growth* (New York, 1960), a pamphlet which reviews and summarizes recent developments in the renewal program.

79. A summary of this activity was presented by Richard L. Steiner, commissioner, Urban Renewal Administration, Housing and Home Finance Agency, at the Arden House Conference on Metropolitan Area Problems, Harriman, New York, Sept. 21-23, 1957. An analysis in depth of the requirements of an effective rehabilitation program in New York City is found in New York City Planning Commission, *Urban Renewal: A Report on the West Side Urban Renewal Study* (New York, 1958).

80. New York State, *Report of the Temporary Commission on the Fiscal Affairs of State Government* (Albany, 1955), Vol. II, Staff Report No. 11, "Low Rent Public Housing and Urban Redevelopment," p. 512. This report provides a succinct and able review of legislative developments in New York State.

81. *Ibid.*, pp. 504, 505.

82. J. Anthony Panuch, *Building a Better New York: Final Report to Mayor Robert F. Wagner* (New York, 1960), p. 49.

83. *Ibid.*

84. Joseph F. Maloney, "Preliminary Report on Reasons for Large Public Housing Program in New York City" (mimeographed, March 1958), p. 4.

85. Committee on Slum Clearance (note 77 above), pp. 30–31.

86. Maloney, p. 2.

87. Committee on Slum Clearance, p. 1.

88. I am indebted to Dr. Luther Gulick, director of the Institute of Public Administration and formerly City Administrator, for personal recollections of the role of the office of the Mayor in housing activities. Confirmatory analyses have also been supplied by Maloney (note 84), and Meyerson and Banfield (note 75), p. 296. For a representative statement of the Comptroller's views, see Laurence E. Gerosa, Comptroller, "Report to the Board of Estimate on Title I Slum Clearance Projects and Tax Exempt Housing Projects" (mimeographed, May 9, 1956).

89. Meyerson and Banfield, p. 296.

90. *Ibid.*, p. 295.

91. See the account of the City's negotiations with the Housing and Home Finance Administrator in *New York Times* (July 24, 1957), p. 1. A summary account of the Lincoln Square project was reported by Maloney, cited above. See also Robert Moses, "A Memorandum at the 'Salute to Lincoln Square' Luncheon" (mimeographed, Oct. 14, 1957).

92. Editorial, *New York Times* (July 24, 1957).

93. *New York Times* (May 4, 1959), p. 1.

94. The most vivid account was contained in the article by Fred J. Cook and Gene Gleason, "The Shame of New York," *The Nation* (Oct. 31, 1959), an analysis cast in the Lincoln Steffens tradition. Subsequent developments brought charges that some of the sources employed in the article were unreliable.

95. Committee on Slum Clearance (note 77 above), p. 20.

96. For an account of typical municipal experiences in the Region and elsewhere, see U. S. Congress, House of Representatives, Committee on Governmental Operations, Sixth Report, *Replies from State and Local Governments to Questionnaires on Intergovernmental Relations,* Union Calendar No. 200: Home Report No. 575—85th Cong., 1st sess., June 17, 1959.

97. State of New Jersey, State Planning Bureau, "The Status of Urban Renewal in New Jersey as of January, 1957," *Jersey Plans* (First Quarter 1957), Vol. VIII, p. 10.

98. "46 Renewal Plans Pressed in New Jersey," *New York Times* (Feb. 7,

1959), p. 1. See also City of Newark, Office of the Mayor, annual reports on "The Progressive Strengthening of the Workable Program for Urban Renewal."

99. *New York Times* (Feb. 7, 1959), p. 1.

100. Joseph Nevins, "Urban Renewal in Newark," *Jersey Plans* (First Quarter 1957), Vol. VIII, p. 8.

101. U. S. Congress (cited in note 96), pp. 15–16.

102 Seymour Stillman, "Words, Time and Urban Renewal," *Jersey Plans* (First Quarter 1957), Vol. VIII, p. 8.

103. Committee on Slum Clearance (note 77, above), p. 20.

104. Herman T. Stichman (see note 22), p. 7.

CHAPTER 5: THE POLITICAL ECONOMY OF THE FUTURE

1. Luther Gulick, *Metro: Changing Problems and Lines of Attack* (Washington, 1957).

2. Otto Eckstein, *Trends in Public Expenditures in the Next Decade,* Supplementary Paper of the Committee for Economic Development (New York, 1959).

3. Harry L. Severson, "The Rising Volume of Municipal Bonds," *The Daily Bond Buyer* (June 10, 1958). This article provides a summary of his analysis. Severson has prepared an extensive review and series of projections for private circulation.

4. Roland I. Robinson, "Postwar Market for State and Local Government Securities," manuscript for National Bureau of Economic Research, dated April 1957.

5. Temporary Commission on the Fiscal Affairs of State Government, *Report,* Vol. II (Albany, 1955), p. 644.

6. Commission on Governmental Operations of the City of New York, *Interim Report* (Feb. 1, 1960), p. 80.

7. City of New York, Planning Commission, *Capital Budget Message* (New York, 1957), p. 5.

8. Merrill Folsom, "Taxes in the Suburbs Heading Up As Demand for Services Keeps Increasing," *New York Times* (Oct. 1, 1959), p. 7.

9. Samuel F. Thomas, *New York City: Its Expenditure and Revenue Patterns* (mimeographed, 1958), pp. 58–59.

10. James E. Allen, Jr., Address to the Columbia University Conference on Problems of Large School Districts (mimeographed, March 17, 1959).

11. State of New Jersey, Commission on State Tax Policy, *Ninth Report* (Trenton, 1958), p. XIX.

12. Jesse Burkhead, "Metropolitan Area Budget Structures and Their Significance for Expenditures," a paper delivered at the 52nd Annual Conference of the National Tax Association, Houston, Texas, Oct. 28, 1959.

13. Eckstein, p. 9.

14. Dick Netzer, "The Outlook for Fiscal Needs and Resources of State and

Local Governments," *Proceedings of the American Economic Association* (May 1958), pp. 317–327.

15. Burkhead.

16. Netzer.

17. State of New Jersey (note 11, above), p. 3.

18. These figures are from a series constructed by the New York Metropolitan Region Study from reports by the Comptroller of the State of New York and by the New Jersey Department of the Treasury, as explained in our Appendix A.

19. Burkhead.

20. On the latest New York consideration of a major tax reform see *New York Times* accounts of Governor Rockefeller's 1960 proposals, Jan. 8, 1960.

21. Note 18, above.

22. Edgar M. Hoover and Raymond Vernon, *Anatomy of a Metropolis* (Cambridge: Harvard University Press, 1959), pp. 59–60.

23. Francis Bator, *The Question of Government Spending: Public Needs vs. Private Wants* (New York, 1960).

24. See Kilpatrick and Drury in J. Frederic Dewhurst and associates, *America's Needs and Resources,* Twentieth Century Fund (New York, 1955), chap. 18.

25. U. S. Government, Special Assistant to the President for Public Works Planning, *Planning and Public Works* (Washington, 1957). See also Department of Commerce, *Survey of Construction Plans of State and Local Government* (April 4, 1955).

26. Note 18, above.

27. For an evaluation of New York City performance specifically, see Commission on Governmental Operations of the City of New York, *Interim Report* (Feb. 1, 1960).

28. See mimeographed statement by Arthur Levitt, comptroller, State of New York, "Financial Circumstances of School Districts and Implications for State Aid Policy" (Dec. 13, 1959).

29. Note 18, above.

30. Lyle Fitch, "Metropolitan Financial Problems," *The Annals of the American Academy of Political and Social Science,* Vol. 314 (November 1957), p. 73.

31. Newspaper comment on the Metropolitan Regional Council has been substantial in the last few years, and the organization publishes a periodic *Bulletin* respecting its activities. Maxwell Lehman, deputy administrator for the City of New York, whose office functions as Secretariat to the Council, and William Cassella of the National Municipal League, who has observed the Council's activities since its inception, have furnished valuable information and observations. A summary evaluation of the Council was made by the Special Committee on Metropolitan Governmental Affairs of the Regional Plan Association in its report published in the *New York Times* (Jan. 9, 1959), p. 16. See also Regional Plan Association, *The Handling of Metropolitan Problems in Selected Regions* (mimeographed, April 1958).

32. *New York Herald Tribune* (Aug. 24, 1959), p. 24.
33. *New York Times* (May 1, 1960).
34. *New York Times* (Nov. 3, 1959), p. 1.
35. *New York Times* (Jan. 8, 1960), p. 1.
36. *New York Times* (Jan. 17, 1959), p. 1.
37. *Bergen Evening Record* (Dec. 3, 1958), p. 1.

Index

DISCHARGED

DISCHARGED

JS
1228
.W6

148598

WISCONSIN STATE UNIVERSITY

LIBRARY

Stevens Point, Wisconsin

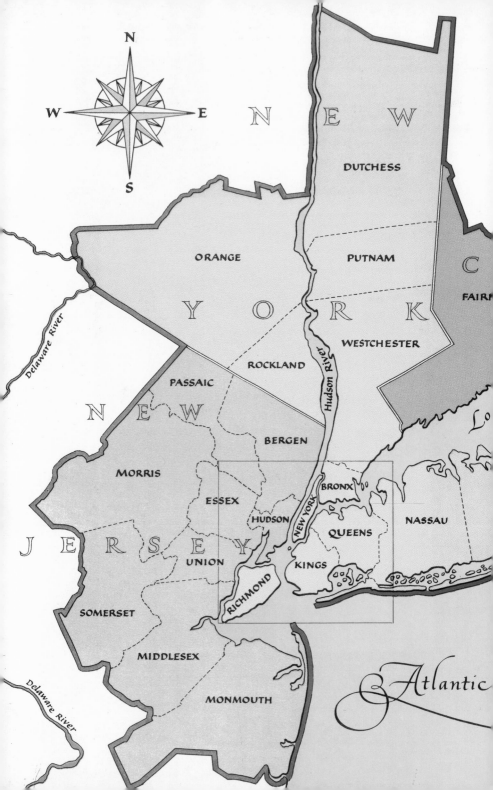